Julian Emperor of Rome, John Duncombe, Libanius

The Works of the Emperor Julian

Vol. II

Julian Emperor of Rome, John Duncombe, Libanius

The Works of the Emperor Julian
Vol. II

ISBN/EAN: 9783337192419

Printed in Europe, USA, Canada, Australia, Japan

Cover: Foto ©ninafisch / pixelio.de

More available books at **www.hansebooks.com**

THE WORKS
OF THE
EMPEROR JULIAN,
AND
SOME PIECES
OF THE
SOPHIST LIBANIUS,
TRANSLATED FROM THE GREEK.

WITH

Notes from PETAU, LA BLETERIE, GIBBON, &c.

TO WHICH IS ADDED,

The HISTORY of the EMPEROR JOVIAN,

From the French of the Abbé DE LA BLETERIE.

By JOHN DUNCOMBE, M.A.

IN TWO VOLUMES.

THIRD EDITION CORRECTED.

Him Poesy, Philosophy, deplore,
The scepter'd Patriot, who distinctions wav'd,
Lord of himself, by Pagan rites enslav'd;
Whom all, but Christians, held their common friend,
Whose very errors had a virtuous end.———IRWIN.

VOLUME THE SECOND.

LONDON,
Printed for T. CADELL, in the STRAND.

1798.

CONTENTS OF VOL. II.

Epistles of Julian	1
The Life of Libanius the Sophist, by Fabricius	216
A Monody, by Libanius, on Nicomedia, destroyed by an Earthquake	227
A Monody, by Libanius, on the Daphnæan Temple of Apollo, destroyed by fire	243
The History of the Emperor Jovian, by the Abbé de la Bleterie	258
An Abstract of an Essay, by the same	365
Additional Notes	381

THE EPISTLES OF JULIAN.

Απασαις μεν απασας νικων, τα δ'αυτε τε των ΕΠΙΣΤΟΛΩΝ.
"Superior, as he was, to all men in all his writings, in
"his EPISTLES he was superior to himself."
LIBANIUS.

*** Of the Epistles of Julian, the nine first were printed in Greek, with other Epistles by various hands, by Aldus, Rom. 1499, 4to. and afterwards in Greek and Latin, at Geneva, 1606, folio. The xth was preserved by Socrates in his History, III. 3. The xith, and those that follow, as far as the xlviith, were in like manner published among the Epistles of various writers. The xlixth was taken from Sozomen, v. 16. The lth, list, and liid were first published in Greek by Peter Martinius, together with the Misopogon, and the other Epistles, illustrated by a Latin translation, Paris, 1567 and 1583, 8vo. Petau therefore first translated those three, and also the liiid, and the following, as far as the lviith, which, together with the Epistle of Gallus to Julian, Bonaventure Vulcanius published at Leyden, 1597, 12mo. at the end of the Epistles and Problems of Theophylactus Simocatta. The lviiith and lixth, but doubtfully blended together, were first published by Nicholas Rigalt, who also added a translation, at the end of his *Funus Parasiticum*, Paris, 1601, 4to. But in the edition of Petau, by the advice of Rigalt himself, it was divided into two, both mutilated, the former having no conclusion, and the latter no beginning. At length the former was supplied from a MS. by the learned and ingenious Lewis Anthony Muratori, in his *Anecdota Græca*, Padua, 1709, 4to. The lxth and the two following were first published by Petau, from a copy of an old MS. lent him by Patricius Junius. The lxiiid, which Martinius and Petau have given in Greek only, but very imperfect and incorrect, Ezekiel Spanheim amended and supplied from the MS. of Allatius, and first added a Latin version. Muratori has also published three other Epistles of Julian, the lxivth, lxvth, and lxvith, from the same MS.

FABRICIUS.

For an account of the other Epistles, see the notes.

EPISTLES OF JULIAN.

Epistle I. To * * * * †.

I THOUGHT that you had long ago arrived in Ægypt; and recollecting what I have often said, "Happy," cried I, "are the Ægyptians in
" the plenty with which they have long been sup-
" plied by the Nile, but happier are they now
" in the possession of your Muse, a blessing, in
" my opinion, superior even to the Nile: That
" river, by flooding, enriches their country; but
" you, by your eloquence, improving the minds
" of their youth, endow them with the treasures
" of wisdom, like Plato and Pythagoras, their
" former visitors."

Such were my reflections, little thinking that you, in the mean time, were not far distant. At the receipt, therefore, of your letter I was at first so much surprised, that I thought it an imposition, and could not believe my eyes. But when I perused the contents, convinced that such elegance could flow from no other pen, how great was my delight! I then entertained hopes of soon seeing you here, and I rejoiced that your own country would soon be blessed with your presence, however short might be your stay. On this subject you seem to have brought a ludicrous charge against

---

† The name of the sage, to whom this Epistle is addressed, is not known.   LA BLETERIE.

me. For though I allow that the air is such as you represent it, that the water is as brackish as the ocean, and that the bread is made of barley; all which, out of regard to your country, you have by no means exaggerated; yet, my good friend, you are much indebted to her for having furnished your mind with philosophy. But beware how you despise the luxuries of Ægypt. Wise Ulysses, though he inhabited a small and rocky island, could not be tempted either by the charms of Calypso, or the promise of immortality, to prefer them to Ithaca. Nor was any Spartan, I imagine, ever induced by the recollection of his coarse domestic fare to complain of Sparta. But I know what has occasioned your bringing this charge against me. You are fond of money, and in that pursuit being disappointed, you sigh with regret, and envy the Nile and the wealth that it produces. This, you say, makes you desert your country, and renders your person as inelegant as that of Chærephon *. But I rather suspect that you are detained by some kind nymph, and are sensible at last of the power of love. Be this as Venus pleases! Mean time, farewell; and may I soon hail you the father of a family!

* Chærephon was a writer of tragedies. He celebrated the actions of the Heraclidæ. But being greatly emaciated by his nocturnal lucubrations, he became a vulgar joke. The name of "owl" was also given him. See *Erasm.* in *Chil.* p 685.

He was a disciple of Socrates. His nocturnal studies procured him the name of νυκτερις, "bat;" and his paleness the epithet of πυξινος, "the man of box." LA BLETERIE.

Epistle

Epistle II. To Prohæresius *.

A. D. 361.

WHY should I not salute the excellent Prohæresius, a man as exuberant in language as a river in water, when it overflows its banks; and in eloquence, the rival of Pericles †, except that he does not embroil Greece? Be not surprised at my adopting the Lacedæmonian brevity. Sages, like you, may make long and verbose orations; but from me to you a little is sufficient.

* One of the Christian professors who shut up their schools in consequence of Julian's edict. [See Epistle XLII.] He taught at Athens, and his reputation extended over the whole empire. The city of Rome had erected a statue to him as large as the life, with this inscription, "The queen of cities to the king of orators." He had received from the Emperor Constans the honorary title of "general of the Roman armies." Julian, it is said, exempted him from the general law, and allowed him to retain his seat without changing his religion. But Prohæresius had the delicacy not to avail himself of a privilege which would have rendered his faith suspected. Eunapius, an admirer and a disciple of this sophist, but a great enemy to the Christians, relates this fact differently.

LA BLETERIE.

On the eloquence of Prohæresius, Eunapius has fully enlarged. But Suidas says, that Julian, in order to pique him, preferred Libanius.

PETAU.

Libanius, in one of his Epistles, recommends him to Maximus, "as an ornament to the world by his eloquence, a good man, and one to whom both Rome and Athens had erected a statue of brass." His death was celebrated in a remarkable epigram by Nazianzen, preserved by Muratori in his *Anecdota Græca*, p. 1.

† As to the oratory of Pericles, see Cicero *de Oratore*, XXXIV.

Know, then, that my affairs are much embarrassed and distracted. With all the reasons of my return, if you intend to compile a history, I will most accurately acquaint you by transmitting the original letters and other authentic evidence. But if you determine to prosecute your present studies for the remainder of your life, you shall have no cause to complain of my silence.

Epistle III. To Libanius *.

A. D. 362.

THOUGH this is now the third day, the philosopher Priscus † is not yet arrived, and a letter from him seems to intimate that he will defer his journey. As you have forgotten your promise, I must remind you of it by demanding my debt. This debt, you well know, it is no less easy for

---

* For an account of this sophist, and some of his epistles, see Vol. I. p. 303.

† A Platonist, whom, at the solicitation of Maximus, sprung from the same school, the Emperor sent for from Greece. He was so reserved and mysterious in what he knew, as even to tax those, who communicated their learning, with prodigality and profaneness. But when he condescended to display his own talents, he discovered a profound knowledge of the systems of the ancients. The court did not corrupt him, and, instead of becoming a courtier himself, he endeavoured to render the courtiers philosopers.

He was one of the philosophers that attended Julian to the Persian war, and with whom he harangued in his last moments on the nature of the soul. He was called in question in the reign of the Emperor Valens; but his innocence was immediately acknowledged. LA BLETERIE.

you to discharge, than it is agreeable to me to receive. Send me therefore your oration, and that divine discourse; but, by Mercury and the Muses, send them soon. For these three days, be assured, you have much wasted me, if what the Sicilian poet says be true,

    Lovers in one day grow old *.

If this be a fact, as no doubt it is, you, my good friend, have trebled my age.

I have dictated this letter in the midst of business. I could not write to you myself, as my hand is more tardy than my tongue. But my tongue also is at present tardy and inarticulate through disuse. Farewell, my dearest and best loved brother!

Epistle IV. To Aristomenes †.

IS an invitation necessary from me to you, and must friendly offices never be anticipated? Let us take care not to introduce such a troublesome custom

A. D. 362.

---

* Theocritus, Idyll. xii. by Fawkes.

† This was, without doubt, a man of learning, and perhaps a philosopher. From the conclusion of the Epistle it may be supposed, that he was zealous for the Pagan religion, and perfectly well acquainted with the ceremonies.

This Epistle seems to have been written by Julian, when he was in Cappadocia; where he staid some time in his way from Constantinople to Antioch. La Bleterie.

In the MS. of Vossius it is addressed " to Aristoxenus."
            Petau.

custom as that of expecting a friend to be as ceremonious as a common acquaintance. If I am asked, "How can you and I be-styled friends, as we are not yet acquainted?" I answer, Why do we profess ourselves friends to those who were born a thousand or even two thousand years ago? Because they were good and virtuous. We wish to resemble them. And though as to myself I am conscious of being in fact far otherwise, in inclination I am certainly not far distant.

But to cease trifling, if you come uninvited, you will be cordially welcome; but if you expect an invitation, you here receive it. Therefore, by Jupiter the Hospitable, hasten hither, I intreat you, as soon as possible, and shew us, among the Cappadocians, a true Greek *. For as yet some

sacrifice

The LXXXIXth Latin Epistle of Libanius, b. III. seems to confirm the former reading, being addressed "to Aristo-" "menes," and much on the same subject. Being short, I will add it in English:

"You wish, I hear, to be known to me. Be assured
"that you have gained your wish, as I am better acquainted
"with nothing than with you. For who can be ignorant
"of the splendor of such a genius? Besides, my love for
"you is such, that I love myself scarce more. Conse-
"quently, command my services, if any thing should offer
"in which I can be useful."

* Ἀληθῶς ἐν Καππαδοκαις καθαρῶς Ἕλληνα. "A pure Greek among the Cappadocians." The restorer of the Greek religion could not but be displeased with Cappadocia. 1. Cæsarea, the capital of the province, was almost entirely Christian. The temples of Jupiter and Apollo, the tutelar deities of the city, had been long destroyed. Even in the reign of Julian, the Christians had just pulled down

the

the temple of Fortune, the only one that remained. This prince, not contented with confiscating the effects, moveable and immoveable, of the churches, enrolling the clergy in the most despicable militia, and putting to death those who had assisted in the destruction of the temple of Fortune, erased the town from the number of cities, subjected it to taxation, and made it resume the name of Mazaca, which it bore before Tiberius gave it the name of Cæsarea.

2. In Cappadocia the Pagans themselves could not be agreeable to Julian. Besides his complaining of their want of zeal, their Paganism was apparently blended with the religion of the Magi. Strabo, a native of the province, says, (*Geogr. l. xv.*) that, in his time, " there was a great " number of Magi, called *Pyræthi*, and several temples of " the Gods that were worshipped in Persia. Large in- " closures were seen there, where those Magi kept up the " sacred fire on an altar," &c. The same author seems to say, that those inclosures, called *Pyræthean*, were appendages to the temples of Anaïtis and Oman. The statue of the latter was carried in procession. More than three centuries after Strabo, St. Basil, a Cappadocian also, and contemporary with Julian, being consulted by St. Epiphanius as to the origin of the Magi, and concerning the Magusæi, replied, that " the former were a nation ori- " ginally transplanted from Babylonia into Cappadocia, " and diffused throughout all the country. They wor- " shipped fire, and condemned the killing of animals, " though they scrupled not to eat them when they had " been killed by others. They had neither any law in " their marriages, nor books, nor teachers, nor any rules " but their ancient customs. They were also unsociable " with all men, and incapable of reasoning." The Magusæi could not be very different from the Hypsistarii, a sect in which Gregory, the father of St. Gregory, Nazianzen, was born. He informs us, that " the Hypsistarii, " or worshippers of the Most High, professed to adore one " God only. They despised idols, and sacrifice," which must probably be understood with some restriction, as the same St. Gregory elsewhere says, that " his father had " been subjected to the idols of animals. They reverenced " fire and lamps; and though they were not circumcised, " they observed the sabbath and the distinction of meats."

From

sacrifice with reluctance, and the few who have zeal, want knowledge *.

Epistle V. To the most honoured THEODORA †.

ALL the books which you sent me, and also your letter, I received with pleasure by the excellent Mygdonius ‡. And though I have little leisure (the Gods know I do not exaggerate) I return you this acknowledgment. Farewell, and favour me with more such letters.

From these testimonies it may be inferred, that the tenets and rites of the Persian religion had made a great progress in Cappadocia, but had undergone several alterations. They were certainly adopted, in some degree, even by those who embraced the Greek religion; a mixture highly offensive to Julian, who thought that the re-establishment of Hellenism, in its purity, was the chief purpose of his existence.

LA BLETERIE.

* Εθελονίας μεν, ουκ ειδοίας δι θυειν, " Willing, but not know-" ing how, to sacrifice." Like those Christians, who, St. Paul says, had *a zeal of God, but not according to knowledge*. Rom. x. 2.

† This literary lady I apprehend to be the same who is addressed by Libanius in the following short Epistle (the MCCXCIXth) " We, in return, invite you to come hither, " and leave the sea. For it is better that you should live " soberly with us than that we should feast with you." By this she appears to have been a person of fortune as well as learning.

‡ This also was a friend of Libanius, as appears from two Epistles to him, the CCCCLXXIst and the DXVIIIth; in the first of which that sophist says, " he was like a pa-" rent to him at Athens."

Epistle VI. To Ecdicius, Præfect of Ægypt *.

T HOUGH you write to me on no other subject †, you ought, however, to have written concerning that enemy of the Gods, Athanasius,

A. D. 362.

---

* It appears from Epistle L, that Ecdicius was very remiss in writing to Julian even on subjects in which he was the most interested. LA BLETERIE.

Ecdicius studied oratory at Athens with Libanius, as appears from several of his Epistles.

† After the tumult of Alexandria had subsided, by the massacre of George [see Epistles ix and x], Athanasius, amidst the public acclamations, seated himself on the throne from which his unworthy competitor had been precipitated. Julian, who despised the Christians, honoured Athanasius with his sincere and peculiar hatred . . . He again banished the archbishop from the city; and he was pleased to suppose, that this act of justice would be highly agreeable to his pious subjects. The pressing solicitations of the people soon convinced him, that the majority of the Alexandrians were Christians; and that the greatest part of the Christians were firmly attached to the cause of their oppressed primate. But the knowledge of their sentiments, instead of persuading him to recall his decree, provoked him to extend to all Ægypt the term of the exile of Athanasius. The zeal of the multitude rendered Julian still more inexorable; he was alarmed by the danger of leaving at the head of a tumultuous city a daring and popular leader; and the language of his resentment discovers the opinion which he entertained of the courage and abilities of Athanasius. The execution of the sentence was still delayed by the caution, or negligence, of Ecdicius, Præfect of Ægypt, who was at length awakened from his lethargy by this severe reprimand. GIBBON.

The death of Athanasius was not expressly commanded; but the Præfect of Ægypt understood that it was safer for him

nafius, especially as you have long been acquainted with our edicts against him. I now swear, by the great Serapis, that if that enemy of the Gods does not leave Alexandria, or rather Ægypt, before the calends of December, the cohort that you command shall be fined a hundred pounds of gold *.

him to exceed, than to neglect, the orders of an irritated master. The archbishop prudently retired to the monasteries of the desert, and lived to triumph over the ashes of a prince, who in words of formidable import had declared his wish, that the whole venom of the Galilean school were contained in the single person of Athanasius. *Ibid.*

" Not contented with banishing Athanasius, the Emperor gave perhaps secret orders to put him to death; or at least Ecdicius, to ingratiate himself with Julian, who seemed dissatisfied with his negligence, took a resolution to deliver Paganism for ever from so formidable an enemy. Be it as it may, Athanasius went up the Nile in order to retire into the Thebais, when he was informed that he was pursued. " Fear nothing," said he to the companions of his flight. " Let us shew, that he who protects us is greater than " he who persecutes us." Saying this, he made the boat steer back towards Alexandria. They soon after met the assassin, who asked them if they had seen Athanasius, and whether he was far off? He is very near, they replied. ' If you make ever so little haste, you cannot fail to over-' take him.' The assassin went on making haste, in vain. Athanasius returned to Alexandria, and there remained concealed. LA BLETERIE.

The three Epistles of Julian, which explain his intentions and conduct with regard to Athanasius, should be disposed in the following chronological order, xxvi, x, vi.
GIBBON.

M. de la Bleterie has, by mistake, placed the xth before the xxvith.

* From the excellent discourse of Mr. Greaves on the *denarius*, the Roman pound of gold, the usual method of reckoning large sums, may be computed at forty pounds sterling. GIBBON.

4000 pounds sterling therefore would have been the fine.
You

You know, that, slow as I am in condemning, when I have once condemned, I am much slower in pardoning *.

P. S. *In his own hand.*

It grieves me extremely to see all the Gods despised by him. None of your transactions will give me so much pleasure as to hear that the wicked Athanasius, who has presumed in my dominions to persuade some Greek women of rank to be baptized, is expelled from all parts of Ægypt †.

Epistle VII. To Artabius ‡.

A. D. 362.

BY the Gods, I would neither have the Galileans put to death, nor scourged, unjustly, nor be in any other manner ill-treated. I think it, never-

---

* Surely this, and the other letters relating to Athanasius, shew that Julian did not practise that indulgence and moderation towards the Christians which he sometimes boasted of. For no fault is alleged against Athanasius, except that he was "an enemy of the Gods," and made convicts to Christianity from among the Gentiles.

LARDNER.

† Mr. Gibbon translates this passage thus: "Under my reign the baptism of several Grecian ladies of the highest rank has been the effect of his persecutions;" and adds, "I have preserved the ambiguous sense of the last word (διαπεισθαι) the ambiguity of a tyrant who wished to find, or to create, guilt."

‡ This Artabius, I imagine, is unknown. What is here given as an Epistle of Julian is perhaps a fragment of some edict. There cannot be a doubt that this prince published such a one at the beginning of his reign, declaring Paganism the religion of the empire, and at the same time forbidding

nevertheless, highly proper that the worshippers of the Gods should be preferred to them. By the madness of the Galileans * the empire was almost ruined †, but by the goodness of the Gods we are now preserved. We ought therefore to honour the Gods, and also religious men and states.

Epistle VIII. To George ‡.

A. D. 362.

"YOU are come, Telemachus §," says the poet. I have now seen you in your letter. I have there seen your divine mind in miniature, like a large statue copied on a small seal. For

forbidding the Christians to be ill-treated. This therefore must have been written in 361. LA BLETERIE.

This edict sufficiently indicates what treatment the Christians were to expect in his reign. LARDNER.

* It was his fancy to call the Christians Galileans. In this appellation there was no reason or argument. But it might answer Julian's purpose to make them appear contemptible in the eyes of weak people. *Ibid.*

† It is certain, that the Arian persecution produced great evils in the state. Constantius, desirous of being a divine, neglected the duties of an emperor. In order to hold councils, he ruined the public carriages, and expended immense sums, &c. But it is unjust to charge the Christian religion with faults which it condemns even when committed for its support. Of all religions it is best calculated to render a state happy. LA BLETERIE.

‡ The procurator, or one of the receivers, of the Cæsar. Epistle LV is also addressed to him, with the addition of Καθολικω, which the MS. of Vossius has annexed to this.

§ Ηλυθες, Τηλεμαχε. In Odyss. XVI. 23. Ηλθες, κ. τ. λ. the beginning of the welcome of Eumæus to that prince on his return from Pylos.

much

much may be expressed in little. The wise Phidias * was not only celebrated for his Olympic and Athenian statues, but also for comprising works of real art in small sculptures. Such, it is said, were his grashopper and bee, and perhaps his fly †, each of which, though the brass was formed by nature, seemed animated by art. But in these, it may be said, the appearances of truth might be owing to the smallness of the insects. Observe then his Alexander hunting on horseback ‡, whose whole dimensions do not exceed the size of a finger-nail: Each figure, however, is so wonderfully executed, that Alexander even wounds the beast, and with his looks terrifies the spectator. But the horse refusing to rear up, even in this

---

* This excellent Greek sculptor, in the year of Rome 323, finished the ivory statue of Minerva, so much extolled by the ancients, and considered as the master-piece of his art. He placed it in the citadel of Athens. Afterwards, being banished from that city, he retired into the province of Elis, where he was killed, after finishing the statue of Jupiter [of ivory also, according to Pliny] which he placed in the temple of Delphi, and which has been reckoned one of the wonders of the world. MORERI.

† These do not occur among the works of this artist enumerated by Pliny, in his Natural History, XXXIV. 8. though he says, that, " in small works Phidias had equal magnificence." Julian does not speak of them as then extant—φασιν is his expression, " it is said." A grashopper and locust of Myron are mentioned by Pliny, as celebrated in the poems of Erinna.

‡ Here Julian seems to refer to some well-known work then in being, (probably at Rome or Constantinople). The expression is Σκοπει, " Behold." A hunting-match of Alexander by Myron, is mentioned also by Erinna, as we learn from Pliny.

theft

theft of motion, moves by art. The same impressions, my excellent friend, you have made on me. For having been often crowned victor in the lists of eloquent Mercury, your writings, though few, are excellent, and remind me of the Ulysses of Homer, who, by only saying who he was, terrified the Phæacians *. Therefore, if my friendship can be serviceable to you, you may freely command it. That even the meanest can be useful, princes may learn from the mouse, whose gratitude preserved the lion †.

* In Odyff. ix. 19. Ulysses tells Alcinous and the Phæacians who he is, by saying, Ειμ' Οδυσευς Λαεῤτιαδης,
Behold Ulysses, fam'd Laërtes' son,
but no terror or confusion, on their part, is mentioned, nor is his narrative discontinued till b. xi. Perhaps Julian has substituted by mistake (trusting to his memory) " the " Phæacians" for " the suitors," who are indeed said (xxii. 42) to have trembled at hearing " who Ulysses was."
——————— confus'd the suitors stood,
F om their pale cheeks recedes the flying blood.
POPE. 53.

† Alluding to the fable of the mouse, who, having been preserved by a lion, in return extricated her benefactor from a net, by gnawing the meshes.
To this fable Libanius also alludes, in his XLVIIth Epistle: " We mice endeavour more to assist you lions, than " you lions, us;" and that proverb, which Synesius uses, " he prefers a mouse to a lion," seems not unknown to the ancients, applied to those who promise much, but perform little. WOLFIUS.

Epistle

Epistle IX. To Ecdicius, Præfect of Ægypt.

SOME delight in horses, some in birds, and others in wild beasts *. I, from my childhood, have always been inflamed with a passionate love for books †. I think it absurd to suffer these to fall into the hands of wretches whose avarice gold alone cannot satiate, as they are also clandestinely endeavouring to pilfer these. You will therefore oblige me extremely by collecting all the books of George ‡ : He had many, I know, on philosophical

A. D. 362.

---

* Ἀλλοι μεν ιππων, αλλοι δε ορνεων, αλλοι θηριων ερωσιν. M. de la Bleterie has translated this, *Les hommes naissent avec des goûts differens*, and says, "Some delight in horses, &c. (as in "the original) would have had no grace in French." The English language is not so fastidiously delicate. Our affected neighbours might with equal reason object to that similar passage of the Psalmist " *Some trust in chariots, and some in horses,*" &c.

† Thus was truly Julian, what Cicero terms himself, *helluo librorum*.

‡ Surnamed, from his parents, or his education, the Cappadocian. He was born at Epiphania in Cilicia, in a fuller's shop. From this obscure and servile origin he raised himself, by the talents of a parasite, first to a lucrative commission, or contract, to supply the army with bacon, and afterwards, by his profession of Arianism, to the primacy of Ægypt, vacant by the expulsion of Athanasius. His entrance was that of a Barbarian conqueror; and he oppressed, with an impartial hand, the various inhabitants of his extensive diocese. Under the reign of Constantius, he was expelled by the fury, or rather by the justice, of the people, and it was not without a violent struggle that the civil and military powers of the

phical and rhetorical subjects, and many on the doctrine of the impious Galileans. All these I would have destroyed *; but left others more valuable should be destroyed with them, let them all be carefully examined. The secretary of George may assist you in this disquisition, and if he acts with fidelity, he shall be rewarded with freedom; if not, he may be put to the torture †.

I am

state could restore his authority, and gratify his revenge. The messenger who proclaimed at Alexandria the accession of Julian, announced the downfall of the archbishop. George, with two of his obsequious ministers, were ignominiously dragged in chains to the public prison (Nov. 30. A. D. 361.). At the end of twenty-four days, (Dec. 24.) the prison was forced open by the rage of a superstitious multitude, impatient of the tedious forms of legal proceedings. The enemies of Gods and men expired under their cruel insults; the lifeless bodies of the archbishop and his associates were carried in triumph through the streets on the back of a camel; and the inactivity of the Athanasian party was esteemed a shining example of evangelical patience. The remains of these guilty wretches were thrown into the sea.

The meritorious death of the archbishop obliterated the memory of his life. The rival of Athanasius was dear and sacred to the Arians; and the seeming conversion of those sectaries introduced his worship into the bosom of the Catholic church. The odious stranger, disguising every circumstance of time and place, assumed the mask of a martyr, a saint, and a Christian hero; and the infamous George of Cappadocia has been transformed into the renowned St. George of England, the patron of arms, of chivalry, and of the garter.   GIBBON.

* It was mean in Julian to wish that all Christian writings might be destroyed. It was beneath a philosopher to entertain such a thought.   LARDNER.

† The deceitful and dangerous experiment of the criminal *question* (as it is emphatically styled) was admitted,

rather

I am not unacquainted with this library; for when I was in Cappadocia, George lent me several books to be transcribed, which I afterwards returned to him.

Epistle X. To the People of ALEXANDRIA *.

IF you do not revere Alexander, your founder †, and more especially that great God, the most holy Serapis ‡, have you no regard for your country,

A. D. 362.

rather than approved, in the jurisprudence of the Romans. They applied this sanguinary mode of examination only to servile bodies, whose sufferings were seldom weighed by those haughty republicans in the scale of justice or humanity; but they would never consent to violate the sacred person of a citizen, till they possessed the clearest evidence of his guilt. GIBBON.

* This public Epistle [occasioned by the massacre mentioned in a note on the last, p. 17.] affords us a very lively proof of the partial spirit of Julian's administration. His reproaches to the citizens of Alexandria are mingled with expressions of esteem and tenderness. " He suffered his " friends," (says Ammianus), " to assuage his anger."
Ibid.

Socrates has transcribed this Epistle, and so has M. Fleury.

In speaking of George, he did not mention the two officers who had been massacred with him; because, not designing to revenge their death, which was most atrocious, he was ashamed to seem to forgive it. His letter is full of noble sentiments. I would not affirm, that, after having written it, he was not in his heart pleased with those who had furnished him with the subject. The Arians circulated a report that the partisans of Athanasius were the authors of the death of George; but the latter need no other apology than the Epistle of Julian himself, which only accuses the Pagans. LA BLETERIE.

country, for humanity, for decency? I will add, for me also, whom all the Gods, particularly the great Serapis, have thought proper to appoint ruler of the world *, and who ought to have been informed of the outrage that you have committed? But anger perhaps has misled you, and rage, which, subverting reason, often instigates the most enormous crimes, has, by a sudden impulse, urged you to perpetrate, as a people, such wickedness as in others you have justly abhorred and detested.

    † Alexander the Great built this city, as one of the most glorious monuments of his conquests, about 330 years before Christ. Its situation was most advantageous, between the sea and one of the arms of the Nile. Alexandria became not only the first city in Africa, after the destruction of Carthage, but in all the world, next to Rome, as Herodian styles it. It is at present subject to the Turks. Selim subdued it in 1517, with the rest of Ægypt, and the country which composed the empire of the Mammelus. The city is almost entirely ruined, and it has no more than 8000 inhabitants. Its haven, however, is very good and commodious, and it has still some trade.   Morerī.

    ‡ A false deity which the Ægyptians adored. The Romans had often forbidden the sacrifices of Serapis to be celebrated in their cities. The idol of which the Emperor Hadrian, and afterwards Julian, wished to have a copy, was composed of all kinds of metals, wood, and precious stones. The temple and statue were demolished in the time of Theodosius the Great, A. D. 389, in consequence of a sedition excited at Alexandria by the Pagans.   *Ibid.*

    * It is observable, that Julian was so addicted to the idolatry of the Ægyptians, that, though he worshipped so many Gods of his own country, he professes himself indebted to Serapis alone even for the empire. On this account perhaps he caused himself to be represented on coins, together with Serapis, or alone, with the name of Serapis inscribed, as if he were that deity.   Baronius.

But

But tell me, I adjure you, by Serapis, what were the crimes that incensed you against George? You will answer, no doubt, " He exasperated " against us Constantius of blessed memory; he " brought an army into the holy city; the king " of Ægypt * seized the most holy temple of " God, despoiling it of the statues, the offerings " and ornaments; being justly provoked, on our " endeavouring to succour the God, or rather to " prevent his treasures being pillaged, he with " equal injustice, wickedness, and impiety, dared " to send against us an armed force, fearing " George perhaps more than Constantius, if he " had treated us with lenity, instead of constantly " acting like a tyrant."

For these reasons therefore, being enraged at George, the enemy of the Gods, you have again

---

* Ο Βασιλευς της Αιγυπτȣ, *rex Ægypti:* so it is expressed in the edition of F. Petau. He thinks, however, that we should read ςρατηγος, (*dux*) or ιπαρχος, and M. Spanheim inserts that correction in the text. But that is not necessary. Julian styles Artemius " king," or tyrant, of Ægypt, in derision, on account of the outrages which he was charged with having committed, and for which the Emperor had just caused him to be beheaded.   La Bleterie.

Some months after the tribunal of Chalcedon had been dissolved, the notary Gaudentius and Artemius, duke of Ægypt, were executed at Antioch. Artemius had reigned the cruel and corrupt tyrant of a great province. His merit, who demolished temples, and was put to death by an apostate, has tempted the Greek and Latin churches to honour him as a martyr. But as ecclesiastical history attests that he was not only a tyrant but an Arian, it is not altogether easy to justify this indiscreet promotion.   Gibbon.

polluted the holy city, instead of bringing him to a legal trial before the judges. In that case, there would have been no murder, no crime; by a just sentence you would have been entirely acquitted, and by punishing the impious author of these incurable evils you would have restrained all who despise the laws, all who dare to insult such flourishing states and cities, and think that their own usurped power is aggrandised by cruelty.

Compare with this epistle that which I sent you not long ago; observe the difference, and recollect how much I then commended you. But now, though I would gladly praise you, by the Gods I cannot, so heinous is your guilt. For the people have dared, like dogs, to worry a man, without being abashed, nor have kept their hands pure to approach the Gods, the purifiers of blood. But " George," you allege, " deserved such a " punishment." Allowed, and one even more severe. " And for us," you say. This also I will grant, but not by you. For you have laws, which you all ought to obey and revere; and though some individuals transgress them, yet still the republic should be well governed; you should obey the laws yourselves, and not violate those which have hitherto been constantly well administered.

"This is nobly done by you, men of Alexandria, in my reign, who, from my reverence towards God, and from a regard to my grandfather*, and

---

* Constantius-Chlorus.

my uncle and namesake *, who governed Ægypt and your city, esteem you with a brotherly affection. The undespised authority of a good and strict government will never suffer the abandoned wickedness of its subjects to pass unpunished. A desperate disease must be cured by rough prescriptions. For the reasons above-mentioned I administer to you, however, the mildest, this epistle and reprimand, which I hope will have the more effect †, as you are by origin Greeks, and the laudable and illustrious stamp of that noble descent still remains in your sentiments and actions.

Let this be communicated to my citizens of Alexandria.

---

* Julian, afterwards Count of the East. See Epistle XIII. Note *.

† I cannot suppose that he flattered himself with correcting the Alexandrians merely by reprimands. Their tumults, which generally arose in the theatre, were so frequent, that the government hardly deigned to take notice of them. It found, no doubt, that they did themselves sufficient justice, for there was always some blood spilt. They were as foolish as the inhabitants of Antioch, and much more wicked.   LA BLETERIE.

EPISTLES OF JULIAN.

Epistle XI. To the Byzantines [*].

ALL your senators we have restored to you, and also those of senatorial families, whether they have attached themselves to the Galilean religion,

[*] This title seems to me faulty. I do not think that any Emperor, especially in a law, has given the name of Byzantium to the city of Constantinople. But this is not my only reason for thinking that this law of Julian was not addressed to the inhabitants of New Rome. Whatever was the city to which Julian wrote, he declares to the citizens that he admits into their senate those who by birth, or any other means, obliged to take their seats there, should allege some exemptions and privileges, by way of excuse. I have often mentioned the zeal of Julian to fill up the council of the cities. But that he had occasion to employ his sovereign authority to retain in the senate of Constantinople, or to recall to it, those who ought to have been members of it, cannot be conceived. I know, that, at least, till the reign of Theodosius the Great, this senate was not in all respects equal to that of Rome, without being able to ascertain in what that inequality consisted. But it was, without doubt, a very august assembly, especially when Constantius and Julian had augmented its prerogatives. With regard to the East, it was considered as the public council of the Roman nation. It there held in the political order the same rank which that of Rome held in the West. The same titles were given to both senates. The Emperors gloried in being members and chiefs of both, &c. Thus, though the place of senator, even in the two capitals, was attended with very great expences, it must have been the object of the ambition of individuals; and we see that one of the methods which was employed to escape municipal dignities, obscure and ruinous honours, was to obtain, when they could, the place or title of senator

either

ligion, or have taken any other method of absenting themselves from the senate, such as have filled any public office in the metropolis * excepted.

either of Rome or Constantinople. One law of Constantius had suffered ecclesiastics, in certain cases and on certain conditions, to quit the *curiæ*, or municipal senates; and it is probable that Julian, as well from hatred to Christianity, as from zeal for the *curiæ*, was desirous to make the ecclesiastics sit there again; as we see by one of his laws, xii *cod. Theod. tit.* I. *De decurionibus l.* 51. *Decuriones, qui ut Christiani declinant munia, revocentur.* But who can be persuaded that he wanted to force them to be senators of Constantinople? That would have been a strange kind of persecution. I could add many other reflections, were I not apprehensive that they would make this note degenerate into a dissertation, perhaps curious, but certainly misplaced. I think I have said enough to prove, that the word Βυζαντιοις, which appears in the title of this Epistle, has been put by mistake, instead of some other similar word, which I will not endeavour to restore, because I should only advance very uncertain conjectures. La Bleterie.

From this Epistle it should seem that the place of senator was considered as a burthen rather than as an honour; but the Abbé de la Bleterie has shewn that this Epistle could not relate to Constantinople. Might we not read, instead of the celebrated name of Βυζαντιοις, the obscure but more probable word Βισανθηνοις? Bisanthe, now Rhodosto, was a small maritime city of Thrace. Gibbon.

* Εν τη μητροπολι. I suppose Rome and Constantinople. La Bleterie.

Epistle XII. To Basil *.

A. D. 361, or 362.

"YOU do not declare war †," says the proverb. But I add, from the comedy, "O messenger of golden words!" Come then, exemplify this, and hasten hither. You will come a friend to a friend. Constant attendance on public business is fatiguing to those who discharge it negligently; but those with whom I act are diligent and industrious, and in every respect deserving. I embrace therefore this opportunity, without neglecting public business, to take some relaxation. For being strangers to the courtly hypocrisy (which you perhaps have experienced) of loading with

---

* There is not a word in this Epistle which can authorise the supposition of its being addressed to Basil the Great. The name of Basil was not uncommon. Who this was is unknown. As to the Epistles of Julian to St. Basil, and from St. Basil to Julian, which are printed with the works of that father, they are unworthy of either, both as to their style and matter. Their spuriousness is visible at the first glance.   LA BLETERIE.

† Ου πολιμον αγγιλλεις. A common saying, when any one brings good news to a town, as war is the most calamitous of all things: and yet with the rumour of it many people at present are delighted; namely, those who feed on the miseries of mankind. Julian has doubled the proverb; as the following expression, χρυσον αγγειλας ιπων, taken from the Plutus of Aristophanes, is also proverbial. They are the words of the old men, who supply the chorus, to Carion, who had informed them of the approach of Plutus. They are also adopted by Plato in his Phædrus; and again in his IIId book *De Legibus*.   ERASMUS.

praises

praises those whom it really detests, with mutual freedom we accuse, when necessary, and blame each other, yet are as cordial as the greatest friends. Hence it happens, envy apart, that I find study a relaxation, and thus studious as I am, I feel no anxiety, and sleep serenely; as when I have watched, I have watched not for myself alone, but also for others. Thus far perhaps I have been trifling with you through mere idleness, and, like Astydamas *, I have praised myself. But I send this to inform you, that the company of a sage like you will be highly serviceable to me. Hasten therefore, as I have said before, making use of a public carriage †, and when you have stayed here as long as you please, you shall be conveyed wherever you think proper.

Epistle XIII.   To his Uncle JULIAN ‡.

IT is now the third hour of the night, and having no secretary, as they are all employed, I with difficulty write you this. I am living, thanks to

A. D. 361.

---

* An actor who, being ordered a statue in the theatre, for his excellent performance of Parthenopæus, inscribed his own elogium; whence the proverb, *Astydamas se ipsum laudat.* See Erasmus *in Chiliad.* p. 627. It is also used by Julian, in his LIXth Epistle, and by Libanius.

† The government furnished carriages to those who travelled by order of the prince; and these were then called public carriages.   LA BLETERIE.

‡ Afterwards Count of the East, the Emperor's maternal uncle. He had also been præfect of Ægypt. (See Epistle X.)

to the Gods, and have been preserved from doing or suffering incurable evils. The sun, whose assistance I particularly requested, and also royal Jupiter, can attest, that I never wished the death of Constantius, but that I rather wished the contrary. Why then did I wage war? Because the Gods expressly commanded me, promising me safety if I obeyed, but, if I hesitated, that which all the Gods avert! By appearing openly in arms I thought I might intimidate him, and thus accommodate matters more easily; or, if a battle should prove inevitable, I determined to rely on Fortune and the Gods, and to wait whatever their goodness should determine.

Epistle XIV. To Libanius *.

I READ yesterday most part of your oration † before dinner; and after dinner, without intermission, I finished the remainder. How happy

At his request, being also an apostate, and hating the Christians with less distinction than his nephew, Julian pardoned the Pagan murderers of George at Alexandria. As soon as Julian had heard in Illyricum of the death of Constantius, he wrote this Epistle to his uncle by the messenger whom he dispatched with the news of that interesting event. La Bleterie.

* One MS. adds Σοφιςη και Κοιαιςωρι, "Sophist and Quæstor." See the first note on Epistle XXVII, which is so superscribed.

† Perhaps this was the oration in praise of Julian, which is mentioned by Suidas; or perhaps one of the two that are published. Baronius.

are you to be able thus to speak, or rather, thus to think! What a discourse! what judgment! what an understanding! what wisdom! what arguments! what an arrangement! what strength! what language! what harmony! what composition!

Epistle XV. To the Philosopher MAXIMUS *.

ALEXANDER of Macedon is said to have slept upon the poems of Homer, that, night and day, he might be conversant with his martial instructions.

A. D. 361.

* The boldest and most skilful master of the Theurgic science, by whose hands Julian (after having imbibed the first rudiments of the Platonic doctrines from Edesius) was secretly initiated at Ephesus, in the twentieth year of his age.

As soon as Julian had taken possession of the palace of Constantinople, he dispatched an honourable and pressing invitation to Maximus; who then resided at Sardis, in Lydia, with Chrysanthius, the associate of his art and studies. . . . His journey through the cities of Asia displayed the triumphs of philosophic vanity; and the magistrates vied with each other in the honourable reception which they prepared for the friend of their sovereign. Julian was pronouncing an oration before the senate, when he was informed of the arrival of Maximus. The Emperor immediately interrupted his discourse, advanced to meet him, and, after a tender embrace, conducted him by the hand into the midst of the assembly; where he publickly acknowledged the benefits which he had received from the instructions of the philosopher. Maximus, who soon acquired the confidence, and influenced the councils, of Julian, was insensibly corrupted by the temptations of a court. His dress became more splendid, his demeanour more lofty, and he was exposed, under a succeeding reign, to an enquiry into the means, by which the disciple of

Plato

instructions *. But I sleep with your epistles as so many Pæonian medicines, and am no more weary of perusing them, than if they were new and just received. To give me therefore in your correspondence a picture of yourself, write, I intreat you, and fail not to write frequently. Or rather come, with auspicious omens; and be assured that, during your absence, I cannot be said to enjoy life, except while I am reading your letters.

Plato had accumulated, in the short duration of his favour, a very scandalous proportion of wealth. Three other Epistles (XVI, XXXVIII, and XXXIX.) in the same style of frendship and confidence, are addressed to this philosopher.
GIBBON.

Maximus and other philosophers accompanied Julian in his Persian expedition; and, when he was mortally wounded, some of his last words were a metaphysical argument with Maximus and Priscus on the nature of the soul, having Socrates no doubt in view. See Ammianus, xxx. 5. He was fined and imprisoned in the reign of Valens, and at last beheaded for magic by Festus, pro-consul of Asia, in 374.

Though Maximus was greatly respected, and much admired by the Emperor Julian, and many learned Heathens, as a great philosopher, and was also reputed to have commerce with the Gods, I do not think he was a wise man.
LARDNER.

* Of all the remains of antiquity, Alexander had the greatest esteem for Homer, who, he thought, was the only writer who had perfectly described that wisdom by which empires subsist; and such was his passion for him, that he was styled "Homer's lover." He used to carry his works always with him; and even when he went to bed, he put them and his sword under his pillow, calling them his "military viaticum, and the elements of martial virtue."
FREINSHEMIUS.

Epistle

Epistle XVI. To the same.

THE fable supposes, that the eagle, when he would try his genuine brood, carries them unfledged into the air, and exposes them to the rays of the sun, that by the testimony of that God he may distinguish the true from the spurious offspring. But I offer my writings to you as to eloquent Mercury: and if they can bear your penetrating ray *, you will judge whether they are fit to be published. If not, throw them away, as strangers to the Muses; or plunge them, as spurious, in the river. Thus the Rhine, the decent avenger of adultery, does justice to the Celts †, by overwhelming illegitimate infants with his

---

* Την σην ακτινα in one MS. which seems preferable to ακοην ("hearing") the common hearing, as it continues the metaphor.

† On examining all the passages in which Julian has used the word *Celtes*, I have observed that he makes it sometimes signify the Gauls, sometimes the Germans, and at other times both of them. I think that it is employed in this latter sense here. Claudian (*in Rufin. l.* 11.) reckons among the Gauls those to whom he ascribes the custom of making their infants undergo the trial of water, by plunging them in the Rhine:

> Thus the fierce Gauls with yellow locks proceed,
> Whom the swift Rhone or flower Arar breed,
> Or whom, new-born, the Rhine's deep current try'd,
> Or whom Garumna washes with his tide,
> When swell'd with torrents from the troubled main,
> The refluent river floats the cover'd plain.
>
> JABEZ HUGHES.

But this poet does not ascribe to them this custom exclusively of the Germans. The nations settled on the two banks of the Rhine must have had nearly the same manners and the same customs, because many of those who inhabited the left side of that river were of German origin. We know also that the Germans plunged their children in cold water as soon as they were born, to ascertain whether they were strong, and to inure them to the cold, as did many other nations, and as, it is said, several in America do at present.

As to the intention of proving the legitimacy of infants, it is probably a fable invented by the Romans. Seeing them plunge in the Rhine those children of whom some perished through weakness of constitution, or by the mismanagement of those who bathed them; and judging, by their own corruption, of that of other nations, they imputed to the Germans some views which they had not, and an anxiety from which the prudence of the women sufficiently preserved their husbands. Be that as it may, the most ancient authors who mention this motive are Julian, Gregory Nazianzen, and Libanius; but many have mentioned it since; among others, Nonnus, Theophylactus, Eustathius, &c. I know not whether Claudian should be added, as he does not mention the object of the trial. According to the author of a Greek epigram, quoted by Cluvier (*German. l. 1.*) infants were exposed on the Rhine in a buckler. When a fable is once invented, circumstances never fail to be added. I shall observe, however, that Julian, who in two passages mentions this trial, speaks of it as a report in his second Panegyric on Constantius; instead of which, in this Epistle to Maximus, subsequent to that discourse, he expresses himself in an affirmative manner: a difference the more remarkable, as in the same Epistle he takes care to relate only as a fable what he says of the eagle and his young ones. Ο μεν μυθος ποιει τον αιτον, κ. τ. λ. *Fabula fingit aquilam*, &c. But, after all, it is probable that Julian was really certain of the fact, that he had seen the nations bordering on the Rhine plunge their children in that river, but that he was mistaken as to the motive. LA BLETERIE.

The other passage, to which M. de La Bleterie alludes, is the following, in the iid Oration: "It is said, that, "among the Germans, there is a river, which is an in- "fallible judge of chastity, which neither sighing mothers,

" nor

his flood; but such as he acknowledges to be of a pure origin he supports above the water, and again delivers into the hands of the trembling mother, rewarding her with the safety of her child, as a testimony of her uncorrupt and irreproachable nuptials.

Epistle XVII. To Oribasius *.

A. D. 358.

WE are told by the divine Homer, that there are two gates of dreams, and that their credit, as to future events, is different †. I think you

" nor fathers dreading the event for their wives and chil-
" dren, can persuade to conceal their shame, being always
" true and sincere."

That in those days of darkness and ignorance such a superstition might prevail, may easily be believed, when we consider, that in much later times female chastity was as absurdly subjected to the test of another element; and that even in our own country, polished as it is, and in our own memory, the aged of the same sex have been exposed to a trial similar to that above-mentioned, and drowning has been deemed the only method of exculpating them from the charge of witchcraft.

* Of Pergamus. He was physician to Julian, and one of the four domestics whom Constantius allowed him to retain when Cæsar. (See the Epistle to the Athenians, p. 78.) Oribasius attended him to the Persian war, and in his last moments tried in vain all the resources of medicine. This letter must have been written in Gaul.

The Christian Emperors afterwards stripped him of all his fortune, and banished him among cruel Barbarians, by whom and their kings he was much esteemed, probably for his skill in physic or surgery. He was then recalled to his native country, had his estate restored to him, and married

Vol. II.   D   a wife

you have had a clear insight into futurity ‡. And a wife with a large fortune. This we learn from his life, among those of the sophists, by Eunapius, who mentions him as living when he wrote, which was about the year 400, above forty years after his going into Gaul with Julian. Suidas says, that Oribasius was of Sardis, and both he and Photius mention several of his works, particularly these four: 1. "An abridgment of the works of Galen," in several books. 11. "The sentiments of other physicians, as well as Galen," in seventy books. Both inscribed to the Emperor Julian. 111. "An abridgment of the other two," in nine books, to his son Eustathius. 1v. "Another compendious representation of the principles of medicine," in four books, inscribed to Eunapius (probably his biographer), at whose desire it was composed. LARDNER.

The Cæsar had rejected with abhorrence a mandate for the levy of an extraordinary tax; a new superdiction, which the præfect [Florentius] had offered for his signature; and the faithful picture of the public misery, by which he had been obliged to justify his refusal, offended the court of Constantius. We may enjoy the pleasure of reading the sentiments of Julian, as he expresses them with warmth and freedom in a letter [the above] to one of his most intimate friends. GIBBON.

† Odyss. xix. 562.
    Immur'd within the silent bower of sleep,
    Two portals firm the various phantoms keep;
    Of iv'ry one, whence flit, to mock the brain,
    Of winged lies a light fantastic train:
    The gate oppos'd pellucid valves adorn,
    And columns fair incas'd with polish'd horn,
    Where images of truth for passage wait,
    With visions manifest of future fate. FENTON.
Virgil has imitated this in Æneid VI. 893.

‡ It is observable, that Julian uses this language to an intimate friend. Can his belief then in dreams be doubted? In what remains of his books against the Christian religion, he affirms that "Æsculapius often cured him by remedies which he had disclosed to him." The Pagans believed that that God appeared to them in their sleep.
LA BLETERIE.

EPISTLES OF JULIAN.

the same I myself also have had to-day *. A lofty tree † grew, I thought, in a spacious room, with its branches bending down to the ground, and from its root sprouted another, small and young, and very flourishing. For this plant I was very anxious, fearing left it should be rooted up, together with the tree. Approaching nearer, I saw the large one fallen to the ground, but the small one not only erect, but raised into the air. Seeing this, I exclaimed, with much concern, "What a "downfall is this! The root, I fear, will perish "also." One, who was a stranger to me, then said, "Observe with attention, and be not afraid! "For as the root still remains in the ground, "the plant is unhurt, and will fix more firm-"ly ‡." Such was my dream; what it portends God knows.

---

* Even in his sleep the mind of the Cæsar must have been agitated by the hopes and fears of his fortune. Zosimus relates a subsequent dream. GIBBON.

† This tree is Constantius, and the shoot Julian himself.
LA BLETERIE.

‡ He here plainly intimates, that he should succeed Constantius. To the same purpose is the following passage of Ammianus, XXI. 2. "As Cæsar Julian was brandishing "a buckler, which he was exercising with various motions "in the field, the pegs, by which it was fastened to-"gether, being shaken out, the handle alone remained, "which he grasped hard in his hand. And all that "were present being terrified by the bad omen," 'Let "'no one,' he said, 'be alarmed: I grasp firmly what "I held!'

As to that wicked and effeminate wretch [*], I am very defirous to learn, when he thus difcourfed concerning me, whether before we met, or fince: inform me as far as you are able. He well knows, that frequently, when he oppreffed the provincials, I was more filent than I ought; not hearing fome things, not admitting others, not crediting a few, and imputing many to his friends and favourites. But when he thought proper to endeavour to brand me with infamy by fending me bafe and fcandalous memorials to fign [†], what was the proper ftep for me to take? To be filent, or to revolt? The former was foolifh, mean, and odious; the latter was juft, manly, and liberal, but, on account of fome prefent circumftances, inconvenient. How then did I act? In the prefence of many, who, I knew, would acquaint him with it, I faid, "He will "certainly alter his plan, its injuftice is fo ap- "parent." Hearing this, inftead of acting with difcretion, he did what, by heaven, a common tyrant would have fcrupled, and that almoft before my eyes. In fuch a fituation, what conduct could one, who is a zealous obferver of the precepts of

---

[*] Τῳ μιαρῳ ανδρογυνῳ. He means Florentius, præfect of Gaul.   LA BLETERIE.

See the Epiftle to the Athenians, p. 92. Petau and others underftand this of the eunuch Eufebius.

[†] A fcheme to augment the capitation.   *Ibid.*

This, in the reign of Conftantius, was in Gaul twenty-five pieces of gold, annually, for every head. The humane policy of his fucceffor reduced the capitation to feven pieces.   GIBBON.
Ariftotle

Aristotle and Plato*, with propriety adopt? Should I abandon the wretched people to the mercy of these extortioners, or should I not, to the utmost of my power, protect them, reduced as they are, by that profligate crew, to the last gasp †? Shall I punish a military tribune, when he deserts his post, with immediate death, and not deem him worthy even of interment; and shall I abandon my own station, when I am called upon to defend the oppressed; a station, in which I was placed by God himself? If disgrace must be my portion, a pure conscience is no small consolation. Would to heaven, that I were still blessed with such an excellent friend as Sallust ! ‡ If, on this account, I should be superseded, I shall not be concerned; as a short time

---

* It is plain that his illustrious actions proceeded from pedantry at least, as much as from virtue. La Bleterie.

† In the original, Το κυκνειον ἀδουσι, "they sing the song "of swans." Julian here adopts the ancient poetical idea of the dying melody of this bird. And the same expression of the "swan-song" is proverbially used to this day, in the same sense, in Sweden. Yet even among the ancients it was doubted by Ælian, denied by Pliny, and ridiculed by Lucian, and by modern naturalists it is generally exploded. Some, however, have supported it. Mr. Jodrell, in his elaborate illustrations of Euripides, after employing thirty-four 8vo pages on the subject, recapitulates the modern evidence on both sides; and a late writer in the Gentleman's Magazine (for 1782, p. 420.) wishes " Mr. Hunter " would ascertain the capabilities of this common b rd for " such enchanting melody," as he has those of the Ouran-Outang for speech; and queries " whether it may not re- " side, like that of bees and other flying insects, in the " motion of the wings."

‡ An officer of great merit, by nation a Gaul. See the Consolatory Oration on his departure, or recall, in Vol. I.

well spent is preferable to a long course of evil *. The Peripatetic philosophy is not, as some think, more pusillanimous than that of the Stoics. In this only, I apprehend, they differ; the former is more sanguine and less systematical; the latter more cool and prudent, urging a tenacious adherence to opinions.

Epistle XVIII. To the Philosopher EUGENIUS †.

DÆDALUS, it is said, formed waxen wings for Icarus ‡; and endeavoured by art to surpass nature. Though I admire his art, I cannot commend his prudence, in venturing to trust the safety of his son to dissoluble wax. But if I had the power, according to the wish of the Teian lyric, to be changed into a bird §, I would not fly to Olympus, or on any amorous pursuit, but to

---

* Such a conduct almost justifies the encomium of Mamertinus: *Ita illi anni spatia divisa sunt, ut aut Barbaros domitet, aut civibus jura restituat; perpetuum professus aut contra hostem, aut contra vitia, certamen.* GIBBON.

† There is great reason to suppose that this Eugenius was the father of Themistius. For he also was a philosopher, and of no small reputation, if the testimony of his son may be credited. See the IId oration of Themistius. -PETAU.

‡ See Ovid. Metam. VIII. Fab. 3.

§ No such passage occurs in any of the Odes of Anacreon that are known to us, or so styled. See a note on the Misopogon, p. 291. The idea is, certainly, Anacreontic,

the

the tops of your mountains, that, as Sappho says,
Thee, my care, I might embrace *.

Nature, however, having confined me in the prison of a human body, and not allowing me to elevate even my words on high, with such wings as I have I pursue you, with my writings, thus endeavouring to be with you as much as possible. Homer styles words " winged †," because they can fly any where, like the swiftest birds, and make what excursions they please. But do you, my friend, write also. For you have an equal, if not a larger, share of the wings of words, to enable you to reach your friends, and, as if you were present, every where to afford them delight.

Epistle XIX.   To Ecebolus ‡.

PINDAR thinks that the Muses are of silver §, comparing the clearness and splendor of their art to the most splendid of all substances. The
wise

---

* Ἴνα σι, τὸ μέλημα τέμον, περιπτύξωμαι.
This also must be in some Ode of Sappho that has not been preserved.

† Ἔπεα πτερόεντα, Il. I. 201. II. 7. and innumerable other places. Thus also Virgil,
——— verbis,
Quæ tuto tibi magna volant. Æn. XI. 380.

‡ The preceptor of Julian, a sophist, whose conscience was so supple, that he was constantly of the religion of the sovereign, and perhaps, in reality, of none. Under Constantius he inveighed against the Gods of the Pagans. Afterwards he declaimed for them, when his pupil Julian had

wise Homer styles silver " shining *," and water " silvery †," as glittering by the bright rays of the sun, and by its own splendid form. Fair Sappho calls the moon " silvery," and says, " on this account all the other stars are obscured ‡." Some therefore may suppose that the Gods abound with silver more than gold. For that silver is more fit for the use of mankind, and better than gold, as being more easily attainable, and much more pleasing and commodious, is not my idea, but that of the ancients,

had opened the temples again. And as soon as he heard of the death of that prince, he acted the part of a penitent by prostrating himself at the doors of a church, and, in a lamentable tone, exclaiming to the faithful, " Trample me " under foot: I am like salt that has lost its favour."

He made Julian promise, with the most dreadful imprecations, never to be the disciple of Libanius; precautions likely to give Julian a greater taste for that sophist.

LA BLETERIE.

§ Pindar, in his VIIIth Isthmian, styles the Muse " golden," (χρυσιαι); but I do not find that the epithet " silver" is so applied in any of his works now extant.

* Αιγληεντα.

† Αργυρεον. Neither of these epithets are to be found so applied in the Index of Homer by Seberus. They must therefore be in some work that has not reached us. Water indeed is often styled " splendid," (αγλαον) both in the Iliad and Odyssey.

‡ This also must be taken from some poem of Sappho that is lost. The only passage in which the moon is mentioned in her few remaining works is in a fragment, and that without the epithet, which the translator has added:

Διδυκε μιν α σιλαινα,
Και Πλειαδις, κ. τ. λ.
The Pleiads now no more are seen,
Nor shines the [silver] moon serene. FAWKES.

Therefore, if for a piece of gold, prefented by you, I return filver, as of equal value, think not the favour lefs, nor imagine, as in the cafe of Glaucus, that the exchange of armour is difadvantageous to you; and even Diomed perhaps exchanged his filver * arms for gold, becaufe he thought thofe much more ufeful and more proper, like lead, to blunt the point of fpears.

What you wrote has occafioned this jocularity. But if you would fend me gifts more valuable than gold, write, and fail not to write inceffantly. For a letter from you, however fhort, will be preferred by me to the moft coftly prefents.

Epiftle XX. To Eustochius †.

THE wife Hefiod thinks, that our neighbours ‡ fhould be invited to entertainments, that they may feaft and rejoice together, as well as lament and mourn together, when they meet with any unexpected misfortune. But I think, that our friends, not our neighbours only, fhould be

A. D. 362.

---

* Αργυρα χρυσων. In Homer the arms of Diomed are of brafs: χρυσια χαλκειων. Il. vi. 236.

M. de la Bleterie has not tranflated this Epiftle.

† A native of Paleftine, an eloquent orator, mentioned by Libanius in feveral of his Epiftles. In one of them he fays, " Euftochius, by his manners, conciliates every one; " they render thofe who are fierce gentle," &c.

‡ Works and Days, I. 340.
  No friends forget, nor entertain thy foe,
  Nor let thy neighbour uninvited go.   COOKE, 457.

invited;

invited; becaufe a neighbour may be an enemy; but a friend cannot, any more than white can be black, or hot cold. That you are my friend, not only now, but have long been fo, and that your regard for me has never varied, if there were no other evidence, my love and efteem for you would fufficiently prove. Come then, and partake the confular feftivity *. The public road will convey you, and you may command one carriage, and a fupernumerary horfe †. To complete your wifhes, I have invited the friendly Enodia and Enodius to meet you.

---

* It was a cuftom for the confuls elect to invite their friends to the confulfhip, which was on the calends of January; this was called *rogare ad confulatum*. And fometimes the confuls elect not only invited their friends by their own letters, but alfo by the letters of the prince himfelf caufed them to be afked to their confulfhip by his agent; which honour, Libanius, in his oration on his own life, p. 67, fpeaking of the conful Richomeres, fays, was firft offered to him. Be that as it may, that the cuftom was frequent in thofe times we learn from the 5th and 6th books of the Epiftles of Symmachus. And of the fame kind is this Epiftle of Julian.   VALOIS.

Julian invited Euftochius both as prince and conful, which he was the fucceeding year. Salluft the fecond was his collegue.

† This παριππος I interpret to be a fingle horfe, a third, in addition to the two that drew the carriage, which horfe, for the greater expedition, king Theodoric, in an Epiftle preferved by Caffiodorus, forbade to carry more than an hundred pounds weight. The fame indulgence is granted by Julian to Ætius, in Epiftle xxxi.   PETAU.

This is alfo omitted by M. de la Bleterie.

Epiftle

Epistle XXI. To CALLIXENE *, Priestess of Ceres.

A. D. 362.

TIME alone evinces men to be just. So we were taught of old. Let me add, pious and religious. But you say, the love of Penelope for her husband was also thus demonstrated. To this I answer, who can prefer, in a woman, conjugal love to piety, without being thought to have swallowed large draughts of mandragora †? And who that

---

* It is plain, by this Epistle, that Callixene had been molested, on account of her religion, for twenty years, that is, during almost the whole reign of Constantius. The date of it may evidently be fixed to the time of the journey which Julian took to Pessinus.   LA BLETERIE.

See note * next page.

The enthusiasm of Julian prompted him to embrace the friends of Jupiter as his personal friends and brethren; and though he partially overlooked the merit of Christian constancy, he admired and rewarded the noble perseverance of those Gentiles who had preferred the favour of the Gods to that of the Emperor. Thus he praises and rewards the fidelity of this priestess, and thus, in Epistle XXVII, he applauds the firmness of Sopater of Hierapolis.   GIBBON.

† Mandragora has such a soporific quality, that, if we credit Pliny, (xxv. 11.) large draughts of it are fatal. It is also called Circean, because its root is supposed to be useful in love-philtres. Therefore those who neglect their duty, and fall asleep, are said " to have drunk much mandragora."
    ERASMUS.

Thus Shakspeare, in Othello:
——— Not poppy, nor mandragora,
Nor all the drowsy syrups of the world,
Shall ever medicine thee to that sweet sleep
Which thou hadst yesterday.   Act III.

considers

considers the times, and compares Penelope, though praised almost universally for her conjugal fidelity, with the pious matrons who lately hazarded their lives, and, in addition to these evils, twice the length of time, can justly put Penelope in competition with you?

Disregard not these praises. All the Gods will reward you. We, for our part, will honour you with a double priesthood, and to that, which you had before, of the most holy Goddess Ceres, we add the priesthood of the great Mother, the Phrygian Goddess at sacred Pessinus *.

* The statue of Cybele had been removed from this temple to Rome by Scipio Nasica many centuries before. See Livy, xxix. 10. and Pliny, v. 32. When Julian arrived on the confines of Galatia, in his way to Antioch, he quitted his route to visit Pessinus. And probably he composed there, in honour of the Mother of the Gods, that hasty discourse which is still extant, as " it cost him," he says, " not a whole night," ἐν βραχει νυκτος μερει, after venting his anger on two Christians, one of whom had pulled down the altar of the Goddess.

The Pessinuntians had such an indifference for the Mother of the Gods, their ancient protectress, that it is no wonder that this priesthood was vacant. Julian confers it as Sovereign Pontiff, the head of the Pagan religion.

LA BLETERIE.

Epistle

Epistle XXII. To Leontius.

THE Thurian historian says, that "mens ears "are less faithful than their eyes *." But as to you I dissent, and my eyes are less faithful than my ears. For though I were to see you ten times, I should never trust my eyes so much as I now trust my ears; having heard, from one of unimpeached veracity, that, as you excell others in every thing else, you excell yourself in acting, as Homer expresses it, both " with hands and " feet †." Allowing you, therefore, the use of arms, we have sent you a complete suit of armour proper for the foot, being lighter than that of the

---

* Thus Horace, in his Epistle to the Pisos,
———————— What we hear
More slowly moves the heart than what we see.

Julian styles Herodotus, the author of this saying, " the " Thurian," because he lived and died at Thurium, in Magna Grecia. It is taken from his Clio, speaking of the queen of Candaules, whom he wished to shew naked to his friend Gyges.

† When we mean to express our utmost endeavours, we say, " with hands and feet." For by the " hands" is declared industry in performing, and by the " feet" swiftness in forwarding, an undertaking. Thus Hom. Il. XX. 360.   ERASMUS.

horse;

horse; and have enrolled you among our domestic guards, who consist of such as have borne arms, and served in the army *.

Epistle XXIII. To HERMOGENES, formerly Præfect of Ægypt.

A. D. 361.

ALLOW me to say, with the poets,
How bless'd beyond my hopes am I!
How much beyond my hopes have I heard of my escape from that many-headed Hydra †! I do not mean my brother Constantius (whatever he was), but the wild beasts who surrounded him, whose eyes nothing could elude, and who made him more severe, who in his own disposition was not the mildest, though he seemed so to many. But he is no more. On him therefore, as the saying is, light lie the earth! As to them, I would not have them, Jupiter knows, treated with the least injustice; but as many charges are brought against them, I allow them a trial ‡. In order to be present,

---

* Symmachus, Epist. 67. l. III. "For to such veterans "a prerogative is due, that they may have the rank of "guards, as a reward for their long services." PETAU. This Epistle is omitted by M. de la Bleterie.

† Πολυκέφαλοι [in one MS. τρικέφαλοι] ὕδρας. Hermogenes was, like himself, conversant with the Greek poets. GIBBON.

‡ To conduct this enquiry, Julian named six judges of the highest rank in the state and army; and as he wished to escape the reproach of condemning his personal enemies,

present, hasten hither, my dear friend, even beyond your strength; for, by the Gods, I have long wished to see you: and as I have had the great satisfaction of hearing that you are well, I now command you to come.

Epistle XXIV. To the most excellent SERAPION *.

SOME present their friends with panegyrics; but I, as a delicious repast, have sent you a hundred of our long-stalked, dried figs †; a gift whose beauty far exceeds its value. Aristophanes says, that "dried figs are the sweetest of all things, "except honey;" and he is afterwards of opinion that not even honey is sweeter ‡. The historian Herodotus thought that a true solitude was sufficiently described by saying, " it has neither figs,

he fixed this extraordinary tribunal at Chalcedon, on the Asiatic side of the Bosphorus, and transferred to the commissioners an absolute power to pronounce and execute their final sentence, without delay, and without appeal. They were a second Sallust, Præfect of the East, President; the eloquent Mamertinus, one of the consuls elect, and four generals, Nevitta, Agilo, Jovinus, and Arbetio. *Ibid.*

* A senator, probably, of Constantinople.

† Pliny (*l.* xv. *c.* 18.) mentions, among the various kinds of figs [twenty-nine in all], those of a purple colour (*porphyritides*) with very long stalks.   PETAU.

‡ The only two passages in which Aristophanes mentions figs, are in his Knights, act II. sc. 2. and his Acharnians, act. III. sc. 3. and in neither of these are they compared with honey. Julian must therefore refer to some play, or work, that is not extant.

" nor

"nor any thing else that is good *." As if no fruit excelled figs, and where there were figs, nothing good could be wanting. Homer praises other fruits for their size, their colour, or their beauty; but to the fig alone he gives the appellation of " sweetness †." Honey he calls " new ‡," fearing lest he should inadvertently style that sweet which often happens to be bitter: on the fig alone he

---

* Herodotus, in the first book of his histories, thus proves the excellence of figs: " You are preparing to " make war, O king, against men who wear breeches, " and other garments, of leather, who feed, not on what " they like, but on what they have, inhabiting a rugged " country; they have no wine, by Jove, but are water-" drinkers; nor have they figs to eat, *nor any thing else* " *that is good.*" ATHENÆUS. The above is part of the speech of Sandanis, a Lydian, who in vain attempted to dissuade Crœsus from invading Persia.

† In the garden of Alcinöus, Odyss. VII. 117. Συκαι τε γλυκεραι. κ. λ. τ.
The blushing fig with luscious juice o'erflows. POPE, 148. And again, XI. 589. among the fruits that torment Tantalus, where though the line in the original is the same, Broome drops the epithet, and substitutes two of his own:
———Figs sky-dy'd a purple hue disclose.
" Homer's epithets," says Eustathius, " are excellent. " For it is observable, that the poet gives every tree an " epithet suited to its peculiar nature. Thus the apple is " " beautiful," and its fruit, as he expresses it, " splendid" " (αγλαος) he therefore styles the apple a " splendid-fruited " tree" (αγλαοκαρπος); among the autumnal fruits, the fig, " by way of eminence, " sweet," and the olive " verdant."

‡ Μελι χλωρον, part of the entertainment given by Nestor, in Il. XI. 630. and by Circe in Odyss. x. 234. Pope renders it in one place by " fresh," and in the other by " new-pressed." The Latin translator of Julian has made it *flavum*.

bestows

bestows this peculiar praise, as on nectar, because of all things the fig only is sweet. "Honey," says Hippocrates, "is sweet to the taste, but quite "bitter when digested *:" and I am of his opinion; for that it breeds bile is generally allowed, and gives the humours a different savour; which shews that it is in its nature rather bitter than sweet. For it would never change to bitter, if it were not so originally, and afterwards became the reverse.

But the fig is not only sweet to the taste, but easy of digestion. It is so useful to mankind, that Aristotle deems it an antidote against all poisons, and says, that "for no other reason it is introduced at "the beginning and close of meals; as, in pre- "ference to every thing else, affording a sacred re- "medy against the injuries of food." That the fig is consecrated to the Gods, and in all sacrifices is placed on the altar, and is better for perfumes than any frankincense, is not merely my opinion; but all who are acquainted with its use know that such also is the opinion of that sage the Hie-

---

* Hippocrates says this, though not in these words, in substance, in his work *de internis affectionibus*, but of honey boiled: " Boiled honey is heating, and adheres to the " belly; but after it is digested, it ferments, and the belly " suddenly swells, and burns, and seems as if it would " burst." Galen also, in his iiid book *de facultate alimentorum*, says, that " honey, in its nature, is subtle, and by " its acrimony swells the belly before it can be digested, so " as to be voided. Therefore by correcting this we render " it fitter for digestion and concoction." And this is done by mixing it with water, and boiling both together. For then, being clarified, it digests easily.   PETAU.

rophant *. The excellent Theophrastus †, in his precepts of husbandry, explaining what kinds of trees can be grafted on others, and the manner of engrafting them, commends, I think, above all, the fig-tree as capable of admitting various sorts, and as being singular in easily bearing at the same time grafts of every kind, if you split any of its boughs, and engraft upon them the shoots of other trees; so that it often resembles a whole orchard, diffusing, like a beautiful garden, the variegated splendor of different kinds of fruit. And while, the fruits of other trees continue but a short time, and attain no age, the fig alone survives the year, and accompanies the growth of the succeeding fruit ‡. Homer therefore says, that, in the garden of

---

* Ἀνδρος σοφου καὶ ἱεροφαντου. I suppose that Julian here means the Eleusinian pontiff, peculiarly styled *Hierophantes*, or a revealer of sacred things. He was obliged to devote himself to the divine service, and lead a chaste and single life. He was attended by three officers, a torch-bearer, a herald, and one who assisted at the altar. (See Epictetus, *l.* III. *c.* 21. and Potter's Greek Antiquities, vol. I. c. 20.) This pontiff was supposed to be more profound even than Maximus in the science of Theurgy. And Julian must have been well acquainted with his sentiments, as he initiated him in the mysteries at Eleusis, and was afterwards invited by that prince to the court of Gaul, to perfect his sanctification. I am not confident, however, that the interpretation which I have given is the true one.

† Theophrastus has treated on figs, and on the grafting of them in the IId book of his *Hist. Plant. c.* 1. and 7. and also in his 1st book *de Causis*, c. VI.   PETAU.

‡ Theophrastus also mentions some wild fig-trees which bore twice, and others thrice, in a year, as in the island of Ceos. The late Mr. Markland, in an ingenious illustration

of Alcinous, some fruits grew old upon others *; which, as to other fruits, perhaps may seem a poetical fiction, but, as to the fig, is consistent with truth, because of all fruits it is the most lasting.

Such, I think, is the nature of the fig in general; but of all figs ours is far the best; as that is superior to all other fruits, ours is superior to all other figs, and though it excells every other kind of fruit, it is, in its turn, excelled by ours. And, to continue the comparison, it not only surpasses, as is fit, all others, but even in those particulars, where it seems inferior, it really excells. Nor is this undeservedly our peculiar lot. For it was just, I think, that the true city of Jupiter, and the eye of the whole East, I mean the holy and most spacious Damascus, as she is pre-eminent in every thing else, in the elegance of her sacred rites, the magnificence of her temples, the happy temperature of her climate, the beauty of her fountains, the number of her rivers, and the fertility

---

tration of Mark xi. 13. adopted from Bishop Kidder, refers "those who will not be convinced that the tree should "have figs on it at the time of the Passover," to the above passage of Julian. See Bowyer's Critical Conjectures and Observations on the New Testament, 4to, p. 65.

* Odyss. vii. 117.
  Each dropping pear a following pear supplies,
  On apples apples, figs on figs arise:
  The same mild season gives the blooms to blow,
  The buds to harden, and the fruits to grow.
         Pope, 154.

of her soil*, should also be unrivalled in this wonderful fruit.

This tree will not bear transplanting, nor will it leave its native soil, disdaining, like an indigenous plant, to grow any where but in the colony. Gold and silver are probably produced in various places; but our country is singular in giving birth to a plant which will not flourish in any other. As the wares of India, and the silks of Persia, and all the valuable productions of Æthiopia, by the law of commerce are exported to all other parts of the world, so this our native fig is transmitted by us into all other countries; nor is there a city, or an island, to which its admirable flavour is unknown. It graces even royal banquets; of every entertainment it is the boast and ornament; nor is there any cake, or wafer, or conserve, or any other kind of confectionary, that is comparable to it in sweetness, so much does it excell all other dainties. Other figs are eaten in the autumn, or are dried for that purpose; ours alone are fit for either purpose; they are good on the tree, and when they are dried they are still better. And were

---

* Damascus is situated in a very fertile plain at the foot of Mount Libanus, being surrounded by hills in the manner of a triumphal arch. It is bounded by a river which the ancients named Chrysorrhoas, as if it flowed with gold, and it is divided into several canals. Damascus has still a great number of fountains, which render it extremely agreeable. Its fertile and delightful meadows, covered with fruits and flowers, contribute also to its fame.

MORERI.

you to observe their beauty when growing, how they hang from every bough by long stalks, like so many cups, and surround the tree in a circular form, thus exhibiting various charms, you would say, that what a necklace is to the neck, such is this appendage to the tree. In the art of preserving them, there is also no less ingenuity than there is pleasure in eating them. For they are not, like other figs, thrown together in heaps, and promiscuously dried in the sun; but, first, they are gathered carefully from the trees, and then they are hung against a wall, by briars or twigs, that they may be bleached by the action of the pure rays of the sun, and may also be secured from the attacks of animals and birds, being protected by the prickles as by so many guards.

In the praise of their origin, flavour, beauty, confection, and use, my epistle has been sportive. Let me now inform you, that the number a hundred is more honourable than any other, and contains in itself the perfection of all numbers. I know indeed that the ancient sages preferred an odd to an even number *..... Homer seems to me

---

* Thus Virgil, *Ecl.* VIII. 75.—*Numero Deus impare gaudet.* Some paragraphs that follow in the original, being only a trifling play on the number a hundred, I have omitted, " as affording," in the words of M. de la Bleterie, " neither " entertainment nor instruction." The French translator indeed has omitted the whole Epistle, and reprobates it in his preface, as one of those " which turn on mere trifles." " I would suppose," he adds, " that this piece is only a

me to have given in his poem, not lightly or inconsiderately, a hundred-folded shield to Jupiter *; as he meant by this obscurely to intimate either that he appropriated the most perfect number, and that which would most honour him, to the most perfect God, or perhaps because, as no number but a hundred describes the world, which, on account of its rotundity, is displayed in the circular form of a shield, that intelligence which is so apparent in the world is also expressed by a century of circles. For the same reason, hundred-handed Briareus is placed near Jupiter, and contends with the Father to give an idea of his perfect strength by a perfect number. Pindar also the Theban,

---

" prostitution of wit and learning, and perhaps a criti-
" cism; for it appears, by the Letter itself, that such
" elogiums were fashionable." Wit and learning, however, are never more displayed than by giving importance and charms to trifles.

* The passage alluded to is in Iliad II. 447.
 The dreadful Ægis, Jove's immortal shield,
 Blaz'd on her † arm, and lighten'd all the field:
 Round the vast orb a hundred serpents roll'd,
 Form'd the bright fringe, and seem'd to burn in gold.
                                                       POPE, 526.

This snaky Ægis, but without the number, is described also in Il. V. 738.

But to make amends (which I wonder Julian should omit) the helmet of the Goddess is described as ἑκατὸν πολίων πρυλέεσσ' ἀραρυῖα, either, as Eustathius says, " because
" it could cover a hundred warriors, or because it had the
" warriors of a hundred cities engraved upon it." Pope adopts the latter, but amplifies the idea:

 So vast, the broad circumference contains
 A hundred armies on a hundred plains.   920.

† Minerva's.

EPISTLES OF JULIAN.

when he celebrates the slaughter of Typhœus in a triumphal song, and ascribes the strength of this greatest of giants to the greatest king of the Gods *, bestows such extravagant applause on him, for no other reason than his being able to destroy this hundred-headed monster with one blow; as if no giant was able to contend with Jupiter but he alone whom his mother had armed with a hundred heads, and as if no God but Jupiter was worthy of the conquest and destruction of such a giant. Simonides, the Lyric poet, thinks it a sufficient commendation of Apollo to style him Εκαῖον, and, in preference to any other title, adorns his name with this sacred distinction, because he flew the serpent Python, it is said, with a hundred arrows; and he delights rather to be styled Εκαῖον than Pythius, being distinguished by that as by a surname †. The island Crete, the nurse of Jupiter, as a reward for his birth and education, is now honoured with a hundred cities ‡. Homer styles Thebes

---

* This must probably be in one of the Olympics that are lost, as no such passage, or "triumphal song", is extant.

† This seems a forced construction. Apollo's name Εκαῖος is naturally derived from his shooting at a distance, like ἑκηβολος, so often applied to him by Homer, and I do not recollect his being any where styled Εκαῖον. The above-mentioned passage of Simonides is not in his few remaining fragments collected by Henry Stephens.

‡ Il. II. 649.
Crete's hundred cities pour forth all her sons. POPE, 790.
It is observable, that in the Odyssey, XIX. 174, only
— Ninety cities crown the sea-born isle. FENTON, 197.

Thebes "hundred-gated *," but gives this praise to no other, becaufe there is a wonderful beauty in a hundred gates. I fay nothing of the hecatombs † offered to the Gods, of the temples a hundred feet wide ‡, the altars with a hundred bafes, the hundred rooms, the hundred-acred fields, and other things, divine and human, which are included in the appellation of this number. This number adorns the eftablifhments both of war § and peace ||, it exhilarates the military centuries, and with its addition honours the title of the judges.

on which Euftathius remarks: "Crete is 'ninety-citied,' in the Odyffey, which is 'a hundred-citied' in the Iliad, from an accidental circumftance; for it is faid that ten cities were deftroyed by Idomeneus, at his return from Troy, when Leucus poffeffed it, whom, being his fon by adoption, he left guardian of the kingdom, "a foftered fnake," as Lycophron ftyles him; but thofe ten cities are faid to have been rebuilt after the Trojan war. Others underftand 'hundred-citied' here not in a determinate fenfe, but merely as 'many-citied.' For 'a hundred' was fometimes fo ufed on account of the diftinction of that perfect number, like 'a hundred fringes,' and the warriors of 'a hundred' cities. Thus 'hundred-citied' Crete is 'many-citied.'" Virgil has followed the Iliad: *Centum urbes habitant magnas.* Æn. III. 106.

* Εκατομπυλοι. Il. IX. 383.
That pours her heroes through a hundred gates.
POPE, 503.

† The facrifice of a hundred oxen.

‡ Εκατονπεδως. Such, as appears from Plutarch, was the temple of Minerva, in the citadel of Athens. SPANHEIM.

§ Centurions, captains over a hundred foot each.

|| *Centumviri*, judges chofen, three out of every tribe, to hear and determine certain civil caufes.

I could

I could add more, did not the rules of epistolary composition forbid. Pardon me, if I have said too much. Should it, in your opinion, attain mediocrity, the laudable attempt shall be communicated to others, such is my confidence in your judgment. But if another hand should be necessary to make it answer its intention, who better than you can polish this epistle so as to enable it to delight its readers?

Epistle XXV. To the COMMUNITY of the JEWS *.

FORMER times were not so grievous to you on account of the yoke of slavery, as on that of your being oppressed by surreptitious decrees, and

A. D. 362.

---

* We are informed by some or all our ecclesiastical historians, who write of Julian, that he sent for some of the chief men of the Jewish nation, and enquired of them, why they did not now sacrifice, as the law of Moses directed. They told him, that "they were not to sacrifice "at any place, except Jerusalem; and the temple being "destroyed, they were obliged to forbear that part of "worship." He thereupon promised to rebuild the temple at Jerusalem. And we still have a letter of Julian, inscribed, "To the Community of the Jews," which, however extraordinary, must be reckoned genuine. For Sozomen expressly says, that "Julian wrote to the patriarchs "and rulers of the Jews, and to their whole nation, de- "siring them to pray for him, and for the prosperity of "his reign." That is an exact description of the letter which is inscribed (as above). It was writ in the year 362, as Bleterie supposeth; in the beginning of that year, say Tillemont and the bishop of Gloucester.   LARDNER.
Aldus

and obliged to pay large fums into the treafury; of which I faw much with my own eyes, and have learned more from the edicts which were preferved

Aldus (*Venet.* 1499.) has branded this Epiftle with an *ες γνησιος*; but this ftigma is juftly removed by the fubfequent editors, Petavius and Spanheim. It is mentioned by Sozomen (v. 22.) and the purport of it is confirmed by Gregory (*Orat.* iv. *p.* 111.) and by Julian himfelf, Fragment, p. 295. GIBBON.

What Gregory Nazienzen, in his fecond invective, tells us of the conference that followed this letter, plainly fhews it to be genuine. "Julian," he fays, "affured the leaders "of the Jews, that he had difcovered from their facred "books, that the time of their reftoration was at hand." It is not a mere curiofity to enquire what prophecy it was that Julian perverted; becaufe it tends to confirm the truth of Nazianzen's relation. I have fometimes thought it might poffibly be the words of the Septuagint in Dan. ix. 27. Συντλεια δοθησεται επι την ερημωσιν, the ambiguity of which Julian took the advantage of (againft helleniftic Jews, who, it is probable, knew no more of the original than himfelf), fignifying *the tribute fhall be given to the defolate*, inftead of *the confummation fhall be poured upon the defolate.* For the letter in queftion tells us he had remitted their tribute, and by fo doing, we fee, was for paffing himfelf upon them for a fecond Cyrus. WARBURTON.

It feems that the Jews, after the deftruction of Jerufalem, preferved a fort of monarchy till the beginning of the Vth century. They had in Paleftine an Ethnarch, or chief of their nation, who, by the toleration of the Romans, was invefted with great power. He ftyled himfelf alfo Patriarch. His place was hereditary, and defcended from father to fon. All the fynagogues of the Eaft and Weft paid him tribute, under the pretence of contributing to the fupport of the Rabbins, who applied themfelves in Judea to the ftudy of the law. Thofe whom he commiffioned to levy this tax were ftyled *Apoftles* or *Envoys.* Thefe patriarchs, who had made themfelves very odious by their extortions and rapines, did not exift in 429. See M. de Tillemont's *Hiftoire des Empereurs*, tome I. LA BLETERIE.

againft

EPISTLES OF JULIAN.

against you. The tribute again ready to be levied upon you I have revoked; this infamous impiety * I have restrained; and the decrees against you remaining in my offices I have destroyed, that none may be able to circulate such an impious report. Of these great oppressions the memorable Constantius, my brother, was less guilty than some men, barbarous in their understandings and wicked in their minds, who frequented his table; whom, arrested by my own hands, and thrown into dungeons, I put to death, that no memorial of their destruction might remain among us †.

Desirous

---

* Ἀσίσημα. Julian, desirous of flattering the Jews, considers them as a sacred nation, who could not be injured without impiety.   LA BLETERIE.

† From this part it appears to have been written early in his reign, on his first coming to Constantinople, when he purged the city and palace of spies and informers, and the like, pests of a corrupted court.   WARBURTON.

The chamber of justice, created by Julian, proceeded against the favourites and ministers of Constantius with the utmost rigour. But that Julian thrust any of them into dungeons "with his own hands," no where appears, and is not even probable. It must therefore be deemed a most extravagant exaggeration; or we must suppose, that the words ιν χερσιν ιμαις λαβομενος were added by some Jew. Though with Messrs de Tillemont and Fleury, I have made use of this Epistle in the Life of Julian, I own nevertheless, that this passage makes me in some measure suspect it, and strikes me much more than the style of the Epistle, which seems to me written with much less purity than the others; for, after all, it is not necessary for it to have been dictated by Julian himself, or that all his secretaries should have been pure writers. It might also, as well as some others, have been written in Latin.   LA BLETERIE.

In

EPISTLES OF JULIAN.

Defirous to fhew you ftill greater favours, I have urged my brother Julus *, your moft venerable patriarch, to forbid the tax which you ftyle apoftlefhip, and no one fhall opprefs you by exacting fuch for the future, that you may enjoy eafe and fafety in all my dominions, and may be ftill more fervent in your prayers for my empire to the moft excellent God, the creator of all things †, who

In the ftrange boaft of his perfonal atchievement in thrufting down the delators into dungeons " with his own " hands" the Imperial character is fo little preferved, that the learned M. de la Bleterie is almoft tempted, on this fingle circumftance, to give up the letter as a forgery. But he here forgets what he himfelf had before mentioned of the ftrange efcapes of this fantaftic monarch: " St. " Gregory Nazianzen fays, that Julian drove away with " cuffs and kicks the poor who came to folicit favours from " him." *Life of Julian*, b. IV. WARBURTON.

* Julian in this refcript forbids the afleflments and tributes which the patriarchs of the Jews ufed to exact by apoftles. Of the Jewifh patriarchs, fee *lib.* xvi. *Cod. Theod. tit.* 8. PETAU.

† This language of Julian is by no means a proof that the letter is forged. We fhall fee, in the conclufion, that he believed that the God of the Jews was the *Demiurgus*, who had created, or rather arranged, the univerfe. The *Demiurgus*, or Λογος, proceeded eternally, fubftantially, and of himfelf, from the firft God, named The Being, the One and the Good. Whether the Platonifts admitted a diftinction of nature between The Being and the *Demiurgus*, or whether they only acknowledged a diftinction of perfons, or laftly, whether they confidered the *Demiurgus* as an attribute of The Being, it is certain that they gave even the *Theurgus* the name of the firft, the Supreme God. It was the *Theurgus* whom Julian worfhipped under the name of the Sun-King, meaning not the orb which ftrikes our eyes, but an intelligence which

pre-

who has condescended to crown me with his own pure hand. Those who labour under any anxiety must necessarily be timid and dispirited, and cannot elevate their hands with confidence in prayer; but those who are utterly free from care rejoice with their whole hearts, and more frequently and more effectually offer their devout supplications to God that the state may be governed in the best manner agreeably to my wishes. In this also you are deeply interested; that, after having happily terminated the Persian war, I may dwell in the holy city Jerusalem *, which you have long desired to see inhabited,

presides over that orb, and holds the same rank in the intelligent world which the material sun holds in the sensible.
LA BLETERIE.

* Julian did not wait so long before he gave the Jews some proofs of his affection, or rather of his hatred to the Christians, by the project which he formed of re-building the temple of Jerusalem; a project, which, as Pagan writers themselves attest, was confounded by one of the most astonishing and best attested miracles mentioned in history. *Ibid.*

On this remarkable event Mr. (afterwards Bishop) Warburton, published, in 1750, his Discourse, entitled, Julian, &c. (occasioned by Dr. Middleton's Free Enquiry into the miraculous Powers) written, it is generally thought, with temper and candour, though Mr. Gibbon brands it " with all " the peculiarities which are imputed to the Warburtonian " school," and charges the author with " revealing the " secret intentions of Julian, and, with the authority of a " theologian, prescribing the motives and conduct of the " Supreme Being."

Dr. Lardner, however, (Jewish and Heathen Testimonies, vol. IV. p. 47—71.) doubts the truth of this miracle. His reasons are drawn from Julian's own writings

(the

inhabited, and in that, restored by my labours, may, with you glorify the Most High *.

(the above passage in particular, which intimates his intention of re-building Jerusalem after his return from the Persian war, which never happened); the improbability of his allotting money for such an expensive work when he was just setting out for Persia, the credulity, in other instances, of Ammianus, the incredible miracles, or pretended miracles, with which the history of this event is loaded by Christian writers, there being no occasion, at that time, for such a miraculous interposition to hinder that undertaking, and the silence of several Christian contemporary writers, particularly Jerom, Prudentius, and Orosius. He concludes thus: "Let not any be offended "that I hesitate about this point. I think we ought not "too easily to receive accounts of miraculous interpositions "which are not becoming the divine Being. There are "many things said of Julian, which all wise and good "men do not believe." But let us hear another excellent writer.

'The interposition certainly was as providential as the attempt was impious. . . There are indeed many witnesses to the truth of the fact, whom an able critic † hath well drawn together, and ranged in this order: "Ammianus Marcellinus an Heathen, Zemuch David a Jew, who confesses that Julian was *divinitus impeditus*, 'hindered by God, in this attempt,' Nazianzen and Chrysostom among the Greeks, St. Ambrose and Ruffinus among the Latins, who flourished at the very time when this was done; Theodoret and Sozomen, orthodox historians, Philostorgius an Arian, Socrates a favourer of the Novatians, who wrote the story within the space of fifty years after the thing was done, and whilst the eye-witnesses of the fact were yet surviving." But the public hath been obliged with the best and fullest account of this whole transaction in Dr. Warburton's Julian, where the evidence for the miracle is set in the strongest light, and all objections are clearly refuted, to the triumph of faith and the confusion of infidelity. BISHOP NEWTON.

* The blind superstition and abject slavery of these unfortunate exiles must excite the contempt of a philosophic

† Whitby's general Preface, p. xxviii.

Emperor;

EPISTLES OF JULIAN.

TO THE PRINCIPAL PHYSICIANS. An Edict *. 12 June, 362. That the medical art is salutary to mankind, experience clearly demonstrates. The philosophers therefore justly teach that it came down from heaven; for the weakness of our nature, and the frequent disorders to which we are liable, are by that corrected. Therefore, as reason and justice require, and according to the example of former princes †, we, from our benevolence, exempt you, for the future, from the senatorial functions.

Dated at Constantinople, on the 4th of the ides of May, in the consulship of Mamertinus and Nevitta.

Epistle

Emperor; but they deserved the friendship of Julian by their implacable hatred of the Christian name. GIBBON.

* This law was, without doubt, written originally in Latin. An abridgement of it is found, with the title and date, in the Theodosian Code, XIII. t. 3. *de medicis et professoribus.* It is addressed *ad archiatros*. The title of *archiatri* was given to the physicians of the Emperor, and to those who practised physic in the two capitals. It is therefore to the physicians of the court, and to those of Rome and Constantinople, that this law of Julian is addressed. LA BLETERYE.

† The Imperial laws exempted the principal physicians from every public office. They could not be obliged to be members of the council, nor to exercise the magistracies in the municipal towns. If they became senators of Rome or Constantinople, they enjoyed some honours and privileges annexed to that office, without being required to discharge its functions, or to bear its burthens, &c. See the Theodocian Code, at the title just quoted, and the notes of Godefroi. These privileges were as early as the reign of Augustus. They had been confirmed by a great number of Emperors, and very recently by Constantine, whose laws are still in being. But it is well known that Julian was the declared enemy of exemptions, and that he loved to undo what Constantine had done. The physicians therefore were uneasy. Julian, however, maintained them

Epistle XXVI. To the Alexandrians. An Edict.*

A. D. 362.

ONE who had been banished by so many Imperial decrees should have waited at least for one edict † before he returned home, instead of contumeliously insulting the laws, as if there were none in being. For we have not allowed the Galileans, who were banished by Constantius, of

in their privileges. The Latin text seems to give them more than is granted to them in the Greek. *Securi à molestiis munerum omnium publicorum reliquum tempus ætatis jugiter agitabitis.* The Greek only says, των βουλευτικων λειτουργηματων. It is remarkable that the exemptions of the professors, though they were the same as those of the physicians, and though Constantine had confirmed them by two laws, were not attacked. It was notorious that Julian's love of literature, and of those who taught it, exceeded his hatred of exemptions, and even of Constantine. LA BLETERIE.

* Athanasius had been banished once by Constantine, and twice by Constantius. He was in his third exile when Julian recalled all those whom Constantius had banished on account of religion. Prudence did not allow Athanasius to avail himself of this recall while his see was occupied by George of Cappadocia. But soon after the death of the usurper (see p. 18.) he returned to his church, where the Pagans did not suffer him to remain long in quiet. They represented to the Emperor that Athanasius would pervert the whole city, and that, if he continued there, not a single Heathen would soon be found there. Their complaints determined Julian to issue this edict. *Ibid.*

† This was not necessary, as Julian had, without distinction, recalled all those whom Constantius had banished for the "madness" of the Galileans. *Ibid.*

blessed

essed memory, to return to their churches *, but only to their countries. Yet I hear that he most audacious Athanasius, with his usual insolence, has again usurped what they call the episcopal throne; and that this has not a little displeased the people of Alexandria †. We therefore command him to depart from the city on the very day that he shall receive the letter of our clemency; and if he remain there, he may expect a much severer punishment.

Epistle XXVII. To the Sophist and Quæstor LIBANIUS ‡.

ON my arrival at Litarbe §, a town in Chlcis, I found a road where were some remains of the Antiochian winter camp. One part of it was morassy;

March, 363.

---

* Whether Julian thought of this distinction at first, or whether it was an after-stroke, that this prince employed it only against Athanasius is glorious to that prelate.
LA BLETERIE.

This explication seems evasive, and perhaps was now first thought of.
LARDNER.

† This was the "pious" people who tore " men in pieces " as if they had been dogs." [See Epistle X.]
LA BLETERIE.

‡ It appears that Julian had given Libanius the honorary title of Quæstor. But Eunapius reports, that Libanius refused the honorary rank of Prætor an Præfect, which one of the successors of Julian would have given him, as less illustrious than the title of Sophist (*in vita Sophist.* p. 135.) The critics have observed a similar sentiment in one of the Epistles (XVIII. *edit. Wolf.*) of Libanius himself.

morassy; the other hilly, and extremely steep; over the morass loose stones were placed by chance, and not artfully cemented, as roads are in a manner built in other places, where, instead of sand, the stones are laid in mortar, as in a wall. Passing this with some difficulty, I reached my first stage *, about the ninth hour, where I saw in the hall the principal part of your senate †. Of the subject of our conversation, though perhaps you may have heard it already, if the Gods permit, I will inform you. From Litarbe I proceeded to Berea ‡, where Ju-

---

In this Epistle Julian gives the journal of his march from Antioch to Hierapolis.   LA BLETERIE.

He informed Libanius of his progress in an elegant Epistle, which displays the fertility of his genius, and his tender regard for the sophist of Antioch.   GIBBON.

§ This place Euagrius mentions, *l.* v. *c.* 12. and says, it was three hundred stadia from Antioch.   PETAU.

* It is singular that the Romans should have neglected the great communication between Antioch and the Euphrates.   GIBBON.

† The martial impatience of Julian urged him to take the field in the beginning of the spring; and he dismissed, with contempt and reproach, the senate of Antioch, who accompanied him beyond the limits of their own territory, to which he was resolved never to return.   *Ibid.*

‡ Now Aleppo. The inhabitants of this place are recorded with honour in the *Acts of the Apostles*, ch. XVII. for the *readiness of mind* with which *they received the word*, preached by Paul, *and searched the scriptures daily whether those things were so.* By Julian's account, they still adhered to their Christian principles, receiving, as Mr. Gibbon expresses it, "with cold and formal demonstrations of respect, the eloquent sermon of the Apostle of Paganism."

St. Basil has addressed two Epistles to the inhabitants of Berea, applauding their piety. See his works, vol. III. p. 1006.

piter,

EPISTLES OF JULIAN.

piter, by the clearest omens, declared all things auspicious. Staying there a whole day, I visited the castle, and royally sacrificed to Jupiter a white bull *. With the senate I conversed a little on matters of religion, but though they all praised my discourse †, a few only were convinced by it; however, they were such as, before I spoke, I thought sensible; the others assumed a kind of licence, and seemed totally destitute of shame. Men are apt to be extremely abashed at qualities that are laudable, such as fortitude of mind and

---

* He was more a superstitious than a legal observer of sacred rites, sacrificing innumerable cattle without parsimony, so that it was thought, if he had returned from Persia, oxen would have been wanting; like Marcus Cæsar, of whom, we are told, it was said, " White bulls to Marcus " Cæsar:" ' If you conquer, we perish.' AMMIANUS. To Capitoline Jupiter white victims only were sacrificed in triumph. See *Turneb. l.* 29. 26.

† The son of one of the most illustrious citizens of Berea, who had embraced, either from interest or conscience, the religion of the Emperor, had been disinherited by his angry parent. The father and the son were invited to the Imperial table. Julian, placing himself between them, attempted, without success, to inculcate the lesson and example of toleration; supported, with affected calmness, the indiscreet zeal of the aged Christian, who seemed to forget the sentiments of nature, and the duty of a subject; and at length, turning towards the afflicted youth, " Since " you have lost a father," said he, " for my sake, it is " incumbent on me to supply his place."
Julian alludes to this incident [above]; which is more distinctly related by Theodoret (*l.* III. *c.* 22) The intolerant spirit of the father is applauded by Tillemont, (*Hist. des Empereurs, tom.* IV. *p.* 534.) and even by La Bleterie (*Vie de Julien, p.* 413.)   GIBBON.

piety; but in the basest actions and sentiments *, in sacrilege and pusillanimity, they have the confidence to glory.

Batnæ next received me, a place to which I never saw any similar but Daphne †. But though Batnæ may now vie with Daphne, not long ago, when the temple and the image were in being, I should, without scruple, not only have compared Daphne to Ossa, Pelion, Olympus, and Thessalian Tempe, but even have preferred it to them all. The place above-mentioned is dedicated to Olympic Jupiter and Pythian Apollo. But on the subject of Daphne you have composed an oration ‡, such as no other mortal,

Of those who live in these degenerate days §, with his utmost efforts, could have written, and, I think, not many of the ancients. Why therefore should I enlarge upon what has so elegantly been described by you? Far be that idea!

---

* Μαλακια γνωμης και σωματος. 'It is not surprising, that by the Pagans that abstraction and contempt of the world, with which the gospel inspires every true Christian, should be deemed meanness of spirit. But why is not Julian ashamed to blame in the Christians those virtues whose very shadow he adored in the philosophers? See his Epistle to Themistius. La Bleterie.

† See an elegant description of Daphne by Mr. Gibbon, in a note on the Misopogon, Vol. I. p. 280.

‡ This lamentation is still extant in the works of Libanius, and composes his IXth Oration. It is entitled, "A Monody on the Temple of Apollo at Daphne, consumed by fire, or, as it is said, by lightning." It is translated in this volume.

§ Hom. Il. V. 304.

At Batnæ (though the name is barbarous, the town is Greek) we inhaled the fumes of incense from all the adjacent country, and saw victims every where prepared. This, though it much pleased me, seemed rather too fervent and foreign to religion *. For sacrifices should be offered in private, far from all public roads and passengers, and all that is required is a supply of victims and offerings. But this by proper care may be easily corrected.

Batnæ is situated on a plain skirted by a grove of cypresses, none of which were old or decayed, but all were equally young and flourishing. My palace was by no means magnificent, being constructed of clay and boards, and having nothing ornamental. Nor could the garden vie with that of Alcinöus †, but rather resembled that of Laërtes ‡. There was also a small grove of cypresses, and a row of those trees was planted along the walls: in the middle were pot-herbs and fruit-trees of every kind. I sacrificed there in the evening, and again early in the morning, as was my constant custom every day; and as the rites were auspicious, we proceeded to Hiera-

---

* He too clearly discerned that the smoke which arose from their altars was the incense of flattery, rather than of devotion.   GIBBON.

† Odyss. VII. 112.

‡ Ibid. XXIV. 204.—Laërtes cultivated land.
  The ground himself had purchas'd with his pain,
  And labour made the rugged soil a plain.
                                        POPE, 235.

polis,

polis *, where we were met by the citizens, and I was received as a guest by one whom, though I had scarce ever seen him before, I had long esteemed. Though you are well acquainted with the reason, I cannot deny myself the pleasure of repeating it; for to hear and speak of these persons is always nectar to me. Sopater, the father-in-law of this, was a disciple of the most divine Jamblichus †. Did I not love all that were connected with him, I should deem myself guilty of the

---

* Hierapolis, situate almost on the banks of the Euphrates, had been appointed for the general rendezvous of the Roman army, who there passed the great river on a bridge of boats, which was previously constructed.
GIBBON.
The ancient and magnificent temple, which had sanctified, for so many ages, the city of Hierapolis, no longer subsisted; and the consecrated wealth, which afforded a liberal maintenance to more than three hundred priests, might hasten its downfall. *Ibid.*

† Of Chalcis, a Pythagorean philosopher, the disciple of Porphyry, and uncle to the philosopher of the same name, to whom Julian has addressed six subsequent Epistles, and whom M. de la Bleterie supposes to have been here meant; but as I understand that the father-in-law of this Sopater (then dead) had been his disciple, it seems rather more applicable to the elder Jamblichus. The elder Sopater was probably that Platonic philosopher who was put to death by Constantine the Great, being styled, by Suidas and others, " a disciple of Jamblichus."
The French translator also styles this Sopater of Hierapolis the " son-in-law" (as well as " pupil") of Jamblichus, for which I can see no authority in the original, or in any other author. Let the reader judge. Ιαμβλιχε τε Σωιλαλε το θειυμα Σωπαιρος, τωιν κηδεστης εξ οσε. In the French, *Sopatre est l'eleve et le gendre du divin Jamblique*, meaning the younger of these philosophers, then living.

worst

worst of crimes. But there is another reason still more cogent. Having often entertained at his house my cousin and my brother *, and, as might well be supposed, being strongly urged by them to apostatise from the Gods, he had the great merit of never being infected with that contagion.

These particulars, immediately relating to myself, I now communicate to you from Hierapolis. As to military and civil transactions, you should be present to see and observe them yourself. For, be assured, if they were distinctly related, they could not be comprised in a letter of twice the length of this. But, as I am writing, I will briefly mention them. I have sent an embassy to the Saracens †, urging them, if they are so inclined, to join us. This is the first article. Next, I have dispatched, as was proper, some observant spies, lest any deserter should acquaint the enemy with our motions. Add to these, I have decided a military dispute ‡, I am persuaded, with lenity and justice.

---

* Constantius and Gallus.

† A wandering people in the deserts of Arabia [who stretched from the confines of Assyria to the cataracts of the Nile], warlike and self-interested, dangerous enemies and burthensome friends. *Nec amici nobis unquam nec hostes optandi*, are the words of Ammianus. The love of rapine and war allured several of them to the imperial standard, though Julian sternly refused the payment of the accustomed subsidies. LA BLETERIE.

‡ Στρατιωτικην δικην. M. de Tillemont suspects that this relates to a fact mentioned by St. Chrysostom. Being ready

justice. I have procured excellent horses and mules, and my army is assembled. The boats are filled with corn, or rather with biscuit and vinegar. What a long letter would it require to tell you how each of these points was accomplished! What was said on every subject you may easily guess. As to the happy omens *, having recorded them in many letters and books, which I every where carry with me, why should I trouble you with the repetition?

ready to pass the Euphrates, Julian made an attempt to gain such of his soldiers as were still Christians. Some suffered themselves to be seduced, but the rest refused, and the Emperor did not dare to cashier them, for fear of weakening his army. *Ibid.*

* Infatuated with his expedition, he saw every thing in the best light, and only kept a register of what he considered as happy presages. He passes over in silence the fatal accident which happened when he made his entry into Hierapolis. Fifty soldiers were crushed to death by the fall of a portico, and many more wounded. Ammianus xxiii. 2. *Ibid.*

Another bad omen is mentioned by Ammianus at Batnæ in Osdroëna (after the date indeed of this letter), fifty men being also killed there by the fall of a stack of straw.

Julian stayed three days only at Hierapolis, and then proceeded to Carrhæ in Mesopotamia, fourscore miles distant.

This is the last Epistle of his writing that is extant.

EPISTLES OF JULIAN.

Epistle XXVIII. To Duke Gregory *.

A SHORT letter from you is sufficient to give me great pleasure. Being much delighted therefore with what you have written, I return you many thanks. The love of our friends should be measured, not by the length of their epistles, but by the extent of their affection.

Epistle XXIX. To Alypius †, the Brother of Cæsarius.

SYLOSON ‡, it is said, came to Darius, reminded him of a cloak which he had formerly given him, and in return requested Samos. Darius

A. D.
361,
or 362.

---

* Though the military Counts and Dukes are frequently mentioned both in history and the codes, we must have recourse to the *Notitia* for the exact knowledge of their number and stations. The second of those appellations is only a corruption of the Latin word, which was indiscriminately applied to any military chief. All these provincial generals were therefore dukes.   GIBBON.

The Greek word is ηγεμων, which M. de la Bleterie translates *Commandant des troupes*.

† Among the friends of the Emperor (if the names of Emperor and of friend are not incompatible) the first place was assigned by Julian himself to the virtuous and learned Alypius. The humanity of Alypius was tempered by severe justice and manly fortitude; and while he exercised

his

Darius afterwards was much elated, thinking that he had returned a great present for a small one.

But

his abilities in the civil administration of Britain, he imitated, in his poetical compositions, the harmony and softness of the odes of Sappho. [See the next Epistle.] GIBBON.

‡ This minister, who is styled by Ammianus "a man of an amiable character," and who, like himself, was a native of Antioch, afterwards received from his master, just before he set out for the Persian war, the extraordinary commission to rebuild, in conjunction with the governor of the province, the temple of Jerusalem. But the attempt was defeated, as Ammianus, a Heathen and a contemporary, relates (XXIII. 1.), by a miraculous interposition, "dread-"full balls of fire (*metuendi globi flammarum*), breaking out "frequently near the foundations, and rendering the place "inaccessible to the scorched and blasted workmen." The truth of this miracle Mr. Gibbon questions, and even Dr. Lardner has doubted. The reasons adduced by the latter have been briefly mentioned, p. 62. "A philosopher (says Mr. G.) "may still require the original evidence of "impartial and intelligent spectators." But Ammianus also was "a philosopher," and therefore, no doubt, "required" and had the "original evidence" of his fellow soldiers, of his friend and countryman Alypius, in particular; and would not rashly have named him, and related a fact, which, if false, must have been immediately contradicted. In the reign of Valens, after having been long in a private station, Alypius and his son Hierocles, a youth of an excellent disposition, were both apprehended on a charge of poisoning. Alypius was deprived of his estate, and banished. And the son, when he was leading to execution, was happily saved. How is not mentioned. Amm. XXIX. 1. Yet Libanius (Ep. xxv. &c.) mentions this Hierocles as perishing in the earthquake at Nicomedia, in 358.

‡ Syloson was the brother of Polycrates, tyrant of Samos. See Herodotus, *l.* III. *c.* 140. and Ælian. *Var. Hist. l.* IV. *c.* 5. He gave his cloak at Memphis to Darius, when that prince was only one of the guards of Cambyses. Julian relates the same story in his IIId Oration.

"The

But Sylofon found it a woeful gift *. Compare my conduct with that of this prince. In one respect I have the advantage. I did not want to be reminded, but retained the remembrance of you unimpaired, and on the first opportunity that God gave me I ranked you, not among my second but my first friends. So much for the past.

As to the future, will you allow me (for I am a prophet) to predict? We shall be more successful, I doubt not, if Nemesis be propitious. For you need not a prince to assist you in destroying a city, but I require the assistance of many in re-building those that have been destroyed †. Such is the pleasantry of my Gallic and barbarous Muse ‡. Come with the auspices of the Gods.

P. S. *In his own hand-writing.*

" The cloak of Sylofon," (η Συλοσονlος χλαμυς) is adduced by Erasmus (*Chil.* p. 352.) as a proverb applied to " those " who boast and pride themselves on their dress." And (he adds) " it may be properly said of those to whom a small " gift, seasonably bestowed, returns with large interest;" and then relates, as the origin of it, the above story from Herodotus.

* Sylofon was put in possession of Samos, but the city being taken, it was pillaged by the Persians, so that he only reigned over a desert.   La Bleterie.

† This perhaps may allude to the forty cities in Gaul, which, Zosimus says, the Barbarians destroyed, and Julian rebuilt. See the Epistle to the Athenians, Vol. I. p. 84.

‡ Julian somewhere says, [Ep. LIV.] that his residence in Gaul had made him a Barbarian, so that he had almost forgotten Greek. He would have been sorry to have been taken at his word.   La Bleterie.

There is ready for you plenty of game, goats and sheep *, which we hunt in our winter-quarters. Come to a friend who loved you before he knew your worth.

Epistle XXX. To the same †.

I WAS just recovering from an indisposition, when I received the geography ‡ that you sent me, nor was the book less acceptable for coming from you. For it contains not only better descriptions than any book of the kind, but you have

---

* Ἄγις ἐρίφων καὶ τῆς ἐν τοῖς χειμαδίοις θήρας τῶν προβατίων.

This passage is obscure and perhaps corrupted. Does Julian mean to say that the winter did not allow hunting; and that there was nothing at his table but butcher's meat? But Julian was not fond of dainties, nor, as I recollect, of hunting. No more might Alypius. The meaning is, that the troops of Julian made incursions, during the winter, on the territories of the enemy, and carried off flocks and herds. If so, this Epistle must have been written in the Gauls before the absolute rupture between Julian and Constantius. Alypius might be then in Britain, where, we know, he was employed before the reign of Julian. *Britannias curaverat pro præfectis*, says Ammianus Marcellinus. LA BLETERIE.

Vice-præfect therefore, or vicar, was his proper title, Britain being one of the dioceses that were governed by a magistrate so named, subordinate to the Præfect of the Gauls.

† La Bleterie has neglected to translate this Epistle. It was probably addressed to Alypius, while he was governor of Britain. GIBBON.

‡ This geography seems to have been the composition of Alypius. Moreri says, " another geographical work " is also ascribed to him, which was a description of the " old world."

also embellished it with Iambics, not "singing a Bupalian * war," as the Cyrenean poet † expresses it, but such as fair Sappho would have thought worthy of adapting to her hymns. Such a work it may be proper perhaps for you to give, but certainly it is most agreeable to me to receive. With your administration of affairs, as you study to act, on all occasions, both with diligence and mildness, I am highly satisfied. For to blend lenity and moderation with fortitude and resolution, and to exert those in encouraging the good, and these in correcting the wicked, requires, I am confident, no small degree of genius and virtue.

May you have these objects always in view, and make both subservient to your own honour! The wisest of the ancients justly thought that this should be the end proposed by every virtue ‡. May health and happiness be your portion as long as possible, my most esteemed and beloved brother § !.

Epistle

* Bupalus, a statuary, made the image of the poet Hipponax, who was very deformed in person, in ridicule; which he resenting, wrote such severe Iambics against him, that he hanged himself. This was the common report, which Horace (Epod. v. 14.) seems to confirm. But Pliny (xxxvi. 5.) says, that report was false. Hipponax is reprobated by Julian in his Duties of a Priest, Vol. I. p. 132.

† Probably Callimachus, born, as Strabo says (*l.* xvii.) at Cyrene in Africa, in the reign of Ptolemy Philadelphus. Thence he is often styled " the Libyan bard." His hymns were translated by Dr. Dodd.

‡ Thus they made the entrance to the temple of Virtue the passage to that of Honour.

§ Little did Alypius imagine, while he was exercising his poetical and political talents in Britain, among a people

Epistle XXXI. To Bishop Ætius *.

A. D. 361.

ALL the rest who were banished by the late Constantius, on account of the madness of the Galileans, I have recalled. As to you, I not only remit your banishment, but, mindful of our old acquaintance, I also invite you hither. Use a public vehicle as far as my camp, and one supernumerary horse †.

---

as insensible to the charms of his poetry as their rocks and forests, that, in a distant age, when the Britons could have relished his verses, he would not have been known as a poet, and scarcely as a governor, eminent as he was in both those characters, had not this accidental billet been happily rescued from the gulph of time.

* A celebrated Arian prelate, who had been sent by Gallus to his brother Julian, while he was reader in the church of Nicomedia, to strengthen him in the Christian religion. See the Epistle from Gallus to Julian, Vol. I. p. 1.

The death of Gallus had been followed by the exile of Ætius, his divine and confident. He was made responsible for some of the faults of that unfortunate prince, and the demi-Arians accused him to Constantius as a very dangerous heresiarch. The rank of bishop, which is given him in the title of the above Epistle, must have been added by the transcribers. Ætius was not a bishop when Julian wrote to him. But he was soon after ordained by the bishops of his party, who then came to an open rupture with the demi-Arians. The credit which Ætius had with the Emperor, who presented him with an estate in the island of Lesbos, no doubt inspired the Anomeans, or pure Arians, with the boldness to complete their schism. It does not appear that Ætius, though a bishop, was ever fixed to any see.   LA BLETERIE.

† See note † on Epistle XX. p. 42.

Epistle

Epistle XXXII. To the Sophist Lucian.

I WRITE, that I may be entitled to an answer. If I offend you by the frequency of my letters, give me, I intreat you, the same offence *.

Epistle XXXIII. To Dositheus †.

I COULD scarce refrain from tears, and with reason, when I heard your name mentioned, recollecting your ‡ beloved, noble, and in every respect excellent father; whom if you imitate, you will be happy, and, like him, render your life honourable; but if you are indolent, you will grieve me, and disgrace yourself, for being useless to the world.

* The length of this letter could not offend. Many scraps, equally insignificant, from Pope, were treasured up by his friend Richardson. But, *le jeu ne vaut pas la chandelle*.

† Dositheus is mentioned by Libanius, in his cxxxIst Epistle, and a short Epistle to him from that sophist is preserved (in Latin) by Zambicari.

‡ In the printed editions it is ημων, a mistake surely for υμων. Julian could scarce remember his own father.

Epistle

Epistle XXXIV.   To the Philosopher
JAMBLICHUS *.

IT was sufficient for Ulysses to say to his son, in order to check his high opinion of him, No God am I; for heaven reserve that name †. But I cannot think myself a man, as the saying is, while I am absent from Jamblichus. I will allow myself, however, to be your admirer, like that father of Telemachus, and though some perhaps may think it unbecoming, that shall not prevent my loving you. For I know that many who have

---

* This Jamblichus must not be confounded with another of the same name, who was more ancient (see p. 70. note †.) This was the disciple of Edesius. Julian has addressed six Epistles to him, [XXXIV, XL, XLI, LIII, LX, LXI.] which I have not translated. To these Epistles in particular may be applied what M. Fleury says, in general, of those which are addressed to the sophists, *Elles sont pleines des louanges outrées, et d'un empressement qui marque plus de légèreté que d'affection.*   LA BLETERIE.

Mr. Dodwell (*Exerc. de Pythag. ætate*) suspects the authenticity of these Epistles, " because they treat on very " trifling subjects, more worthy of a sophist than a prince, " and shew a greater attention to style than becomes even " a philosopher." As to his argument drawn from a mistake in chronology, in regard to Sopater, that may easily be obviated by supposing there were also two of that name, as Julian seems to intimate   See note †. on Ep. XXVII. p. 70. Libanius has addressed seven Epistles to this younger Jamblichus, of which one is preserved by Fabricius, Bibliotheca Græca, vol. IV. p. 384.

† Odyss. XVI. 187. Broome, 222.

admired

admired fine statues, far from detracting from the praise of the artist, have by their passion for them added fresh honour to the work. As to your humorously ranking me among the ancient sages, that I am far distant from them is as certain as that you are one of them. But you unite not only Pindar, and Democritus, and the most ancient Orpheus, but almost all the Greeks, who are said to have gained the summit of philosophy, as the various notes of vocal and instrumental music combine in a perfect concert. And as Argus, who guarded Io, is described by the poets as surrounded with eyes, so you, the genuine guardian of virtue, are enlightened by eloquence with the pure eyes of learning. It is said, that Proteus, the Ægyptian, assumed various forms, fearing lest he should inadvertently appear wise to those who questioned him *. But as Proteus was really wise, and, as Homer says, had much knowledge, I praise him for his knowledge; but I do not admire his virtue, as he acted not like a benevolent being, but an impostor, in concealing himself to avoid being useful to mankind. But who, my noble friend, does not admire you, not only for equalling Proteus in wisdom, but also for never invidiously withholding from any one that virtue and perfect knowledge, which you possess, of all things excellent? Thus, like the splendid sun, the radiance of your wisdom enlightens all, both by

* See Virg. Georg. IV. and Ovid. Metam. XI.

instructing the present, and by your writings, as far as possible, improving the absent. In this you excell even the illustrious Orpheus, since he wasted his music in the solace of brutes, but you, as if born for the good of mankind, imitate the hand of Æsculapius, and every where diffuse your eloquent and salutary precepts. So that Homer, I think, if he were to return to life, might with much more reason apply that line to you,

— One still living traverses the world *.

For to those who are of ancient stamp, to us in particular, a certain sacred spark, as it were, of true and fertile learning is by you alone rekindled and revived. And, O Jupiter the Preserver, and eloquent Mercury, grant, in return, that, for the general good of mankind, the life of the excellent Jamblichus may be prolonged to the utmost extent! If for Homer, Plato †, and all that are worthy of their society, just vows were of old suc-

---

* Homer. Odyss. iv. 198. Proteus speaking of Ulysses to Menelaus,

Εις δ' ἔτι που ζωος κατερυκεται ευρει ποντω,

Otherwise, ευρει κοσμω.

Not so well. For the word κοσμος does not occur in Homer in that sense.   CLARKE.

This various reading may perhaps rest on no better foundation than the above passage of Julian, in which his insertion of κοσμω may be accidental, by his quoting (as usual) from memory, or intentional, as better suiting his purpose.

† The Latin translator has added " Socrates," but without any authority from the original; and indeed Julian would hardly have mentioned him on this occasion, as his life, though in an advanced age, was shortened by violence, and the prayers of the virtuous were therefore in that respect unsuccessful.

cessfully

cefsfully offered, and their lives were thus prolonged, why should not a contemporary of ours, their equal both in virtue and eloquence, be transmitted by similar vows to the extremest old age, and endowed with every blessing?

Epistle XXXV. For the ARGIVES *.

IN favour of the city of the Argives much may be said by any one who would celebrate their actions ancient and modern. Of the glory acquired at Troy they are justly entitled to the greatest share †, as are the Lacedæmonians and Athe-

---

* The Argives being oppressed by the Corinthians, and subjected to new exactions, contrary to law, Julian recommends them, as I imagine, to the Pro-consul, saying it was unjust that a city, so flourishing of old, and, on account of the expence of the sacred games, exempted from taxes, should pay a tribute to Corinth towards the amphitheatral sports. Corinth was made a Roman colony by Augustus, who, at the desire of Julius Cæsar, raised that city from ruins. Under this title she claimed authority over several cities that were not colonies. That this was not an edict of the Emperor, but a petition of Julian, then a private man, appears by an observation made in a subsequent note. PETAU.

This Epistle, which illustrates the declining state of Greece, is omitted by the Abbé de la Bleterie.

The eloquence of Julian was interposed, most probably with success, in behalf of a city which had been the royal seat of Agamemnon, and had given to Macedonia a race of kings and conquerors. GIBBON.

† It seems strange that he should ascribe the greatest share in the Trojan war to the Argives, in the same manner as he does afterwards to the Lacedemonians and Athenians.

Athenians afterwards. For though both those wars were waged by all Greece, of praise, as well as of cares and labours, the generals may claim a large proportion. But these are of ancient date. After the return of the Heraclidæ, the birth-right taken from the eldest [*], the colony sent from thence into Macedonia, and the constant preservation of the city, free and independent, from the neighbouring Lacedæmonians, were proofs of no moderate or

For they attempted nothing afterwards against the Trojans; but by the appellation of "Trojan" he means some other expeditions which were undertaken by the Greeks against the Persians, as if Τρωικα were the same as Βαρβαρικα.

PETAU.

Agamemnon, the " king of men," was king of Argos (in Achaia), as well as of Mycenæ, but is not so styled by Homer in his catalogue of the ships, the troops of Argos being there subdivided from those of Mycenæ, and led by Diomed, acting as their general under Agamemnon. "Di-"omed" (as Mr. Wodhull observes, in his notes on the Orestes of Euripides), "though he derived his title of "king from Ætolia, never possessed that throne, but re-"sided chiefly at Argos (about six miles only from My-"cenæ), till he settled in Italy. Euripides, it has been "observed, perpetually confounds those two cities."

[*] Temenus. The origin of the Macedonian kingdom was derived from the Argives by Caranus (their first king), brother to Phidon, king of the Argives. On which account, he says, the ancestors of Philip and Alexander sprung from Argos.

PETAU.

This pedigree from Temenus and Hercules may be suspicious, yet it was allowed, after a strict enquiry, by the judges of the Olympic games (Herod. *l. v. c.* 22.) at a time when the Macedonian kings were obscure and unpopular in Greece. When the Achaian league was declared against Philip, it was thought decent that the deputies of Argos should retire. GIBBON.

common

common fortitude. Actions similar to those of the Macedonians against the Persians may also be ascribed to this city; as this was the country of the latter ancestors of Philip and Alexander. In later times it obeyed the Romans, not as a vassal, but rather as an ally; and, I think, partook with the rest of the freedom and other privileges which the Emperors have always indulged to the cities of Greece. But now the Corinthians *, prone to oppression, compell that city, which is annexed to theirs (for thus it should properly be expressed) by the reigning city †, to be tributary to them; and this innovation, it is said, they have now

---

* Argos, he says, was made tributary to Corinth by the authority of the reigning city, because when the Achaians were subdued by Mummius, and Corinth destroyed, all Greece, being assessed under the name of Achaia, received a magistrate from the Romans, who, under the Emperors, was styled a Pro-consul, and resided at Corinth, which was therefore the metropolis of Achaia, nay of Peloponnesus, and consequently of all Greece. See Pausanias, *in Achaicis, p.* 222. and Pliny, *Ep. ult. l.* VIII. Seven years before Julian wrote this Epistle, the Corinthians had begun to exact a tribute from the Argives towards their wild beasts and hunting-matches. PETAU.

† Rome. Julian gives her the same appellation in his 1st Oration, p. 5. Eunapius, who flourished after the death of Julian, styles her η Βασιλευσα Ρωμη, in his Prohæresius. Themistius, though he was ambassador from Constantinople to Constantius at Rome, in his IId Oration, p. 41. styles the one "the queen of cities," and the other "the second." For the same reason, Rome is represented on ancient coins, and those struck even under Constantine or his sons, as a woman sitting, and holding a globe in her right hand. SPANHEIM.

practised for seven years, not considering that Delphi and Elis are by agreement exempted from tribute on account of their celebrating the sacred games. For since there are, as is well known, four great and most illustrious games in Greece, the Eleans furnish and direct the Olympic, the Delphians the Pythian, the Corinthians the Isthmian, and the Argives the Nemean. Why then should those retain the exemptions formerly granted, and these, who, on account of the like expences, were formerly exempted, or perhaps not taxed originally, now be deprived of a privilege with which they were once honoured? Besides, Elis and Delphi *, for those highly celebrated games every fifth year, are used to contribute only once; but at Argos there are two Nemean, as there are two Isthmian at Corinth. And at this time also two other games

---

* The Olympic and Pythian games were celebrated once in five years; the Nemean and Isthmian, twice. For the Nemean were kept at the beginning of the first, and, in like manner, at the close of the third year; the one being in winter, and the other in summer. Besides the two Nemean, the Herean also were defrayed by the Argives. Four solemnities therefore, in the whole, were exhibited by them, on which account they ought justly to have been exempted from tribute. PETAU.

The first institutor of the Olympic games is unknown, though it is generally supposed to have been Pelops. They were consecrated to Jupiter, and were performed in the neighbourhood of Olympia, in the district of Pisa. The Pythian were celebrated at Delphi in honour of Apollo; the Nemean at Nemea, in Peloponnesus, in honour of Hercules; and the Isthmian in the Isthmus of Corinth, in honour of Neptune.

are

are added to those at Argos, so that there are four games in four years. Is it proper then that those who exhibit them only once should be exempted, and that these who exhibit them four times at home should be obliged to contribute to others, especially as they are not ancient nor accustomed in Greece? For the Corinthians do not require these large sums for the support of gymnastic or musical performances; but for hunting-matches, which they often exhibit in the theatres, purchasing, for that purpose, bears and panthers; an expence which they easily defray by means of their wealth and large revenues; and as many others contribute also towards it, they reap the advantage of their own institution. But do not the Argives, who are extremely indigent, by thus being made to contribute to a foreign entertainment in another country, suffer unjustly and illegally, and in a manner unsuitable to the ancient power and glory of their city? And as they are neighbours, they ought on that account to be more esteemed, if that saying be true,

" —— Bad must be your neighbours,
" If an ox perish *."

But

---

* Ουδ' αν βυς απολοιο, ει μη δια κακιαν γειτονων.
Taken from one of the moral maxims of Hesiod,
Ουδ' αν βυς απολοιτ', ει μη γειτων κακος ειη.
Works and Days, ver. 346.
A corresponding Latin proverb occurs in Plautus:
— *Verum illud verbum esse experior vetus,*
Aliquid mali esse propter vicinum mal·*m.*
Mercator, Act. IV. Sc. 4. 31.
Juvenal

But the Argives do not bring this charge against the Corinthians through their solicitude for one ox only, but for many and great expences with which they are unjustly burthened. The Corinthians might also be asked, whether they would choose to adhere to the ancient laws of Greece, or adopt those which they have since received from the reigning city? For if they approve the majesty of the ancient laws, the Argives are no more bound to pay tribute to the Corinthians, than the Corinthians are to pay it to the Argives. But if the Corinthians adopt the modern laws, and, because they are made a Roman colony, contend that they

---

Juvenal, in his XVIth Satire, ver. 36. expresses his apprehension of similar dangers from bad neighbours:

—— *Convallem ruris aviti*
Improbus, aut campum mihi si vicinus ademit,
Et sacrum effodit medio de limite saxum.

If any rogue vexatious suits advance
Against me for my known inheritance,
Enter by violence my fruitful grounds,
Or take my sacred land-mark from my bounds.
                                             DRYDEN.

Many other parallel passages might be adduced both from the Latin and Greek writers.

I am indebted for this note to a writer in the Gentleman's Magazine for 1783, p. 215.

Similar humanity to animals and good neighbourhood are inculcated in the Levitical law. *Thou shalt not see thy brother's ox or his sheep go astray, and hide thyself from them: thou shalt in any case bring them again unto thy brother. Thou shalt not see thy brother's ass or his ox fall down by the way, and hide thyself from them: thou shalt surely help him to lift them up again.* Deut. XXII. 1, 4. &c.

have

have the dominion over Argos, we will humbly intreat them not to be more assuming than their fathers, nor to new model, or subvert, to the detriment of their neighbours, those customs which their ancestors with sound judgement observed, relying on the decree which they lately obtained, and meanly taking advantage of the ignorance of the advocate who pleaded for the Argives *. For if this cause had been removed out of Greece, the Corinthians would have had much less influence, and its merits, discussed by many skilful advocates, would have been more apparent; on which account it is probable, that the judge, abashed by the established dignity of Argos, would have made a just decree. Concerning the rights of the city, if you will only hear the orators, and they may be allowed to speak, you shall be acquainted with the cause from the beginning, and, from their arguments may form a judgement of the whole. On what is said, that we ought not to credit those who are sent hither as petitioners †, it may now be proper to add a few words.

---

* In the reign of Constantius this dispute between the Corinthians and Argives had been litigated, and the latter lost their cause through the inexperience of their advocate in law-affairs. PETAU.

† It appears from this passage that Julian, then a private man, had been requested by the Argives to use his interest with the pro-consul of Achaia in their behalf: otherwise he would have commanded with authority, instead of presenting a petition; as he himself would have put an end to the dispute. *Ibid.*

EPISTLES OF JULIAN.

If there are any philosophers in these times, Diogenes and Lamprias are such. They decline the legislative and lucrative offices of the state; but if their country wants their assistance, they serve her to the utmost of their abilities; when the city is in any emergency, they plead causes, assist in the government, engage in embassies, and liberally expend their money, thus confuting by their conduct the scandalous aspersions on philosophy, and disproving that vulgar notion, that those who study philosophy, are useless to their country. For their country employs them in those functions, and they endeavour to defend the cause of justice by our assistance; but we employ yours.

All that remains for the defence and safety of the oppressed is the appointment of a judge both willing and able to make a just decree. If either of these be wanting, if he be either mistaken or unfaithful, justice must absolutely perish. But though we should have a judge agreeable to our wishes, we have not the liberty of speaking *, as we have not appealed; this, they request, may first be allowed them, and that the indolence of him who then pleaded for the city, and managed her cause, may not entail such a burthen on posterity. Nor can there be any impropriety in granting a new trial. It is sometimes expedient to forego

---

* The advocate of the Argives, when he lost the former cause, neleted to appeal; therefore the city could not bring a new action, nor demand another trial. PETAU.

some present advantages and opportunities, for the sake of future security. And as life is short, they wish to pass that short space with tranquillity. But that the cause should sink before the judgement-seat, and be transmitted to posterity undetermined, is dreadful; so that, the hazard being so great, it seems better to accept half the advantage, than, by contending, to lose the whole. But those immortal cities, unless a just decree be made, and their mutual animosities terminated, must necessarily be at perpetual variance. For enmity gains strength by time.

I have said *, as the orators express themselves. May justice direct your determination!

---

* Εἰρῆται ὡς πρὸς λόγος, analogous to *Dixi*, in Latin.

Epistle

Epistle XXXVI. To Porphyry*.

THE library of George was large and copious †. It was stocked with books of philosophy of all kinds, and with many of history; on other subjects not a few; and with various writings of the Galileans. Examine therefore carefully the whole, and send it to Antioch. Be assured, that, unless you make a diligent scrutiny, you shall be severely fined; and as to those who are in the least suspected of having secreted any of these books, if you cannot induce them, by all kinds of arguments, and adjurations, and in particular by putting their slaves to the torture, let them be compelled by force to restore them all ‡.

---

* Treasurer-general of Ægypt. Libanius mentions him in one of his Epistles as an excellent friend; and says, that he was calumniated and oppressed by two Ægyptians, a race " more savage than all the wild beasts of Libya."

† See Epistles IX. and X.

‡ This is by no means an instance of cruelty in Julian. A considerable robbery had been committed, and of property much more valuable than it is at present. The Romans, on the slightest suspicions, put their slaves to the torture.   La Bleterie.

EPISTLES OF JULIAN.

Epistle XXXVII. To Amerius *.

YOUR letter, in which you mention the death of your wife, and express your extreme affliction, filled my eyes with tears. Painful would it have been to hear that any wife, young, chaste, and engaging, and also an excellent mother, was prematurely snatched away; but that you have sustained such a loss gives me peculiar concern. For, of all my friends, Amerius least deserved such a calamity; a man whose understanding is superior to most, a man whom I highly esteem.

If I were writing on this subject to any other person, I should be more prolix in telling him that such is the lot of human nature, that submission

---

* I know not that this man of letters, apparently a sophist and a Pagan, is elsewhere mentioned. One MS. styles him "Himerius." We are acquainted with a celebrated professor of that name, the rival and the collegue of Prohæresius, and who, like him, taught eloquence at Athens when Julian was there. Himerius left some discourses, of which there are some extracts in the Bibliotheca of Photius. It might be supposed that this Epistle was addressed to him, if the MS did not style him " Præfect of Ægypt."
In the reign of Julian that province was governed by Ecdicius; and this Epistle is certainly written to one who was a teacher: but it might not be impossible for the title of Præfect to be here no more than an honorary title. In those times honorary titles of the greatest employments were sometimes given to men of letters. I would not venture, however, to assert, they had that of governor of any particular province. La Bleterie.

is necessary, that the most poignant grief admits of consolation *, and, in short, should use, as to a novice, all the arguments that are likely to alleviate affliction. But as I am ashamed of employing to one who instructs others those arguments which are used to teach and improve the ignorant, waving every thing else, I will relate to you a fable, or rather a true story, of a certain wise man, not new perhaps to you, but probably unknown to many, whose only medicine, mirth, you will find as effectual a remedy for sorrow as that cup † which the fair Lacedæmonian is supposed, on a similar occasion, to have given to Telemachus.

It is reported, that Democritus ‡ of Abdera, finding nothing that he said could console Darius for

---

* Thus the three remedies which Pliny prescribes are, "Length of time, the necessity of submission, and satiety of grief."

† In the IVth book of the Odyssey, ver. 220, &c. when Menelaus gives an entertainment to Telemachus, Helen puts into the wine a drug which had the virtue to induce an oblivion of the most cruel anxieties.   LA BLETERIE.
Julian refers to the same passage in his Consolatory Oration, Vol. I. p. 32, where it is quoted in the notes.

‡ Demonax comforted Herod the philosopher under affliction by a similar fable, as Lucian relates in his life.
PETAU.
This story is no where found. Though Democritus had travelled into Persia, and was acquainted with the secrets of magism, his discourse with Darius has all the appearance of being only a philosophical novel. At the time of the death of Darius, the son of Hystaspes, Democritus was, at most, 28 years old; perhaps he was no more than

for the loss of a beautiful wife, promised to restore her to life, if the king would supply him with all things necessary for the purpose. Darius ordered him to spare no expence, but to take whatever was requisite to perform his promise. Soon after, Democritus told him, that " every thing was " ready for the completion of the work, one only " excepted, which he knew not how to procure; " but that Darius, as he was king of all Asia, " would perhaps find no difficulty in providing " it." On his asking what this important matter was, Democritus is said to have replied, " If you " will inscribe on the tomb of your wife the names " of three who have never known affliction, she " shall immediately return to life, this ceremony " being irresistible *." Darius hesitating, and not being able to recollect any one who had not experienced some sorrow, Democritus laughed, as usual, and said to him, " And are not you, the ab- " surdest of men, ashamed still to lament, as if

23, or even nine. This philosopher was on his return to Greece, when Darius II. surnamed Nothus, ascended the throne, in the year before Christ, 423.   LA BLETERIE.
See Vol. I. p. 21. note †.

* It is in the Greek Ευθυς αυτην αναβιωσεσθαι τω της τελευτης νομω δυσωπουμενη, which Martinius has translated thus: *Illam ab inferis esse redituram; fore enim ut ejus mortis consuetudine erubesceret.* I think that it may be restored by leaving out a single letter. Instead of της τελευτης, we should read της τελετης, and translate it, *fore ut statim revivisceret, ejus ceremoniæ ritu exorata.* The word δυσωπισθαι signifies not only " to blush, to be ashamed," but also, " to suffer oneself " to be persuaded, to be moved."   *Ibid.*

" you

"you alone were involved in such distress, when you cannot find one that ever lived exempt from some domestic misfortune?"

That Darius, an illiterate Barbarian, a slave both to joy and grief, should be told this, was highly proper; but you, a Greek, who cultivate true literature, should learn from yourself to govern your passions. For it is shameful that reason should not anticipate the certain effects of time *.

Epistle XXXVIII. To the Philosopher Maximus †.

A. D. 360.

MY ideas crowd so fast upon me, that they choak my utterance, some hindering the passage of others. Whether this be frigidity, or any thing else, you will determine. But let me now arrange them in order, and first return my

---

* If Julian had read the Latin authors (and why should he not have read, at least, some of them?) I should say that he has copied this passage of the letter of Servius Sulpicius to Cicero: *Nullus dolor est quem non longinquitas temporis minuat atque molliat. Hoc te expectare tempus turpe est, ac non ei rei tuâ sapientiâ te occurrere.* La Bleterie.

† This Epistle was written in Illyricum at the time when Julian was preparing to march against Constantius.
Ibid.

Among the philosophers, Maximus obtained an eminent rank in the friendship of his royal disciple, who communicated, with unreserved confidence, his actions, his sentiments, and his religious designs, during the anxious suspence of the civil war. Gibbon.

See the first note on Epistle XV. p. 29.

EPISTLES OF JULIAN.

thanks to the Gods, whose goodness still allows me to write *, and perhaps will permit us to meet.

When I was first made Emperor (the Gods know, and I, as far as possible, declared to them, with what reluctance), I was waging war against the Barbarians. After passing three months in that service, as I was returning to Gaul, I looked round, and enquired of those who came from thence whether any philosopher, any scholar, or any one clad in a woollen coat or cloak, had arrived there. At length I approached Vesontio †. This small town, now rebuilt, was formerly a large city, adorned with magnificent temples, and fortified both by strong walls and its natural situation, being surrounded by the river Dubis ‡, and elevated, as if in the sea, on a high rock, almost inaccessible even to the birds, except where an isthmus joins it to the continent. Near this town I met a Cynic philosopher, with his cloak and staff.

---

* It is probable that Julian, after his taking the title of Augustus, wrote seldom to Maximus, for fear of embroiling that philosopher, who dwelt in Ionia, or Greece, and consequently under the dominion of Constantius.

LA BLETERIE.

† Now Besançon, the capital of Franche-Comté. Julian passed through this town, which had suffered severely from the fury of the Barbarians, after his fourth expedition beyond the Rhine, A. D. 360, in his way to Vienne, where he fixed his head-quarters for the ensuing winter. See Ammianus, xx. 10. Of the citadel of Vesontio, on a high mountain, see Cæsar, de bell. Gall. *l.* 1. F. Martinius translates it "*Danubius*."

‡ Now the Doux.

At a distance I thought it was you *, and on his nearer approach I imagined that he came from you. He proved to be also a friend of mine, but not such as I hoped and expected. He was useful to me therefore in one instance only, that of giving me reason to conclude that your anxiety on my account had prevented your leaving Greece. Witness Jupiter, witness great Sun, witness Minerva, and all ye Gods and Goddesses, how much, in my return from Illyricum to Gaul, I trembled for you! And I enquired of the Gods, not that I dared myself (for I was not able † to see or hear any thing of the situation in which you then might be), but I entrusted that office to others. The Gods clearly shewed, that some troubles would befall you, but that nothing terrible should ensue, nor any wicked device prevail.

I omit, you observe, many important events. You are chiefly interested to know how soon we experienced the manifest assistance of the Gods, and

---

* This clearly shews that Maximus was of the sect of the Cynics. A Cynic was as vain of his staff and cloak as if he had been decked with all the ornaments of dress. But this Maximus must be distinguished from another Cynic of the same name, under the Emperor Theodosius, who was of Alexandria. BARONIUS.

† He means the danger to which Maximus was exposed under Constantius, and affirms, that he did not venture himself to consult the Gods concerning him, lest he should be compelled to hear some inauspicious tidings, as was highly probable. PETAU.

After this, can there be a doubt of Julian's belief in theurgy? LA BLETERIE.

escaped

escaped such a multitude of traitors, killing none and spoiling none, but only imprisoning those who were apprehended in the very fact *.

These things perhaps it might have been better to speak than to write. I am certain, however, that they will give you pleasure. We worship the Gods publickly, and all the troops that are returning with me profess the true religion. We openly sacrifice oxen. We have made our grateful acknowledgments to the Gods in several hecatombs †. They command me to restore their worship with the utmost purity ‡. Most willingly I obey them. They promise me great rewards, if I am not remiss. Euägrius § is arrived.

* Soon after Julian was proclaimed Augustus, an eunuch, suborned by the partisans of Constantius, attempted to assassinate him. Julian pardoned him. We learn from hence, that this was not the only conspiracy which threatened his life. *Ibid.*

† The legions of Gaul devoted themselves to the faith, as well as to the fortunes, of their victorious leader; and, even before the death of Constantius, he had the satisfaction of announcing to his friends, that they assisted, with fervent devotion, and voracious appetite, at the sacrifices, which were repeatedly offered in his camp, of whole hecatombs of fat oxen. " So that the soldiers," says Ammianus (xxii. 12.) " living grossly on fat meat, and " greedy of drink, were carried through the streets on the " shoulders of passers-by, from the public-houses.... " to their quarters." The devout prince, and the indignant historian describe the same scene; and in Illyricum, or Antioch, similar causes must have produced similar effects. GIBBON.

‡ He had no doubt of his being raised up by the Gods to be the restorer of Paganism. LA BLETERIE.

§ See the first note on Epistle XLVI.

Epistle XXXIX. To the same.

WELCOME the coming, speed the parting guest *.
Such is the law of the wise Homer. But our friendship is superior to that of hospitality, being founded on learning and religion. So that no one could justly charge me with transgressing this law of Homer, if I should think proper to detain you longer with me. But as, I see, your diminutive frame † requires more attention, I allow you to go into your own country ‡, and have provided for the convenience of your journey, by giving you the use of a public carriage. May Æsculapius, and all the Gods, conduct you, and bring you safely back to us again!

---

* This is said by Menelaus (Odyss. xv. 74.) when Telemachus, after visiting him at Lacedæmon, was going to take his leave. LA BLETERIE.
Pope, 84. He has adopted this line in his imitation of the 2d satire of the 1st book of Horace. Thus also Theocritus, Idyll. xvi. 27. as translated by Fawkes:
With prudent hospitality they spend,
And kindly greeting speed the parting friend.

† Σωμάτιον, corpusculum. As from ἀνθρωπίσκος, homuncio, applied to Athanasius in Epistle LI. it has been inferred, that the primate of Ægypt was a little man, the same conclusion perhaps may be drawn from the above expression in regard to Maximus; though, in this instance, the diminutive is a term of affection, and, in the other, of contempt.

‡ Ephesus. Maximus probably took this journey while the Emperor was at Constantinople. LA BLETERIE.

Epistle XL. To Jamblichus *.

I AM so sensible of the good-nature with which you blame me, that I think myself equally honoured by your letters, and instructed by your reproofs. But were I conscious of the least failure of attention to you, I would certainly endeavour, if possible, to palliate the fault, or I would not scruple to ask your pardon, especially as I know that, whenever your friends indiscreetly violate the laws of friendship, you are not implacable. Now then (since negligence, or indolence, generally prevents my accomplishing what I ardently desire), ascend, as it were, a tribunal, while I plead my cause before you, and shew that I did not treat you with impropriety, or act with tardiness or neglect.

Three years ago I left Pannonia †, with difficulty escaping those snares and dangers of which you are well apprised. But when I had crossed the Chalcedonian strait ‡, and approached the city of Nicomedia §, to you first, as to the God of my country, I paid due offerings for my safety, by sending you a message as a token of my approach,

A. D. 363.

---
* See the first note on Epistle XXXIV.
† Now Hungary.
‡ Now the Bosphorus.
§ This city was then in ruins by an earthquake, which happened in 358. See a note on an epistle of Libanius, vol. I. p. 304. and his Monody on that event, in this vol.

or a kind of sacred present. The letter was consigned to the care of one of the Imperial guards, by name Julian, the son of Bacchylus, a native of Apamea *, to whom I the more readily entrusted it, as he was going thither, and declared that he knew you perfectly well. After this, I received, as from Apollo, a sacred epistle from you, expressing that you had heard with pleasure of my arrival. Wise Jamblichus, and a letter from Jamblichus, were to me a happy omen, and the dawning of good hopes. Need I say how much I rejoiced, and how greatly I was affected by your letter? For if you have received what I wrote on that subject (which was sent to you by one of the letter-carriers that came from thence), you certainly know the great satisfaction that it gave me. And again, when the man who nursed my children † returned home, I sent you another letter,

in

---

* The metropolis of Phrygia.

† Τω τροφιμω των ιμαυτε παιδων. M. de Tillemont, who takes in its most rigorous sense that suspicious passage in the Misopogon (p. 244.) in which Julian ironically urges the reproach of the people of Antioch, that "he almost always (ὡς ἐπιπαν) lay alone," and considers it as a confession that Julian himself makes of his incontinence, observes, in order to strengthen this pretended confession, that Julian, in this Epistle (which is one of those that I have not translated), speaks of " the man who had nursed his children." "Now," says M. de Tillemont, " he never had any le-
" gitimate, except a son who perished by the wickedness
" of the midwife, whom the Empress Eusebia, the wife of
" Constantius, had suborned. The fact is certain, there-
" fore he had some illegitimate."

But

in which I expressed my acknowledgments for your former, and also requested a repetition of the favour. Afterwards the distinguished Sopater * came to us on an embassy, and, as I knew him, I instantly sprung forward to embrace him, and shed

> But we must not conclude from this passage, as M. de Tillemont does, that there was actually a man who was charged with the care of the children of Julian. Helena had a son. After her first lying-in, she never went her full time. But at every pregnancy a nurse was provided. The same perhaps was frequently chosen. It was probably the husband of that nurse whom Julian styles " the nurse " of his children." I say probably, because a number of other plausible reasons may be supposed for Julian's having given some one that name. Who knows, for instance, but that it was a man whom he had destined for the care of the children that he hoped to have? Whether he did not cause some children that did not belong to him to be educated with the tenderness of a father? Or whether it was not a joke which Jamblichus perfectly understood?
> LA BLETERIE.
> When Julian speaks of " the tutor of his children," who is not named, the expression must be understood figuratively. For Julian had no children, legitimate or illegitimate. Historians are quite silent about them, excepting that one which he had by his wife Helena, who was not suffered to live. If Julian had any children out of lawful marriage, and therefore illegitimate, can it be supposed that Christian writers would have been silent about it ? By no means. Eumenius, in his Panegyric, recommends to Constantine not only his five children of whom he was the parent, but his other children likewise, as he calls them, whom he had educated for the bar or the court. In some such figurative sense Julian must be understood. He intends some young persons under his special care. LARDNER.

* See Epistle XXVII. p. 70. note †. That this was the same Sopater who entertained Julian afterwards at Hierapolis, though probable, I cannot affirm.

tears of joy, dreaming of nothing but you and a letter from you. As soon as I received it, I kissed it, held it to my eyes, and strained it close, as if I had feared, that, while I was reading it, the features of your face should secretly escape me. I immediately wrote an answer, not only to you, but to the excellent Sopater, his son, telling him, in joke, that I had accepted a common friend from Apamea as an hostage for your absence.

From that time to the date of my present writing, I have received no letter from you, but that, in which you seem to chide me. If by this appearance of a charge you mean only to urge me to write, I accept the whole charge with the utmost joy, and the very letter which I have now received I deem the highest favour. But, if you really accuse me of having given you the least offence, who can be more miserable, than I in having been prevented by the negligence of letter-carriers from giving you the satisfaction that I wish? However, though I were not to write very frequently, I might justly claim your indulgence, not on account of the business in which I am engaged (for I am not such a wretch as not to prefer you, as Pindar says, to all my affairs *); but, because there is more

---

* Ἀσχολίας ἁπάσης τὰ καλὰ σὲ κρεῖττον ἡγεῖσθαι. The sense, but not the words, of Pindar.

———— τὶν τίοι, χρυσάσπι Θήβα,
Πρᾶγμα καὶ ἀσχολίας ὑπέρτερον
Θήσομαι ———— Isthm. I. 1.

Your business, golden-shielded Thebes,
To all my own I willingly prefer.

wisdom

wisdom, in being loth to write to such a man as you, who cannot be recollected without veneration, than in being too presumptuous. For as those who venture to gaze stedfastly on the light of the sun, unless they are in a manner divine, and can behold his rays like the genuine off-spring of eagles*, cannot see what is unlawful to be seen†, and the more they endeavour it, the weaker are their efforts; so he, who presumes to write to you, clearly shews that the bolder he is, the more he ought to fear. But you, distinguished sage, who I may say, were created for the total preservation of Gentilism, judged right in sending me frequent letters, and thus, as far as possible, checking my indolence. For as the sun (again to compare you with that deity), when he shines perfectly bright, with full radiance, is regardless whether all the objects that he illuminates perform their respective functions with propriety‡; you, in like manner, should liberally diffuse the light of your knowledge among all the Gentiles, and not secrete it because fear or modesty prevents your hearers from making a reply. Æsculapius does not heal diseases from interested motives, but every where displays his humanity, like a kind of doctrine. You, being the physician of noble souls,

* See Epistle XVI. p. 31.

† Ουδε α μη θεμις οφθηναι Not unlike St. Paul, α ουκ εξον ανθρωπω λαλησαι, *not lawful for a man to utter*: 2 Cor. xii. 4.

‡ This passage in the original being corrupted and mutilated, I can only guess at the meaning.

I   should

should do the same, and in every thing observe the precepts of virtue; like a good archer, who, though he has no adversary, always exercises his art against a proper opportunity. Our views are not the same, as we wish to enjoy your auspicious letters, and you to receive ours. But we, though we should write a thousand times, resemble the playful children in Homer, who erect clay-buildings on the shore, and then soon overwhelm them with sand *: While your letter, however short, is preferable to the most copious stream. And in truth, I had rather possess one epistle of Jamblichus than all the gold of Lydia.

If you have any regard for your friends (and some regard you have, or I am much mistaken); do not neglect us, who, like poultry, are always in want of your sustenance; but write frequently, and forbear not to nourish us with your good cheer. And if we have been deficient, discharge at once two friendly offices, that of writing to us, and also of writing for us. For such a pupil of eloquent Mercury as you are, should employ his rod, not in exciting, but in banishing and dispelling sleep, and in this particular, above all, let him be your model.

* Il. XV. 362, where the poet describes the Grecian turrets nodding, and the bulwarks falling, when shaken by Apollo;

Easy, as when ashore, the infant † stands,
And draws imagin'd houses in the sands,
The sportive wanton, pleas'd with some new play,
Sweeps the slight works and fashion'd domes away.

POPE.

† Julian, quoting by memory, substitutes παιδὸς for παις.

Epistle

Epistle XLI. To the same.

IN obedience to the Delphic oracle, we should have known ourselves, and not presumed to stun the ears of a sage like you, whose very looks it is difficult to encounter, much more to contend with him in genius, as he combines all the powers of philosophic harmony. Every musician, Aristæus * not excepted, must yield to Pan, when he breathes sweet melody; and when Apollo warbles to his lyre, all, though they had the musical powers of Orpheus, would be silent. Conscious, as we are, of our own inferiority, it is just that the less should submit to the greater. But he who would put human in competition with divine harmony must be unacquainted with the catastrophe of Marsyas † the Phrygian, and with the river named from him, which flows as a punishment to the mad musician.

---

* The son of Apollo by Cyrene, the daughter of Peneus, king of Arcadia. He is said to have discovered the use of honey, milk, rennet, and other useful things. Just. Hist. XIII. 7. This the poets have turned into a fable. See Virg. Georg. IV. 317, &c. One MS. instead of Αρισταιος, has αριστος, ("the best" musician.) The fable of Aristæus is also in the IVth book of the Odyssey.

† A satyr, who challenged Apollo, and, being overcome by him, was flead alive, and changed into a river. See Ovid, Metam. VI. and Liv. XXVIII. 13.

Nor

Nor can he have heard of the fate of Thamyris *, who unsuccessfully contended in singing with the Muses. Not to mention the Sirens †, of whom such of the Muses as conquered them still bear a wing in their foreheads. All these now suffer, and will long suffer, for their presumption; we therefore, as I said before, ought to have remained within our own bounds, and to have been quietly satisfied with your strains; like those who silently receive the oracle of Apollo issuing from the sacred

---

* Superior once of all the tuneful race,
Till, vain of mortals empty praise, he strove
To match the seed of cloud-compelling Jove.
Too daring bard! whose unsuccessful pride
Th' immortal Muses in their art defy'd.
Th' avenging Muses of the light of day
Depriv'd his eyes, and snatch'd his voice away.

POPE.

† This contest of the Sirens with the Muses is thus mentioned by Spenser:

They were fair ladies, till they fondly strew'd
With th' Heliconian maids for maisterye,
Of whom they overcomen were, depriv'd
Of their proud beauty, and th' one moiety
Transform'd to fish, for their bold surquedry.

Fairy Queen, b. XI. c. 12. ſt. 31.

which Mr. Spence justly quotes as one instance (among many) of this great poet's misrepresenting the stories and allegorical personages of the ancients. The Sirens being "never represented in antiques with a fish-tail, but with "the upper part human, and the lower like birds." See *Polymetis*, p. 30.

Ovid, in his Metamorphoses, v. 552, ascribes their transformation to another cause.

‡ Presumption.

shrines.

shrines. But since you lead our song, and by your eloquence, as with the rod of Mercury, rouse us from sleep, we, in the manner of those enthusiasts, who with dances meet Bacchus, when he celebrates his orgies, will join in unison with your harp, as they in tune and measure accompany the leader of the dance. Accept therefore the orations *, which, by the command of the Emperor †, I lately composed on the celebrated junction of the straits ‡; a small work, if compared with yours, and brass for your gold §; but such presents as we have ‖, we offer to our Mercury. Theseus by no means despised the coarse fare of Hecale **; but, urged by necessity, was satisfied with little. And the shepherd Pan disdained not to apply to his lips the pipe of a young herdsman. Such as it is, then, receive it, and scorn not to bestow great attention on a small poem ††. If it have any merit, both the work and its author will be fortunate in receiving such a token of esteem from Minerva.

* These orations are not extant.
† Constantius.
‡ Does he mean the Hellespont joined by Xerxes?
PETAV.

§ Il. VI. 236. Julian seems particularly fond of this passage, this being the third time of his quoting or alluding to it in these Select Works.

‖ Οις δε εχομεν ξενοις—ισωίλις. Not unlike that expression of St. Peter, Acts III. 6. Ο δε ιχν, τυιο σοι δίδωμι. *Such as I have, I give thee.*

** A poor old woman mentioned by Callimachus, as having entertained Theseus with wild lettuce. See Plin. Hist. Nat. XXII. 22. and XXVI. 8.

†† Ολιγω μελει. Could this be one of those which before were styled λογων ("orations?")

And

And should a finishing hand be necessary to complete it, disdain not, I intreat you, to supply its defects. Thus of old the God appeared to the archer * who invoked him, and directed his shaft, and thus the harper who was playing the Orthian † tune was answered by Apollo in the form of a grass-hopper ‡.

An Edict relating to Professors §.

17 June, 362.

PROFESSORS and masters should be distinguished first by their manners, and in the next place by their talents. We therefore forbid any,

---

* Paris probably, when Apollo guided his arrow against Achilles. See Ovid. Metam. XII.

† A kind of loud music used by Arion, according to Herodotus. It is introduced by Homer, Il. xi. 11. where

         Discord
————— ————— Through the Grecian throng,
With horror sounds the loud Orthian song.
           POPE, 13.

‡ I am aware that the Greek word τιτιξ, and the Latin *cicada*, mean a different insect from our grass-hopper; for it has a rounder and shorter body, is of a dark green colour, sits upon trees, and makes a noise five times louder than our grass-hopper. It begins its song as soon as the sun grows hot, and continues singing till it sets. Its wings are beautiful, being streaked with silver, and marked with brown spots; the outer wings are twice as long as the inner, and more variegated; yet, after the example of Mr. Pope (see Il. III. 300.), I retain the usual term.
         FAWKES *on Theocritus*.

§ I have taken this Epistle from the Theodosian Code, XIII. t. 3. *De medicis et professoribus*. It is not known from what

any, whoever they be, to intrude hastily or rashly into this important office. He who would keep a school must be approved by the council of the town, and also have the sanction of the principal inhabitants; and, as I * cannot be every where personally present, let the decree be sent to me for examination, that the candidate may have the additional honour of seeing the suffrages of his fellow-citizens † confirmed by our opinion.

Given at * * * * on the fifteenth of the calends of July. Received at Spoleto on the fourth of the calends of August, in the consulship of Mamertinus and Nevitta.

what place it was dated, nor to whom Julian addressed it. It only appears that he wrote it on the road from Constantinople to Antioch, as he left Constantinople in the month of May, and was at Antioch towards the end of July. It was made, without doubt, on account of some professor of Spoleto, a city of Picenum, and consequently was addressed either to the Præfect of the Prætorium of Italy, or to the Præfect of Rome, or perhaps to the Consular of Picenum (now the march of Ancona), or, lastly, to the inhabitants of Spoleto. The intention of Julian is plain. He reserves to himself the right of confirming or annulling the election of professors, in order to exclude the Christians from all literary offices. This law might perhaps be part of the following edict. I have therefore placed it here.

LA BLETERIE.

* The Emperors generally speak in the plural in their laws; Julian, however, here uses the singular. *Sed quia singulis civitatibus adesse ipse non possum, jubeo,* &c. *Ibid.*

† The original is, *Hoc enim decretum ad me transferendum deferetur* ‡, *ut altiore quodam honore nostro judicio* (M. de la Bleterie thinks we should read *nostrum judicium*) *studiis civitatum accedat.*

‡ In Gothofred's edition, *referatur.*

Epistle

Epistle XLII. An Edict, forbidding the Christians to teach polite Literature *.

A. D. 362.

TRUE learning, in my opinion, consists not in words, in elegant and magnificent language, but in the sound dispositions of a well-formed

---

* Two motives induced Julian to restrain the Christian professors from teaching: 1. He flattered himself, that, in order to keep their chairs, they would change their religion. In this, he did not succeed, if, as Orosius says, almost all rather chose to quit them. This, in particular, is affirmed of Prohæresius, the sophist, of Athens, and of Marius Victorinus, who professed eloquence at Rome. 2. Julian knew, by his own experience, that masters, when they shewed their scholars the ancient authors, never failed to insist on the weakness and folly of Paganism. He was sensible how much a Christian master can contribute to the progress of religion, when he explains profane authors christianly, and equally avails himself of the truth and the falshood which he finds there in order to conduct his pupils to God and Jesus Christ. This is what he wished to prevent. But, instead of discovering his true motives, he employs the most lamentable pretext that can be; so that this piece of eloquence is a master-piece of sophistry. M. Fleury has inserted most of it in his Ecclesiastical History.

LA BLETERIE.

His most illiberal treatment of the Christians was, his forbidding the professors, who were of that religion, to teach humanity and the sciences in the public schools. His more immediate design in this was to hinder the youth from taking impressions to the disadvantage of Paganism; his remoter view, to deprive Christianity of the support of human literature. His own historian, Ammianus Marcellinus, passes a severe sentence on this edict, XXI. 10.

WARBURTON.

His

formed mind, and in just notions of good and evil, of virtue and vice. Whoever therefore thinks or teaches otherwise seems no less destitute of learning than he is of virtue. Even in trifles, if the mind and tongue be at variance, it is always esteemed a kind of dishonesty. But if in matters of the greatest consequence a man thinks one thing

---

His driving from their schools such teachers of rhetoric and grammar as professed the Christian religion, was severe *(inclemens)*, and should be buried in eternal oblivion.
AMMIANUS.

He enacted no oppressive laws . . . . a few excepted; among which was that severe one, which forbade Christian masters to teach rhetoric and grammar, unless they conformed to the worship of the Gods. *Ibid.*

Ammianus has twice mentioned this Edict, and always with dislike, as a great hardship. Orosius says, that " when Julian published his edict forbidding the Chris- " tian professors of rhetoric to teach the liberal arts, they " all in general chose rather to resign their chairs than " deny the faith." And Jerom, in his Chronicle, assures us, that " Prohæresius, the Athenian sophist, in particular, [see Epistle II.] " shut up his school, though the Em- " peror had granted him a special licence to teach." Augustine records the like steadiness of Victorinus, who had long taught rhetoric with great applause at Rome. But Ecebolus, a Christian sophist at Constantinople [see Epistle XIX.], who had been Julian's master in rhetoric, was overcome by the temptations of the times, and with great humiliations intreated to be reconciled to the church.
LARDNER.

This Edict may be compared with the gross invectives of Gregory (*Orat.* III. *p.* 96.). Tillemont (*Mem. Eccl. tom.* VII. *p.* 1201—1204.) has collected the seeming differences of ancients and moderns. They may be easily reconciled. The Christians were *directly* forbid to teach; they were *indirectly* forbid to learn, since they would not frequent the schools of the Pagans. GIBBON.

and teaches another [*], does he not resemble those mean-spirited, dishonest, and abandoned traders, who generally affirm what they know to be false, in order to deceive and inveigle customers?

All therefore who profess to teach ought to be strict in their morals, and should never entertain opinions opposite to those of the public; such, especially, ought to be those who instruct youth, and explain to them the works of the ancients, whether they are orators, or grammarians; but particularly sophists, as they affect to be the teachers, not only of words, but of manners, and insist that civil philosophy is their peculiar province. Whether this be true or not I shall not at present consider. I commend those who make such specious promises, and should commend them much more, if they did not falsify and contradict them-

---

[*] If the Christian professors, when they explained in their schools Homer, Hesiod, &c. had canonised the doctrine of those writers, the reproaches of Julian would have been just; yet perhaps he would not have made them. A book may be esteemed in some respects, and condemned in others. No one is deceived by this. To explain the classic authors, to commend them as models of language, of eloquence and taste, to unveil their beauties, &c. this is not proposing them as oracles of religion and morality. Julian is pleased to confound two things so different, and to erect, under favour of this confusion, the puerile sophistry which prevails through his whole edict.

LA BLETERIE.

Thus Homer's Achilles, Il. ix. 312.
Who dares think one thing, and another tell,
My soul detests him like the gates of hell.   POPE.

selves

selves by thinking one thing, and teaching their scholars another. What then? Were not Homer, Hesiod, Demosthenes, Herodotus, Thucydides, Isocrates, Lysias, guided in their studies by the Gods, and esteemed themselves consecrated, some to Mercury, and others to the Muses? It is absurd therefore for those who explain their works to despise the Gods whom they honoured.

I do not mean (I am not so absurd *) that they should change their sentiments for the sake of instructing youth; I give them their option, either not to teach what they do not approve, or, if they choose to teach, first to persuade their scholars, that neither Homer, nor Hesiod, nor any of those whom they expound, and charge with impiety, madness, and error, concerning the Gods, are really such as they represent them. For as they receive a stipend, and are maintained by their works, if they can act with such duplicity for a few drachms, they confess themselves guilty of the most sordid avarice.

Hitherto, I allow, many causes have prevented their resorting to the temples; and the dangers that every where impended were a plea for their disguising their real sentiments of the Gods. But now, when the Gods have granted us liberty, it seems to me absurd for any to teach what they do not approve. And if they think that those

---

* Petau thinks that something is wanting here to perfect the sentence.

writers whom they expound, and of whom they sit as interpreters, are truly wise, let them first zealously imitate their piety towards the Gods. But if they think their ideas of the most holy Gods erroneous, let them go into the churches of the Galileans, and there expound Matthew and Luke *. In obedience to your rulers, you forbid sacrifices. I wish that your ears and your tongues were (as you express it) regenerated † in those things of which I wish that myself, and all who in thought and deed are my friends, may always be partakers.

* Let all the moral truths which are found, or are supposed to be found, dispersed here and there in the Pagan writers, be collected; let all profane antiquity, if I may so express myself, be laid under contribution; the system which can be drawn from it will be far less valuable than what we are taught in a few words by the authors of whom Julian affects to speak with contempt, and will so far only be rational, as it resembles their doctrine.
LA BLETERIE.

A just and severe censure has been inflicted on the law which prohibited the Christians from teaching the arts of grammar and rhetoric. The motives alleged by the Emperor to justify this partial and oppressive measure might command, during his life-time, the silence of slaves, and the applause of flatterers. GIBBON.

† He ridicules the Christians by the trite application of an expression used by them. Ἀναγέννησις is commonly understood of baptism, the reformation of the new man, and the change of studies and manners. Therefore forbidding the Christians to read the books of the Heathens, he says, he would have their ears and tongues cleansed from all acquaintance with their writings, that what is deposited in them may in a manner be born again. PETAU.

EPISTLES OF JULIAN.

To masters and teachers let this be a general law. But let no youths be prevented from resorting to whatever schools they please *. It would be as unreasonable to exclude children, who know not yet what road to take, from the right path, as it would be to lead them by fear, and with reluctance, to the religious rites of their country. And though it might be proper to cure such reluctance, like madness, even by force †, yet let all be indulged with that disease. For the ignorant should, in my opinion, be instructed, not punished.

---

* This was fair, but would by no means be accepted. Here the bait was half off the hook, and discovered, that to draw them to the schools of the Pagan professors was one end of the edict, which he imagined would necessarily reduce things to this state, either to dispose the Galileans, during their youth, in favour of Paganism, or to disable them, in their adult age, to defend Christianity. So that it appears from hence, his forbidding Christian professors to *explain* Pagan writers to any audience whatsoever, amounted to a prohibition of *learning* them.   WARBURTON.

Mr. Gibbon has adopted the same idea in a former note, p. 113.

† He derides the μωρια Γαλιλαιων (Epist. VII.) and so far loses sight of the principles of toleration as to wish (Epist. XLII.) ακοντας ιασθαι.   GIBBON.

Epistle XLIII. To Ecebolus *.

A. D. 362.

SO mild and humane have been my decrees concerning the Galileans, that none of them can suffer any violence, or be dragged to the temples, or be exposed to any other injury. But they who are of the Arian church, being pampered with riches †, have attacked the Valentinians, and have dared to perpetrate such outrages at Edessa as can never be tolerated in a well-governed city. Therefore, as they are taught, in their wonderful law, the most easy method of entering into the kingdom of heaven, for this pur-

---

* This is not the sophist under whom Julian had studied, and to whom he addressed Epistle XIX. This, no doubt, was the chief magistrate of Edessa, the capital of Osrhoëna, a province beyond the Euphrates and the Tigris.
LA BLETERIE.
About the same time that Julian was informed of the tumult of Alexandria, he received intelligence from Edessa of the disorders which occasioned this mandate. GIBBON

† The Arians were put in possession of the church of Edessa, under Constantius. They must necessarily therefore be great persecutors to retain it under Julian. The Valentinians derived their name from the heresiarch Valentinian, who lived in the second century after Jesus Christ, and who, by a mixture of the gospel, of Platonism, and the theogony of Hesiod, formed a system so compounded, so extravagant, that we do not understand it, perhaps he did not understand it himself. Some remains of the Valentinians still existed in the Vth century.
LA BLETERIE.

pose

pose co-operating with them *, we have ordered all the wealth of the church of the Edessenes † to be confiscated and given to our soldiers, and the lands to be annexed to our demesnes. Thus being poor they may become wise, and not fail of that heavenly kingdom to which they aspire ‡.

We also command the inhabitants of Edessa to refrain from all tumults and seditions §, lest, if they provoke my humanity, you yourself should be punished for the public disorders by exile, fire, and the sword.

Epistle

---

* Julian might boast as much as he pleased of not being a persecutor. Those profane and cruel railleries, which fell from the pen of the sovereign, were in themselves a cruel persecution, and must expose the Christians to the fury of the idolaters, wherever they found themselves the strongest. In order to ill-treat those who are not of their religion, the populace only wait for the least signal from the prince, and frequently not even for that.

LA BLETERIE.

† The effects of the church of Edessa were probably returned to it by the successors of Julian. At least, it was very rich in the vth century. Ibid.

‡ Doubtless Julian refers to divers texts of the gospels; perhaps to Matth. v. 3. Luke vi. 20. Matth. xix. 21. or some other parallel places. But few will allow him to be a good interpreter of scripture, or that he deduces right conclusions from it. LARDNER.

§ These divisions might perhaps be occasioned by the Arians having seized the church and its revenues, though the greater part of the inhabitants was inviolably attached to the Catholic faith. It is notorious, that, nine years after the death of Julian, in the reign of Valens, the bishop, the clergy, and the laity, strictly deserved the glorious title of confessors. The women, and even the children, shared the glory of this confession. The Edessenes pretended

Epistle XLIV. To Libanius *.

RECOVERING lately from a severe and dangerous illness, by the providence of the Supervisor of all things, your letter was delivered to me on the day that I first bathed. Reading it in the afternoon, I can scarce express how much it confirmed me in my opinion of your pure and disinterested benevolence, of which I wish I were worthy, that I may not disgrace your friendship. I immediately began your Epistles †, but could not finish them: those from Antony to Alexander I postponed to the next day. A week after, my health, by the providence of God, improving to my wish, I wrote you this. May you be preserved, my most esteemed and beloved brother, [by God, who regards all things! may I see you, my best friend! With my own hand, by your safety and my own, by God the superintendant

---

that their city had the honour of being the first that dedicated itself to Jesus Christ, and shewed in their archives a letter which they believed to have been written to one of their kings by Jesus Christ himself in the course of his mortal life. We may judge to what degree Julian hated them, and we must no longer be surprised at his writing to Ecebolus, or rather to the whole senate of Edessa, so bitter and so threatening a letter.   LA BLETERIE.

* This, in one MS. is addressed " to Priscus."

† What these " Epistles" were we know not. Possibly some in assumed characters (now lost), such exercises being common with this sophist.

of all things, I have written what I think. Excellent man, when shall I see and embrace you? For now, like a disappointed lover, I am enamoured even of your name *.]

Epistle XLV. To Zeno †.

BESIDES many other proofs of your having attained the summit of the medical art, to which you have added propriety of behaviour, good-nature, and regularity of life, this testimony now crowns all, your having turned the whole city of Alexandria towards you in your absence; such a sting, like a bee, you have left behind you. And with reason; for Homer well observes,

A. D. 362.

 A wise physician, skill'd our wounds to heal,
Is more than armies to the public weal ‡.

And you are not merely a physician, but also a master to all who practise physic, so that you are to physicians what physicians are to others. For this reason you are re-called from exile, and with great splendor. If you were obliged to quit Alex-

---

* The words between [ ] are added in one MS.

† Some MSS. give Zeno the title of " Chief Physician," (αρχιητρω). He was, it appears, a celebrated professor of physic, a Pagan without doubt, as Julian expresses to him so much esteem and affection.

         La Bleterie.

‡ Il. xi. 514. Pope, 636. The words of Idomeneus on Machaon. It is needless to observe that the ancient physicians were surgeons.

andria

andria by the Georgian * faction, as the process was unjust, you may most justly return. Return therefore to your former honour, and let acknowledgements be paid to us by both; by the Alexandrians for restoring Zeno to them, and by Zeno for restoring to him the Alexandrians.

Epistle XLVI. To Euagrius †.

I INHERITED from my grandmother ‡ a small estate in Bithynia, consisting of four farms, and with it I reward your affection to me. It is too inconsiderable to elate a man with wealth, or to confer

---

* George had equally persecuted the Catholics and the Pagans. He must have procured by surprise some order of Constantius to banish Zeno; for if George had only driven him out by force, this physician, so dear to the city of Alexandria, would not have waited for an order from the successor of Constantius to return thither. La Bleterie.

† It is not known to whom this Epistle is addressed. It is very well written; nevertheless, it is tinctured with pedantry. *Ibid.*

The name of " Euägrius" occurs in the Index to Petau's edition. I have therefore added it. He is probably the same who is mentioned in the conclusion of the xxxviiith Epistle.

Libanius has two Epistles to one of this name, and mentions him in several others. He held, it appears, some office under the government, and being accused of some mismanagement in it, was brought to trial, but was acquitted by the interest of Sallust, whom Libanius thanks for his good offices.

‡ In the Duties of a Priest, p. 122, Julian mentions his inheriting the whole estate of his grand-mother, which had been forcibly with-held from him.

felicity,

felicity, but its endowments are by no means unpleasing, as you may judge from the particulars. And there is no reason why I should not be jocular to you who abound with elegance and wit.

It is twenty stadia * distant from the sea, and is therefore undisturbed by trafficking merchants and clamorous or quarrelsome sailors. Yet it is not entirely destitute of the graces of Nereus; for it can always supply a gasping fish fresh-caught, and an eminence near the house commands a view of the Propontic sea, the islands, and the city which bears the name of a great prince †; and instead of being disgusted by sea-weed, and various other kinds of filth that shall be nameless, which are often thrown on the beach and the sands, ground-ivy, thyme, and other aromatic herbs, will afford you a constant regale. When with tranquil attention you have pursued your studies, and wish to relax your eyes, the prospect of the ships and the ocean is delightful. In this retirement I found many charms when I was a boy, for it has fountains also far from despicable, a beautiful bath, a garden, and an orchard; and when I grew up, I was still so fond of it, that I frequently resorted to it, and therefore my obtaining it seemed a fortunate circumstance. It affords too a small memorial of my agriculture, a sweet and fragrant wine, which is

* About two miles and a half.
† Constantinople.

good even when it is new *. In short, you will there see Bacchus and the Graces. The grapes, both when they hang on the vines, and are pressed into the vat, are as odoriferous as roses. But as soon as the wine is in the casks, to speak in the language of Homer, it is

A rill of nectar, streaming from the Gods †.

Why then, you will say, did I not plant many more acres with such vines? Because I was not a very keen husbandman; and besides, as mine is a temperate cup, and the neighbourhood abounds with nymphs, I provided enough for myself and my few male friends. Such as it is, my dear friend, you will now accept it: however trifling the

---

* In the original, Ουκ' αναμενοιλα τι παρα τυ χρονυ προσλαβων, literally, "not waiting to receive any thing from time." But the Latin translator has affixed a meaning no less opposite to the intention of Julian, than to fact and observation: *neque temporis diuturnitate vitii quicquam assumit*. Though our Imperial author was no votary of Bacchus, his "cup" (as he says) being "temperate" (νηφαλιος), he must have known, and meant to intimate, that, in general, old wine is proverbially good, and *vice versâ*. *A new friend*, says the wise son of Sirach, *is like new wine; when it is old, thou shalt drink it with pleasure*. Eccl. IX. 10.

† Τυ νεκταρος εστιν απορρωξ. *Odyss*. IX. 359. POPE, 426.

The elogium of Polyphemus on the rich Maronean wine given him by Ulysses. This wine also, like that of Julian,

Breath'd aromatic fragrances around, ver. (210.) 245.

Julian, it appears, had several female friends whom he occasionally mentions, viz. Areta, Theodora, Enodia, &c. but here, to avoid any misconstruction, he takes particular care to specify, that though " there were many nymphs " there" (πολυ των νυμφων δε εστι), those whom he entertained were " a few of the other sex" (ολιγοι δε εστι το χρημα των ανδρων.)

present,

present, it is pleasing to a friend both to give and receive, "from house to house," according to the wise Pindar *.

This is a hasty epistle, written by lamp-light. Whatever therefore may be its faults, do not criticise them with the severity of one orator towards another †.

Epistle XLVII. To the Inhabitants of Thrace ‡.

TO a prince who was avaricious your request would seem unreasonable, nor should the public revenue ever be injured through any favour to individuals. But as it is our view not to collect from our subjects as much as possible, but rather to do them the utmost possible good, we remit you what is due. Not indeed the whole, but it shall be divided; one moiety you shall retain, and the other shall be given to the soldiers. Of

* Οικοθεν οικαδι. I have not found these words in Pindar. If I have searched well, it must be supposed that Julian took them from one of the works of that poet which has not been transmitted to us. La Bleterie.

M. de la Bleterie has not "searched well." They are both in the vith and viith Olympics.

† This conclusion favours more of the author than the prince. *Ibid.*

‡ He remits them the arrears of taxes till a certain time, namely, till the third indiction, or levy, which began in the year of Christ, 359. This used to be styled "an indulgence." See *Cod. Theod. l.* xi. *tit.* 28. *De indulgentiis debitorum.* Petau.

this

this no inconsiderable part will also be yours, as they preserve you in peace and safety. We remit you therefore, till the third indiction*, all that is in arrear; after that, you must pay it as usual. For what we have remitted to you is fully sufficient; and the public revenue we must not impair. I have written on this subject to the præfects, that the favour intended you may have its full effect.

I pray the Gods always to preserve you †.

---

* The name and use of the indictions, which serve to ascertain the chronology of the middle ages, were derived from the regular practice of the Roman tributes. The Emperor subscribed with his own hand, and in purple ink, the solemn edict, or indiction, which was fixed up in the principal city of each diocese, during two months previous to the first day of September. And, by a very easy connection of ideas, the word "indiction" was transferred to the measure of tribute which it prescribed, and to the annual term which it allowed for the payment.

The proportion, which every citizen should be obliged to contribute for the public service, was ascertained by an accurate *census*, or survey, and from the well-known period of the indictions there is reason to believe that this difficult and expensive operation was repeated at the regular distance of fifteen years. The cycle of indictions, which may be traced as high as the reign of Constantius, or perhaps of his father Constantine, is still employed by the papal court; but the commencement of their year has been very wisely altered to the first of January. GIBBON.

† This sentence is added in one MS.

Epistle XLVIII. To ****.

MY body is on many accounts in an indifferent state of health *; my mind, however, is pretty well. An epistle from one friend to another cannot, I think, have a better preface. Of what then does this preface consist? Of a petition, I suppose. For what? An epistolary correspondence; which, I hope, will confirm my wishes, and bring me intelligence of your health and happiness.

Epistle XLIX. To Arsacius, High-priest of Galatia †.

THAT Hellenism ‡ does not yet succeed as we wish is owing to its professors. The gifts of the Gods are indeed great and splendid, and far superior

A. D. 362. or 363.

---

* From this and several other passages, which the reader must have observed, it appears, that Julian had frequent returns of illness, owing probably to his great and constant fatigue of mind and body, and to his rigid manner of life.

† This pontiff is not known. I imagine this Epistle was written, at the soonest, towards the end of the year 362, as it supposes that some time had been employed in endeavouring to re-establish Hellenism. Sozomen and M. Fleury have thought the whole worth being inserted in their Ecclesiastical History. Indeed it would be impossible to produce a more honourable and less suspicious testimony in favour of our religion. But I will not deprive the reader of the pleasure

superior to all our hopes, to all our wishes. For (be Nemesis propitious to my words!) not long ago no one dared to hope for such and so great a change in so short a time. But why should we be satisfied with this, and not rather attend to the means by which this impiety § has increased, namely, humanity to strangers, care in burying the dead, and pretended sanctity of life? All these, I think, should be really practised by us.

It is not sufficient for you only to be blameless. Intreat or compell all the priests that are in Galatia to be also virtuous. If they do not, with their wives, children, and servants, attend the worship of the Gods, expell them from the priestly function; and also forbear to converse with the servants,

---

of making himself all the useful reflections which the perusal of this piece supplies. LA BLETERIE.

The pastoral letters of Julian, if we may use that name, still represent a very curious sketch of his wishes and intentions. GIBBON.

‡ This was the style at that time. *Hellenism* is Heathenism, or Gentilism. And Heathens are called *Hellenes*, and Hellenists, by our Ecclesiastical historians, Socrates, Sozomen, and Theodoret, especially in their history of Julian's reign. LARDNER.

§ A singular kind of impiety, which renders man the friend of man, and makes him practise all virtues! To charge good men with hypocrisy is the usual resource of extravagant prejudice and wickedness. Julian, with all his genius, did not and would not see that a society, so numerous as the Christians then were, does not carry on and cannot even conceive such a design. Hypocrisy will never be a popular vice. The multitude, be it what it may, is always honest. LA BLETERIE.

children

children, and wives, of the Galileans *, who are impious towards the Gods, and prefer impiety to religion. Admonish also every priest not to frequent the theatre, nor to drink in taverns, nor to exercise any trade or employment that is mean and disgraceful. Those who obey you, honour; and those who disobey you, expell. Erect also hospitals in every city, that strangers may partake our benevolence; and not only those of our own religion, but, if they are indigent, others also.

How these expences are to be defrayed must now be considered. I have ordered Galatia to supply you with thirty-thousand bushels of wheat † every year; of which the fifth part is to be given

---

* Ἀλλὰ ἀνέχεσθε τ ι οικεῖων, ἢ υἱέων, ἢ τῶν Γαλιλαίων γαμέων, κ. τ. λ. I have attempted a new translation of this passage, not being satisfied with any other which I have met with. In Spanheim's edition the Latin version is, *ne patiantur servos, aut filios, aut conjuges Galilæorum impiè in Deos se gerere, et impietatem pietati præponere.* And much to the same purpose is the Latin translation of this Epistle in Sozomen, made by Valesius, which would be commanding every Heathen priest and his family to become persecutors: which cannot be supposed to be probable. Cave, in the introduction to his History of the Fathers of the ivth century, p. 34. "not suffering their servants, children, or " wives, to be Galileans, who are despisers of the Gods, " and prefer impiety before religion," which cannot be right. For it is a tautology, saying over again the same thing which had been said just before. And yet Bleterie's translation is much to the same purpose: *s'ils souffrent dans leur famille de ces impies de Galiléens.* LARDNER.

I have adopted this construction.

† The Latin and French translations add here " and " sixty-thousand *sextarii* (or *septiers*) of wine," words, for which there is no authority in Petau's or Spanheim's edition.

VOL. II. K to

to the poor who attend on the priests, and the remainder to be distributed among strangers and our own beggars. For when none of the Jews beg, and the impious Galileans relieve both their own poor and ours, it is shameful, that ours should be destitute of our assistance *.

Teach therefore the Gentiles to contribute to such ministerial functions, and the Gentile villages to offer to the Gods their first-fruits. Accustom them to such acts of benevolence, and inform them that this was of old the regal office. For Homer puts these words into the mouth of Eumæus:

———. It never was our guise
To slight the poor, or aught humane despise;
For Jove unfolds our hospitable door,
'Tis Jove that sends the stranger and the poor †.

Let us not suffer others to emulate our good actions, while we ourselves are disgraced by sloth ‡,

lest

---

*. Julian beheld with envy the wise and humane regulations of the church, and he very frankly confesses his intention to deprive the Christians of the applause, as well as advantage, which they had acquired by the exclusive practice of charity and benevolence.   GIBBON.

See the conclusion of the Duties of a Priest, Vol. I. p. 142, &c.

† Odyss. XIV. 56. Pope, 65. This passage is quoted by Mr. Harris, on the subject of the Arabian hospitality. See his *Philological Enquiries*, part III. ch. 7.

‡ Who doubts but that, before Christianity appeared in the world, the Pagans performed some humane actions, and that some among them practised some moral virtues? But it was not as Pagans, it was as men that they practised them: In that they only followed the impressions of the law and religion of nature. It was because the corruption

ruption of the heart, the strange idea which the idolaters, at least the people, formed of the divinity, and that monstrous collection of senseless opinions, of scandalous traditions, and of ridiculous superstitions, in which Paganism consisted, had not absolutely extinguished the *light which shineth in darkness.*

The Pagans had a morality, but Paganism had none. It is no less absurd to appropriate virtues to it, as Julian does, than it would be to ascribe to infidelity some virtuous actions, of no consequence, which escape from infidels. Supposing that they have some probity, it is from temper, from interest, from caprice, because they are men, and often because they have preserved some remains of a Christian education. This epistle of Julian shews, how many virtues, even those which by the pleasure that attends their practice carry with them their reward, were rare among the Pagans. Could the finger of God be mistaken in a religion which renders all virtues common; which, founded also on all the proofs of which a fact is susceptible, brings into the world a system of morality the most perfect that can possibly be imagined, supports it by the most powerful motives and examples, regulates even the most secret motions of our souls; in a word, which re-establishes, unfolds, and perfects the principles of the law of nature, almost effaced in the minds of men, and still more in their hearts?

Let us judge of the necessity of Christianity by the horrid crimes which were committed, and are still committed, in the best-governed Pagan nations. To the disgrace of Philosophy, it will, for instance, be always true to say, that mankind are indebted to the gospel of Jesus Christ for the abolition of the barbarous custom of exposing infants. In this respect the most savage animals rise up in judgement, even at the tribunal of reason, against the Greek, the Roman, and the Chinese.

To deprive our religion of a glory which is peculiar to it it would be useless to say, that Mahometanism has been equally serviceable to humanity. Who knows not, that this false religion supposes and acknowledges the mission of Jesus Christ, and is only a corruption of Christianity and Judaism? No one can deny, that the Christian religion has at least sweetened the manners, civilised the barbarous people who have embraced it, enlightened, as to his duties,

lest by negligence we lose our reverence for the Gods. If I hear that you practise this, I shall overflow with joy.

Visit the dukes * seldom at their houses, but write to them often. Whenever they enter a city, let none of the priests go to meet them; but when they resort to the temples, let them be received within the vestibule. When they enter, let none of

the rudest Pagan, diffused every where some delicacy of conscience, and, even among those whom it does not alter, a tincture of probity. A Christian, moderately instructed, and of common virtue, knows more in point of morality, and is more philosophical than a philosopher. Those who, like Julian, but with less splendor than he, have abandoned the Christian religion, are more indebted to that religion than they imagine. They, as well as Julian, are indebted to it for the exactest and purest notions of certain moral virtues. It is from that that some have retained those maxims of rigid probity of which they would not have made parade, if Christianity had not given them reputation. It has already been said, that if, which is impossible, the gospel were false, it would be for the interest of mankind to believe it true. LA BLETERIE.

* Or commanders of the troops. See note on Epistle XXVIII, p. 73. Julian, in what follows, seems very attentive to the dignity of the priesthood, by endeavouring to prevent those who were ordained to any holy office from degenerating into mere secular politicians, party zealots, and danglers at the levees (as we now call them) of the great. What so proper to impress them with a just opinion of their own rank and importance as to forbid their mixing in popular assemblies and tumultuous processions, even when intended to give honour where honour was due, and paying idle or even ceremonious visits, and rather to confine them within the precincts of their own temples, where, without offence, they had an undoubted precedence? In the Duties of a Priest, in like manner, the priests are allowed to " visit the dukes and præfects." See Vol. I. p. 138.

their

their guards precede them; but let who will follow them. For as soon as they enter the door of the temple, they become private persons. You yourself, you well know, have a right to precede all who are within it, that being agreeable to the divine law. Those who are truly pious will obey you, and none will oppose you but the proud, ostentatious, and vain-glorious.

I am ready to assist the people of Pessinus *, if they can render the Mother of the Gods propitious to them. But if they neglect her, they will not only be culpable, but, which is more harsh to say, will incur my displeasure †.

No law requires that they my care should prove,
Or pity, hated by the powers above ‡.

There-

---

* See Epistle XXI. p. 43.

† An ungenerous distinction was admitted into the mind of Julian, that, according to the difference of their religious sentiments, one part of his subjects deserved his favour and friendship, while the other was entitled only to the common benefits that his justice could not refuse to an obedient people. GIBBON.

‡ See Odyss. X. 73. What Julian says here does not seem to agree with the order which he has just given to establish some hospitals, where all might be received, Christians as well as Pagans. This contradiction, if such it were, would not have been the only one of which he had been guilty. But it is only apparent. The duties of humanity are strictly just. They are obligatory with regard to all men. But favours are due to none; and it was some favour that the inhabitants of Pessinus had asked of the Emperor. LA BLETERIE.

These two lines, which Julian has changed and perverted, in the true spirit of a bigot, are taken from the speech of Æolus, when he refuses to grant Ulysses a fresh supply of winds.

Therefore assure them, that, if they wish for my protection, all the people must supplicate the Mother of the Gods.

Epistle L. To Ecdicius, Præfect of Ægypt *.

A. D. 362.

"YOU tell me my dream †," says the proverb. But I am going to tell you what you have seen waking. The Nile, I am informed, has

---

winds. Libanius (*Orat. Parent. c.* 59. *p.* 286.) attempts to justify this partial behaviour by an apology, in which persecution peeps through the mask of candour. GIBBON.

† The lines in Homer are,

Ου γαρ μοι θεμις εςι κομιζεμεν, ουδ' αποπεμπειν
Ανδρα, τ' ος κε θεοισιν απεχθηται μακαρεσσιν.

His baneful suit pollutes these bless'd abodes,
Whose faith proclaims him hateful to the Gods.

POPE, 85.

Julian has altered them thus, at the expence of a false quantity, and a jingle:

Ου γαρ μοι θεμις εςι κομιζεμεν, η' ελεαιρειν
Ανδρας, οι και θεοισιν απεχθωντ' αθανατοισιν.

In the last word, probably, his memory might deceive him, as απεχθωνται μακαρεσσιν would have suited his purpose and metre as well. The other alterations (και perhaps excepted) must have been intentional.

* This Epistle is a good piece of pleasantry on the negligence of Ecdicius. That governor, I fancy, would rather have received a serious reprimand. Nothing was more interesting to the Emperor and the empire than an account of how many cubits the Nile had risen in the autumnal solstice, as on that depended the fertility of Ægypt, and the subsistence of Constantinople. Where the waters rose too much, or too little, the lands could not be sown. " If the increase," says Pliny, (*l.* v. *c.* 9.) " be only
" twelve

has risen several cubits, and overflowed all Ægypt. If you wish to know the number, it was fifteen on the twentieth of September. This intelligence I received from Theophilus, præfect of the camps. If you had not heard it before, rejoice at hearing it now from me.

" twelve cubits, the province is afflicted with famine; if
" it be only thirteen, it still suffers. Fourteen give joy;
" fifteen safety; sixteen absolute plenty." The Nile swells from the middle of July to the solstice. When it is at its greatest height, the canals are opened, to let it in upon the lands. It returns to its bed in the month of November. The seeds are then sown. The corn is reaped in May. LA BLETERIE.

The cubit, by which the rising of the Nile in Ægypt was measured, had been usually lodged in the temple of Serapis [at Alexandria]. Constantine removed it into a Christian church. But Julian ordered it to be replaced in the temple of Serapis. His statue and temple having been demolished, by order of Theodosius I. in the year 391, it was given out by the Gentiles that the Nile would no longer overflow. Nevertheless it rose the following year to an uncommon height. The cubit was then again restored to the Christians. LARDNER.

Thales, the Milesian, accounted for the inundation of this river by the Etesian winds blowing against the mouth of it at that season. But the same would probably then happen to other rivers where the like winds are known to blow. The true cause is probably the melting of the snows on the mountains of Ethiopia, when the sun comes over them. Yet these winds may contribute to make the overflow more regular and lasting, as they are an equal balance to the waters, and prevent their running into the sea after these have sufficiently fertilised the land.

† Τὸ σὸν ὄναρ σοι διηγοῦμαι, " I tell you your dream." That is, " I tell you what you yourself know better than I." In Suidas this proverb is quoted from some unknown author, and also in Plato *De Republ. l.* VIII. It seems derived from those who consult interpreters of dreams; whom some also require to guess what they have dreamed. ERASMUS.

Epistle LI.   To the ALEXANDRIANS *.

A. D. 362.

IF your city had had any other founder, any one of those who, transgressing their own laws †, had justly suffered punishment for leading a wicked life, and introducing a new doctrine, a new religion, even then it would have been unreasonable for you to wish for Athanasius. But now, as the founder of your city is Alexander ‡, and your ruler and tutelar deity king Serapis, with the virgin his associate, and the queen of all Ægypt, Isis, * * * *, you do not act like a healthy city, but the distempered part dares to arrogate the

---

* The Catholics, who were, without doubt, the most numerous, presented, in the name of the city, a petition to the Emperor, requesting the repeal of the order which he had issued against Athanasius. The Emperor answers their petition by this new Edict. M. Fleury quotes the whole of it.   LA BLETERIE.

† Those whom Julian here treats as apostates (a reproach strange enough in his mouth), had not abandoned the God of their fathers, to run after strange gods. They believed in the second revelation, which was only the object, the sequel, and the accomplishment of the first. By dying for the doctrine of their master, they have proved that they were not deceivers. The proofs of the fact which determined them to embrace it are of such a nature, that it is impossible for them to have been deceived. Could Julian allege any thing similar in justification of his change? He has here given us a very remarkable sketch of his reasons in the pathetic discourse which he addresses to the inhabitants of Alexandria.   *Ibid.*

‡ See Epistle X. note †, p. 20.

name

name of the whole. By the Gods, men of Alexandria, I am ashamed, that any of you should avow himself a Galilean.

The ancestors of the Hebrews were formerly slaves to the Ægyptians. But now, men of Alexandria, you, the conquerors of Ægypt (for Ægypt was conquered by your founder), sustain a voluntary servitude to the despisers of your national rites, in opposition to your ancient laws *; not recollecting your former happiness, when all Ægypt had communion with the Gods †, and enjoyed many blessings. But tell me, what advantage ‡ has accrued to your city from those who now introduce among you a new religion? Your founder was that pious man § Alexander of Macedon, who did

---

* The Hebrews were subjected to the ancient kings of Ægypt; the Alexandrians therefore ought to prefer the Greek religion to the doctrine of the Apostles: What a singular complication of bad arguments! LA BLETERIE.

† If they recollected it, they recollected but little of it.
Ibid.

Julian makes intercommunity the distinguishing character of the Pagan religion. For the Imperial sophist, writing to the people of Alexandria, and upbraiding them with having forsaken the religion of their country, in order to aggravate the charge, insinuates them to be guilty of ingratitude, as having forgotten "those happy times when "all Ægypt worshipped the Gods *in common*" (ηνικα ην κοινωνια). WARBURTON.

‡ The Christian religion does not promise temporal blessings; but, if men practise it, they will be as happy as they can be on earth. LA BLETERIE.

§ In matters of religion, what authority was that of Alexander? What conquests were his, compared to those
of

did not, by Jove, resemble any one of these, or any of the Hebrews, who far excelled them. Even Ptolemy, the son of Lagus *, was also superior to them. As to Alexander, if he had encountered, he would have endangered, even the Romans. What then did the Ptolemies, who succeeded your founder? Educating your city, like their own daughter, from her infancy, they did not bring her to maturity by the discourses of Jesus, nor did they construct the form of government with which she is now blessed by the doctrine of the odious Galileans.

Thirdly, after the Romans became its masters, taking it from the bad government of the Ptolemies †, Augustus visited your city, and thus addressed the citizens: " Men of Alexandria, I ac-
" quit your city of all blame, out of regard to
" the great God Serapis, and also for the sake of
" the people and the grandeur of the city. A
" third cause of my kindness to you is my friend

---

of the Apostles? I beg the reader to recollect that passage in the epistle to Themistius (p. 24.), where Julian raises Socrates above Alexander; and to determine whether the just reasons which he has given for preferring the former are not infinitely more striking and decisive in favour of the disciples of Jesus Christ. Here Julian speaks like a true sophist. He was well acquainted with Alexander, and would not have wished to resemble him in every thing.
LA BLETERIE.

* Ptolemy, the son of Lagus, was one of the generals of Alexander, who shared his empire. He founded the kingdom of Ægypt.   *Ibid.*

† The family of the Lagides terminated in the person of Cleopatra, after having reigned 300 years.   *Ibid.*

" Areus."

" Areus *." This Areus, the companion of Augustus Cæsar, and a philosopher, was your fellow-citizen.

The particular favours conferred upon your city by the Olympic Gods were, in short, such as these. Many more, not to be prolix, I omit. Those blessings which the illustrious Gods bestow in common every day, not on one family, nor on a single city, but on the whole world, why do you not acknowledge? Are you alone insensible of the splendor that flows from the sun †? Are you alone ignorant that summer and winter are produced by him, and that to him all things owe their life and origin? Do you not also perceive the great advantages that accrue to your city from the moon, from him and by him the disposer of all things? Yet you dare not worship either of these deities; and this Jesus, whom neither you, nor your fathers have seen, you think must necessarily be God the Word ‡, while him, whom, from eternity, every

---

* The same who is mentioned in the Cæsars, (Vol. I. p. 193.) and in the Epistle to Themistius, (p. 25.)
La Bleterie.

† All nature, and the heavenly bodies, in particular, prove the existence of a Supreme Being, and declare his power, his wisdom, and his goodness. But their splendor, the regularity of their motions, and the uses which they render to mankind do not prove that they are governed by some particular intelligences, and much less that they deserve to be worshipped. *Ibid.*

‡ I have already said that Julian placed the *Logos*, or Demiurgus, in the Sun. *Ibid.*

Θεος λογος. Taken from St. John, i. 1. Θεος ην ὁ λογος, *The Word was God.*

generation

generation of mankind has seen, and sees, and worships, and by worshipping lives happily, the great sun, I mean, a living, animated, rational, and beneficent image of the intelligible Father *, you despise. If you listen to my admonitions †, * * * *, you will by degrees return to truth. You will not wander from the right path, if you will be guided by him, who, to the twentieth year of his age, pursued that road, but has now worshipped the Gods for near twelve years.

If you will follow my advice, my joy will be exuberant. But if you will still persevere in that superstitious institution of designing men, agree, however, among yourselves, and do not desire Athanasius. There are many of his disciples who are abundantly able to please your itching ears ‡; desirous as they are of such impious discourses. I wish that this wickedness were confined to Athanasius and his irreligious school. But you have

---

* In another place (*apud Cyril. l.* 11. *p.* 69.) he calls the sun " God, and the throne of God." Julian believed the Platonician Trinity, and only blames the Christians for preferring a mortal to an immortal Logos.   GIBBON.

Though the Alexandrians saw the sun, they by no means saw that he was a divinity; but without having seen the MAN GOD, they had certain proofs of his mission; proofs which, all united, form, in fact, a complete demonstration. It is worth observing, that Julian, in one and the same phrase, speaks the language of Pyrrhonism and that of credulity.   LA BLETERIE.

† Something here is wanting.

‡ Τας ακοας υμων κνηςιωσας. Similar to that expression of St. Paul, 2 Tim. iv. 3. κνηθομενοι την ακοην.

among

among you many, not ignoble, of the same sect, and the business is easily done. For any one whom you may select from the people, in what relates to expounding the scriptures will be by no means inferior to him whom you solicit. But if you are pleased with the shrewdness of Athanasius (for, I hear, the man is crafty), and therefore have petitioned, know, that for this very reason he was banished. That such an intriguer should preside over the people is highly dangerous; one, who is not a man, but a puny contemptible mortal, one who prides himself on hazarding his life*, cannot but create disturbances. That nothing of that kind might happen, I ordered him formerly to leave the city, but I now banish him from all Ægypt.

Let this be communicated to our Alexandrians.

---

* I cannot convey all the energy of the Greek : Μηδὲ ἀνηρ, ἀλλ' ἀνθρωπισκος εὐτελης, καθαπερ οὑτος, ὁ μεγας (it should be τὸ μεγα) οιομενος; περι της κεφαλης κινδυνευει. *Ne vir quidem, sed homuncio nullius pretii, qualis iste est, qui de capite periclitari magnum aliquid existimat.* La Bleterie.

The present translator may say the same.

M. de Tillemont concludes from this text, that Athanasius was a little man, and that his person had nothing that announced the grandeur and elevation of his mind. The most, I think that we can conclude from this expression of Julian is, that, Athanasius was not of a proper height. I say, the most; for it must be observed, that it is an Emperor who speaks of one of his subjects, and who affects to speak of him in a tone of contempt. Gregory Nazianzen (*Orat.* xxi.) says, that Athanasius " had the form of an angel," ἀγγελικος τὸ ἠδος. It even appears, that, when he went to meet the Emperor Constantine the younger, in Gaul, that prince was struck with his advantageous appearance. *Ibid.*

Epistle LII. To the BOSTRENIANS *.

Aug. 362.

I THOUGHT that the prelates of the Galileans had been under greater obligations to me than to my predecessor. For in his reign many of them were banished, persecuted, and imprisoned; and numbers of those, who are styled heretics, were put to death, particularly at Samosata and Cyzicus; and in Paphlagonia, Bithynia, Galatia, and many other provinces, whole villages were laid waste and entirely depopulated †. In my reign the re-

---

* Bostra, or Bosra, as it is styled in scripture, was a Roman colony, and the capital of Arabia. It had then for its bishop a man equally well versed in polite literature, and the doctrine of the church, named Titus.
LA BLETERIE.

In this very remakable Epistle to the people of Bostra, Julian professes his moderation, and betrays his zeal; which is acknowledged by Ammianus, and exposed by Gregory, (*Orat.* III. *p.* 73.) GIBBON.

† The successor of Constantius has expressed, in a concise, but lively, manner, some of the theological calamities which afflicted the empire, and more especially the East, in the reign of a prince, who was the slave of his own passions, and of those of his eunuchs. *Ibid.*

Under Constantius the Arians, who pretended to be the Catholic church, had persecuted not only the orthodox, but also the sectaries, especially the Novatians, who, without receiving the council of Nice subsequent to their schism, were no less zealous than the orthodox for consubstantiality. They were the subsisting and unsuspected proof of the novelty of Arianism; which made them much regarded by the Catholics, and more odious to the Arians than the Catholics themselves. LA BLETERIE.

verse.

verse has happened. For they who had been banished are allowed to return, and to those whose goods had been confiscated, all have been restored. Such, nevertheless, are their madness and folly, that, because they can no more tyrannise, or perpetrate what they had projected, first against their brethren, and then against us, the worshippers of the Gods, enraged and exasperated, they move every stone, and dare to alarm and inflame the people *; impious towards the Gods, and disobedient to our edicts, humane as they are. For we suffer none of them to be dragged to the altars against their will. We also publickly declare, that, if any are desirous to partake of our lustrations and libations, they must first offer sacrifices of expiation, and supplicate the Gods, the averters of evil. So far are we from wishing to admit any of the irreligious to our sacred rites before they have purified their souls by prayers to the Gods, and their bodies by legal ablutions †.

The populace therefore, deluded by those who are called the clergy, as the severity above-mentioned is abolished, grow tumultuous. For they who have been used to tyrannise, not satisfied with impunity for their past crimes, but ambitious of their former power, because they are no

---

* The Arian clergy, who were in possession of a great number of churches, gave occasion to the invectives of Julian.   LA BLETERIE.

† One who speaks in this manner was very capable of having endeavoured to efface his baptism.   *Ibid.*

longer permitted to act as judges *, or make wills †, or embezzle the estates of others, and appropriate every thing to themselves, all, if I may so say, pull the ropes of sedition, and, as the proverb expresses it, heap fuel on the fire, and scruple not to add greater evils to the former by urging the multitude to commotions.

It is my pleasure therefore to declare and publish to all the people, by this edict, that they must not abet the seditions of the clergy, nor suffer themselves to be induced by them to throw stones, and disobey the magistrates. They may assemble together, if they please, and offer up such prayers as they have established for themselves. But if the clergy endeavour to persuade them to foment disturbances on their account, let them by no means concur, on pain of punishment.

---

* Julian had revoked all the privileges granted to the church, and, among them, the law by which Constantine allowed those who had law-suits to decline the ordinary jurisdiction, and to apply to the bishops, whose sentences were to be executed like those of the Emperor himself.

La Bleterie.

† Γραφειν διαθηκας, *scribere testamenta*, may here have three meanings; 1. to make wills; 2. to receive wills in a public capacity; 3. to dictate or suggest wills. Julian had not deprived the clergy of the right of making wills. This is proved by the silence of Christian writers. Among the Romans, to the making of the most solemn will no public person was requisite: there only wanted a certain number of witnesses. The third sense therefore remains. A law of Constantine, which is still in being, allowed wills to be made in favour of the church. Julian having abrogated that law, the ecclesiastics could no longer engage any one to give his estate to the church by will, and consequently to their advantage, as Julian pretends they had.

Ibid.

I thought proper to make this declaration to the city of Bostra in particular, because the bishop, Titus *, and the clergy †, in a memorial which they have presented to me, have accused the people of being inclined to raise disturbances, if they had not been restrained by their admonitions. I will transcribe the words which the bishop has dared to insert in that memorial: " Though the Christians " are as numerous as the Gentiles, they are re- " strained by our exhortations from being tumul- " tuous." These are the words of the bishop concerning you. Observe, he does not ascribe your regularity to your own inclination; unwillingly, he says, you refrain, " by his exhortations." As your accuser, therefore, expell him from the city ‡. And,

for

---

* This Titus, bishop of Bostra, taught that we do not die in consequence of the sin of Adam, but by the necessity of nature; and that Adam himself would have died, if he had not sinned. In this he was followed by Pelagius.

PRIESTLEY.

† It seems as if there was an apprehension of some commotion in the city of Bostra. Julian had threatened to make the bishop, Titus, and his clergy, responsible for the whole. The bishop had presented, or caused a memorial to be presented, to the Emperor, accounting for his conduct.

LA BLETERIE.

‡ If we did not know how much the mind is narrowed by the spirit of party, it would be inconceivable that an Emperor, a man who piqued himself on reasoning, and who published this himself, should be capable of such a trick [*tracasserie*.] I use this word, because it is a low one, and I know none more proper to characterise the artfulness of Julian, who was determined, at any rate, to prejudice in the minds of the people an irreproachable

Vol. II.   L

for the future, let the people agree among themselves; let no one be at variance, or do an injury to another; neither you who are in error, to those who worship the Gods, rightly and justly, in the mode transmitted to us from the most ancient times; nor let the worshippers of the Gods destroy or plunder the houses of those who rather by ignorance than choice are led astray. Men should be taught and persuaded by reason, not by blows, invectives, and corporal punishments. I therefore again and again admonish those who embrace the true religion in no respect to injure or insult the Galileans *, neither by attacks nor reproaches.

proachable prelate, who employed his authority to maintain the public tranquillity. This philosophical Emperor, in an edict which breathes the principles of mutual support, foments the flame, which he pretends it is his wish to stifle. If he had banished the bishop, his orders would have been peaceably obeyed. But does not his advising the people to drive him out indicate a design to excite a tumult? Some might consider the advice of the Emperor as an order, and others only as an advice. History does not inform us what was the consequence of this affair.

LA BLETERIE.

After this, no instance of baseness, or injustice, will be thought strange. It is remarkable that the author of the Characteristics has given us a translation of this letter, for " a pattern," as he tells us, " of the humour and genius, " of the principles and sentiments, of this virtuous, gallant, " generous, and mild Emperor." p. 87, &c. 4th edition. It is true, his translation drops the affair of Titus, their bishop. So that nothing hinders his reader from concluding but that the Emperor might be as " gallant and generous" as he is pleased to represent him. WARBURTON.

* How irreconcileable is this with the above Edict, [Epistle XLII.] for which he deserved no small reproof from

proaches. We should rather pity than hate those who in the most important concerns act ill. For as piety is the greatest of blessings, impiety, certainly, is the greatest of evils. Such is their fate, who turn from the immortal Gods to dead men *, and their relicks. With those who are thus unhappy we condole, but them who are freed and delivered by the Gods we congratulate †.

Given at *Antioch* on the calends of *August*.

Epistle

(in other respects) his chief panegyrist! "It was very unmerciful in him (as that excellent writer expresses it) to forbid the masters of grammar and rhetoric to teach the Christians, unless they embraced the worship of the Gods." Amm. Marc. xxv. 4.   SPANHEIM.

* Απο Θιων ετι τυς νεκρυς μιlαlιlεαμμενυς. An expression similar to that of St. Paul, Επιςρεψαlι προς τον Θιον απο των ειδωλων: *Ye turned to God from idols, to serve the living God.* 1 Thes. i. 9.

† From this Edict, as well as from other things, it appears that Julian was very fond of Hellenism, or Heathenism. And Sozomen's observations appear to be very pertinent. Julian was very ready to lay hold of every pretence, and to improve every occasion, to rid himself of the Presidents of Christian churches; especially such as had an influence with the people. We see three instances of this, in Athanasius of Alexandria, Eleusius of Cyzicum, and Titus of Bostra, all of them men of great distinction.

Julian here makes repeated professions of moderation and equity toward the Christians. But the letter bears witness against him. Titus was one of the most learned men of the age. His people were peaceable, and he had exhorted them to be so. And yet Julian commands his people to expell him out of their city; under a pretence, that his exhortations to a peaceable behaviour implied an accusation of an unpeaceable temper.

Julian was a man of great ingenuity, sobriety of manners, and good-natured in himself. But his zeal for the religion which he had embraced was excessive, and degenerated

EPISTLES OF JULIAN.

Epistle LIII. To the Philosopher JAMBLICHUS *.

O JUPITER! can it be true that we reside in the middle of Thrace, and winter in its caverns, while from the excellent Jamblichus, as from some eastern spring, letters greet us, instead of swallows, though we are not yet allowed to go to him, nor he to come to us? Who but a Thracian, or one like Tereus †, can with equanimity support this?

> O royal Jove! from Thrace the Grecians free ‡,
> Dispell these fogs, and give us but to see

---

generated into bigotry and superstition; insomuch that with all his pretensions to right reason, and all his professions of humanity, moderation, tenderness, and equity, he has not escaped the just imputation of being a persecutor. LARDNER.

This learned writer has given an English translation of the above Epistle in his Jewish and Heathen Testimonies, Vol. IV. p. 108.

* See Ep. XXXIV. note *, p. 80.

† Tereus was a king of Thrace, but seems here introduced for his cruelty and brutality. See Ovid. Metam. VI.

‡ Ζευ ατα' αλλα συ ρυσαι απο Θρηκηθεν Αχαιων, altered from Il. XVII. 645. Ζευ πατερ, αλλα συ ρυσαι υπ' ηερος υιας Αχαιων, the beginning of the celebrated prayer of Ajax, applauded by Longinus and others. The other line is the same as in Homer. Pope has thus translated them:

> ——————————— Lord of earth and air!
> O King! O Father! hear my humble prayer!
> Dispell this cloud, the light of heaven restore,
> Give me to see, and Ajax asks no more.

EPISTLES OF JULIAN.

sometimes our Mercury, and to salute his shrine, and embrace his images, as Ulysses is said to have done, when, after his wanderings, he at last saw Ithaca *; though the Phæacians departed, after laying him out of the ship, like a bale of goods, in his sleep †. But sleep does not seize us till we are allowed to see the great blessing of the world. You too are jocose in saying that I and my companion Sopater ‡ have transported all the East into Thrace. For if the truth must be spoken, while Jamblichus is absent, I seem involved in Cimmerian § darkness. Besides, you desire one of these alternatives,

---

* Ulysses, at his return to Ithaca, Odyss. XIII.
————————With joy confess'd his place of birth,
And on his knees salutes his mother earth; Pope, 403.
but where Julian found the two other circumstances mentioned above, I cannot say.

† Odyss. XIII. 116.
Ulysses sleeping on his couch they bore,
And gently plac'd him on the rocky shore, &c.
Pope, 138.

‡ Could this be the Sopater, who afterwards entertained him at Hierapolis, (see p. 70.) whom he " had (then) " scarce ever seen before ?"

§ The Cimmerians were a people of Italy who dwelt in a valley, between Baiæ and Cumæ, so surrounded with hills, that it is said they never saw the sun. There was the Sibyl's grot, and there was supposed to be the descent to hell.

Great obscurity, or darkness, of the mind, is called " Cimmerian darkness." This adage arose from the prodigious darkness of the Cimmerian region, which Strabo describes in his first book of his Geography, and quotes the following passage from the Odyssey of Homer, XI. 14."

alternatives, either that I would go to you, or that you may come to me; one of which, namely, that I would return to you, and enjoy your advantages, is very desirable to me. The other exceeds all my wishes. But as this is not only inconvenient to you, but also impracticable, remain at home, fare you well, and continue to enjoy your present tranquillity. As to me, whatever the Gods shall allot, I will bear with fortitude: for it is the character of the virtuous to cherish good hopes, and to perform their duty; but always to submit to fatal necessity.

> There, in a lonely land, and gloomy cells,
> The dusky nation of Cimmeria dwells;
> The sun ne'er views th' uncomfortable seats,
> When radiant he advances, or retreats:
> Unhappy race, whom endless night invades,
> Clouds the dull air, and wraps them round in shades.
> BROOME, 15.

Tully also mentions the Cimmerians in the 1vth book of his Academic Questions. And in this country Ovid, in the 11th book of his Metamorphoses, has built a temple to the God of Sleep. ERASMUS.

Epistle LIV. To George, the Catholic *.

LET Echo be, as you say, a Goddess, and talkative, and also, if you please, the wife of Pan †. I say nothing to the contrary. Though Nature would teach me, that Echo is the sound of the voice reverberated by the percussion of the air, and reflected back to the ear, yet, by the opinion both of ancients and moderns, as well as by yours, I am induced to think that Echo is a Goddess. But what is this to me, who in love to you far exceed Echo? For she does not reply to every thing she hears, but only to the last words of the voice, like a coy mistress, who receives the salute of her lover on the extremity of her lips. In this as I gladly lead the way, so again challenged by you, like a tennis-player, I return the stroke. You shall not escape, but shall be convicted by your own letter; and in that image you may discover a resemblance of yourself, as you re-

* Epistle VIII. is addressed to the same.
† The Mythologists fable, that Echo was desperately beloved by Pan. See, among others, Hephæstion in the Writers of poetic history, published by Thomas Gale, p. 333.
WOLFIUS.
And thus Libanius says to his friend Demetrius, "You have transmitted me so sweet a voice by your epistle, that I was quite captivated by it, and enamoured of its charms, admiring the beauty of the words no less than Pan admired the Goddess!" Ep. ccccxlii.

ceive much and return little, not of me, who endeavour to excell in both. But whether you return with the same measure that you receive, or not, whatever I receive from you is agreeable to me, and shall be deemed a full and satisfactory answer.

Epistle LV. To Eumenius and Pha- rianus*.

A. D. 359.

WHOEVER has persuaded you that any thing is more pleasing and beneficial to mankind than philosophising in ease and security, is deceived himself, and deceives you. If you retain your former spirit, and, like a sparkling flame, it be not suddenly extinguished, I deem you happy. Four years have now elapsed, and almost three months more, since we parted. I would gladly therefore learn what progress you have made in that time. As to me, it is a wonder that I can even speak Greek, such barbarism I have contracted in this country †. Despise not oratory,

---

* These were probably two of Julian's fellow-students, whom he left with regret at Athens, in 355, when he was summoned to court by Constantius, and created Cæsar. I have therefore dated this Epistle as above. I know not that their names occur any where else.

Among the Epistles of Libanius, preserved (in Latin) by Zambicari, are two to Eumedius, (III. 237, S.) which probably means this Eumenius, especially as in one of them Andromachus, an Athenian, is recommended to him.

† This expression shews, that Julian was then in Gaul. It is similar to one in Epistle XXIX. p. 75.

nor neglect rhetorick, nor be inattentive to poetry. But let your principal study be philosophy; and in this bestow all your labour on the maxims of Aristotle and Plato. Be this your chief work; be this the base, the foundation, the walls, the roof. Let the rest be no more than offices; which, however, you may finish with more skill than some can build a mansion.

This advice is given you by one, who, by divine Nemesis, loves you both with a brotherly affection, as having been his school-fellows and intimate friends. If you retain a regard for me, my affection will increase. If not, I shall grieve. And what at length may be the consequence of continual grief, for the sake of a better omen, I suppress.

Epistle LVI. To Ecdicius, Præfect of Ægypt.

IF any thing particularly deserves our serious attention, it is sacred music. Selecting therefore from among the Alexandrians some youths of good families, order two *artabæ* * to be distributed every month to each; and some oil, wheat, and wine. The præfects of the treasury shall supply them with cloaths. They shall be chosen by

---

* Among the Ægyptians, that an *artaba* made twenty *modii* we are told by Jerom on Isaiah, ch. v.
 Among the Persians it was different, as we learn from Herodotus, *l.* 1.   Robertson.

their

their voices. Mean time, let those who are proficients in that art be informed, that we have allotted rewards for their labours. And, besides these encouragements from us, they may also be assured by those who have a right judgement in these things, that they will profit their souls by purifying them with divine music. So much for these youths. As to what relates to the scholars of the musician Dioscorus, let them cultivate that art with more attention, and they shall receive from us all possible assistance *.

Epistle LVII. To the Philosopher ELPIDIUS †.

THE pleasure even of a short letter is great, when the friendship of the writer is measured, not by the concisenefs of his epistle, but by the greatness of his mind. Therefore if my present mental salutation be rather short, do not from thence form a judgement of my regard. But as you well know the extent of my love for you, excuse the brevity of this address, and answer it with-

---

* This Epistle is a proof of the Emperor's great esteem for music. And indeed it is impossible to read his works without being convinced, that he was ignorant of nothing which was then necessary to be known to render a man an universal scholar.   LA BLETERIE.

It is omitted, however, by this translator.

† This philosopher, and the Emperor's kindness to him, are mentioned by Libanius in one of his Epistles to Julian. See Vol. I. p. 305.

out delay. For whatever you send me, though it be small, I esteem as a specimen of every thing that is good.

Epistle LVIII. To the ALEXANDRIANS.

YOU have a stone obelisk *, I am informed, of a proper height, but that, as if it were worthless, it lies on the shore. Constantius, of blessed memory, had constructed a vessel on purpose to convey it to my country, Constantinople †. But as he, by the will of the Gods, has taken a fatal departure from hence, that city now requests this present from me, being my country, and consequently more nearly connected to me than to him. His was a brotherly, but mine is a filial, love ‡; for

A. D. 362.

---

* In a remote but polished age, which seems to have preceded the invention of alphabetical writing, a great number of these obelisks had been erected in the cities of Thebes and Heliopolis, by the ancient sovereigns of Ægypt, in a just confidence that the simplicity of their form and the hardness of their substance would resist the injuries of time and violence.   GIBBON.

† Constantius caused one of the obelisks that are still seen at Rome to be transported thither from Ægypt. It is that which was erected by Sixtus V. Constantius was desirous of procuring a like decoration for New Rome.
    LA BLETERIE.

A vessel of uncommon strength and capaciousness was provided to convey this uncommon weight of granite from the banks of the Nile to those of the Tyber.   GIBBON.

‡ Julian, I think, might have said that *Constantine* loved the city as his " daughter;" and then he would have had no

for I was born there, I was educated there, and therefore I cannot be ungrateful to her *.

As your city is no less dear to me than my own country, instead of a triangular stone engraved with Ægyptian characters, I allow you to erect the colossal statue †, which has lately been made, of a man whose resemblance you desire. And as it is generally reported that some persons repose on the top of that obelisk, and pay it adoration ‡, it

---

no occasion to magnify his affection for that place above *Constantine's*. However, the more to satisfy the Alexandrians, he promises them a column of brass, of a large size, in the room of the Ægyptian obelisk of stone. And thus Julian does what had been blamed in *Constantine*. He robs and strips Alexandria to enrich and adorn Constantinople.

LARDNER.

. This learned writer, it is observable, has here mistaken "Constantine" for "Constantius." Yet he refers to Spanheim's edition, where we read ὁ μακαρίτης Κωνστάντιος.

* In the editions of Julian the Epistle ends here. M. Muratori found the conclusion in a MS. of the Ambrosian library; and has published it in his *Anecdota Græca*, from whence M. Fabricius has inserted it in his *Bibliotheca Græca*.

LA BLETERIE.

† I imagine this was a statue of Julian himself. *Ibid.*

‡ Τινὲς εἰσιν οἱ θεραπεύοντες καὶ προσκαθεύδοντες αὐτῷ τῇ κορυφῇ. M. Muratori translates it, *quosdam esse therapeutas qui obelisci hujus vertici indormiunt.* He thinks that these *therapeutæ* were some monks, who, no doubt in the spirit of mortification, slept on that obelisk. M. Fabricius adds, that these were certainly some Stylites. But, 1. in order to find *therapeuts* here, a force must be put upon the text, and no regard paid to the conjunction copulative which connects the two verbs: *cultum adhibentes et indormientes ejus vertici*. 2. The Stylites were entirely unknown before the illustrious St. Simeon, who did not ascend his pillar till about the year 423; and it is remarkable that the anchorets

it should, I am convinced, on account of that superstition, be removed. For those who see them sleeping there, amidst the filth which must sur-

chorets of Ægypt sent and declared to him, that they separated themselves from his communion, because they could not approve so new a kind of life. Nor did they again unite with this saint till they had had proofs of his obedience and humility. It is better therefore to translate it as I have done, and to say that some Heathens paid adoration to this obelisk. It is well known, that all the obelisks were dedicated to the sun, a reason sufficient to mislead some Christian anchorets; and the hieroglyphics which were seen on this might render it still more respectable to idolaters. Some, hoping no doubt to have divine dreams, went to sleep on the point, or rather near the point, of this obelisk, which lay on the sea-shore. The heat of the climate will not admit a doubt that this was in the night; and this nocturnal superstition served as an occasion and a pretext for some disorders which completed the discredit of Paganism. Julian, if I may be allowed the expression, was desirous of removing that *stone of offence*, and of preserving from this ridicule his unhappy religion, which had already too much of it. *Ibid.*

This obelisk might be that which Spon saw at Constantinople in the square of the Armeydan, where was formerly the Hippodrome. It is of Ægyptian granite, fifty feet high, and covered with hieroglyphics. The inscription on the base relates that " Theodosius undertook to erect " this monument, which lay on the ground, and that Pro- " clus accomplished the work in thirty-two days." Julian, no doubt, was dead before his obelisk was erected, and Valens had neglected it. In the reign of Theodosius they were far from giving the honour of it to Julian, or from saying that it had been transported from Ægypt by the orders of that apostate. It may be objected that the obelisk of Spon is square, but that this which Julian mentions was triangular, τρίγωνον. But this word is a correction of M. Muratori, as the MS. gives τρίτων, which has no meaning. Probably we should read τετράγωνον, especially as, according to M. Muratori himself, all the other obelisks are square. *Ibid.*

found

round the place, and the shameful actions there committed, can by no means regard this stone as sacred, and the superstition of those who dwell on it confirms unbelievers in their infidelity. You should therefore second me in my undertaking, by sending this obelisk to my country, which, when you navigate our seas, receives you with such hospitality, and thus contributing your assistance to the outward embellishment of that city. Nor can it be disagreeable to yourselves to have something of your own extant among us, which, as you sail towards the city, you may hereafter view with pleasure.

Epistle LIX *. To Dionysius †.

[MORE prudent was your former silence than your present defence;] for then, though perhaps you devised scandal, you did not utter it. [But now, teeming, as it were, with slander against us, you pour it forth most abundantly; unless I ought not to deem slander] and abuse your thinking

---

* For an account of this Epistle and the former, see p. 2. In the editions of Rigalt, Petau, and Spanheim, it is imperfect. The above is translated from a copy in the *Lux Evangelii* of Fabricius, p. 326. collected by Rostgaard. The additions are inserted within { }.

† The Medicean MS. has this inscription: Ιελιανος και Νωλυ. The beginning of the Epistle is wanting in the editions. FABRICIUS.

me like your friends; to each of whom you offered your services unasked *, but particularly unasked by the first, and the second only hinting that he should be glad of your assistance, you immediately complied. Whether I resemble Constns and Magnentius †, facts, as the saying is, will shew. But you, like Astydamas in the comedy, are your own panegyrist ‡; and this is evident from what you have written. For those expressions, " intrepidity," and " great boldness," and, " I wish you knew who " and what I am," and the like, for shame! what boasting and ostentation do they exhibit! But, by Venus and the Graces, if you are so bold and noble-minded, [why were you so fearful of being under the necessity of offending a third time? For those who have incurred the displeasure of princes, if they are wise, find an ease, and perhaps a pleasure, in

---

* Suidas: ακλητος, ανωνυμος, δεδωκας σεαυτον ακλητον τω δευτερω. He alludes to the words of Julian. By προτερον (" the " former,") understand Constans (" the second,") o δευτερος, is Magnentius.   FABRICIUS.

† Constans, the youngest son of the great Constantine, was engaged in a civil war with his eldest brother Constantine, who was killed in the course of it. Magnentius revolted against Constantius, and usurped the West. By comparing Julian to them, Dionysius perhaps meant to stigmatise him with the murder of Constantius and usurpation of the empire.

‡ In the MS. σεαυτον επαινεις, not σαυτης επαινεις, γυναι, as even Rigalt to Onosander, in his edition, p. 90. It refers to Philemon, the comic poet, as appears from the Proverbs of Apostolius, Centur. xvii. 30. and Suidas on σαυτην επαινεις. See also Zenobius, v. 100. Julian quotes the same proverb in his xiith Epistle.   FABRICIUS.

being

being difcharged from bufinefs; or if they muft be fined, they fuffer in their fortunes; or the utmoft effect of refentment is that incurable evil, as it has been called, the lofs of life. All thefe things are fcorned and defpifed by you, who have renounced your friend, a man, from common and general report, well known to us, dull as we are. Inftead of this, you fay, you invoke the Gods that you may not offend a third time. My anger therefore will not from being good make you wicked. He that could do this would be a prodigy indeed. According to Plato, it might indeed have the contrary effect *. But virtue being perfectly free, you ought to have no fuch ideas. You, however, think it a great matter to flander all men, to utter the bittereft farcafms, and to convert the temple of peace into a brothel.]

Do you think that your paft faults are in general excufed, and that your late courage has atoned for your former cowardice? You know the fable of Chabrias †. A cat was once in love with a handfome youth ‡. Learn the reft from the book. What-

---

* De Legibus, vi.

† The words τον Χαβριυ are in the Medicean and Barroc. MSS. and this is in the xvith fable of Chabrias, or Babrias, a Greek poet, who has put the fables of Æfop into Iambic verfe.

‡ Rather, according to our fables, a young man was in love with a cat. Dionyfius could no more diveft himfelf of his natural pufillanimity, &c. than the cat (tranf-formed to a woman) could forego her purfuit of mice. The Latin tranflator renders it *muft.la* ("a weafel"); but γαλη fignifies alfo "a cat."

ever you may say, you will persuade no one that you were not what you were, and what many have long known you to be. But your unskilfulness and temerity are owing, not to philosophy, the Gods forbid! but rather to what Plato calls "a double ignorance *." For though experience might have taught you, as it has me, that you know nothing, yet you think yourself the wisest of all men, past, present, or to come; so great is your ignorance, so abundant your self-conceit.

But enough concerning you. Some apology perhaps is necessary to others for so readily giving you a share in the conduct of my affairs. I am not the first, nor the only one, Dionysius, who has been mistaken. Your name-sake also deceived Plato †. [And so did Callippus the Athenian ‡, whom, he said, he knew to be wicked, but that he was profligate to such a degree he never could have suspected.] And need I add, that the greatest of physicians, Hippocrates, said, " in my opinion of " the sutures of the head I was mistaken §? Thus they were deceived in what they ought to have known,

---

* The one is when men acknowledge their ignorance, the other when they think they know that of which they are ignorant. *In Alcib.* I.

† Dionysius the younger sent for Plato into Sicily, to instruct him in philosophy. See the Life of Dion in Plutarch.

‡ A hearer of Plato, who murdered Dion.

§ The following is doubtless the passage to which Julian alludes: " Autonomus of Omilus died of a wound on his " head, on the sixteenth day, having received a hurt by a " stone

known, and even a physician was ignorant of a theorem of his own art. Is it strange then that Julian, hearing that Nilöus *, or Dionysius, had on a sudden behaved bravely, should be mistaken?

You have heard of Phædon † of Elis, and you know his history. If not, read it with attention. He thought that no one is so depraved that philosophy cannot cure him, and that it purifies human life from the passions, desires, and all such disorders. For that it should be serviceable to those who are well born, and well educated, is not at all extraordinary. But if it brings back into the light those whose minds are ever so much darkened by depravity, this seems to me truly admirable. And on that account, as all the Gods know, I began by degrees to form a more advantageous opinion of you.

" stone on the sutures. I did not think it necessary to " open it; for that the sutures themselves were injured by " the blow escaped me." (εκλεψαν δε μα την γνωμην αι ραφαι, κ. τ. λ.) *Hipp. de morb.* V. 7. 27. The words above quoted, as from Hippocrates, are, εσφηλαν δε μα την γνωμην αι περι την κεφαλην ραφαι. But though in a particular case (as above) this great physician had the candour to own himself mistaken, it does not follow, nor does it appear, that he was ignorant of the nature of the sutures in general. Julian trusted to his memory, which, though good, was not infallible.

This candid confession of Hippocrates is mentioned also with applause by Celsus, VIII. 4. and Plutarch *de profectu in virtutem*, p. 82.

* Τον Νειλωνν. MS. Τον Νειλον. FABRICIUS.

† A scholar of Socrates, so much beloved by Plato, that he inscribed his divine book, on the immortality of the soul, *Phædon*.

Not that I placed you in the first, or even in the second, rank of worthies, as you yourself perhaps may know. If not, ask the excellent Symmachus *,] for he, I am persuaded, being naturally disposed to speak truth, will never utter a wilful falshood.

[But if you resent my not raising you to the highest, I reproach myself for not degrading you to the lowest, rank. And I thank all the Gods and Goddesses for preventing me from forming an intimacy with you, and making you privy to my counsels, as a bosom friend. Though the poets have said many things of Fame, as a Goddess; she is rather, if you please, a Dæmon. For Fame is not always to be credited; and therefore her nature is dæmoniacal, being not absolutely pure or perfectly good, like that of the Gods, but allayed with some degree of evil †. And though it may not be proper to say this of the other Dæmons, I know I may safely affirm of Fame, that she utters many falshoods, as well as many truths ‡. For I

---

* A Roman orator and præfect, well known by his epistles still extant, and by his writings against Christianity, refuted by Prudentius and St. Ambrose. Three epistles to him are extant from Libanius, to whom, it appears, he wrote in Latin, as his letters required an interpreter. He was consul in 391.

† And had not the Gods, as well as Fame and the Dæmons, of Julian and the Heathens, much evil in their nature? Not to mention the notorious vices of Mars, Bacchus, Apollo, and the rest of them, in what was their Jupiter, their Supreme, so pre-eminent as in his debaucheries?

‡ *Tam falsi pravique tenax quam conscia veri.*   Virg.

would by no means be accused of bearing false witness.]

You value your freedom of speech at four *oboli* *, as the saying is. [But know you not, that Thersites, among the Greeks, was also a free-speaker, and in return was chastised by the wise Ulysses with his sceptre †? and that the drunkenness of Thersites was less regarded by Agamemnon than the flies in the proverb were by the tortoise ‡?]

What avails our reproaching others? We should rather be irreproachable ourselves. If you are so, convince me of it. [When you were young, you told fine stories of yourself to your elders. These adventures, with the Electra of Euripides §, I pass

---

* That is, at ever so high a rate. Suidas on Τετlαρων οβολων, quoting this passage of Julian. FABRICIUS.

He quotes it, as usual, without naming his author. An *obolus* was a small Athenian coin of silver, weighing about twelve grains; in our money five farthings.

† Il. II. 199.
  ———— Cowering as the dastard bends,
 The weighty sceptre on his back descends. POPE, 336.

‡ Suidas quotes these words from an author to me unknown, τω δε Αγαμεμνονι. κ. τ. λ. Flies cannot hurt a tortoise, on account of the shell with which it is furnished. Similar to this is, " an elephant does not regard a fly." It would be more pleasant if applied to the mind. A mind fortified by virtue and philosophy no more fears the attacks of fortune than "a tortoise flies." ERASMUS.

The passage above quoted by Suidas is this of Julian, which has been brought to light long since the time of Erasmus. It is also quoted anonymously by Apostolius, in his Centur. XX. proverb. 66.

§ Eurip. Electr. ver. 946. 1122.
 I never with the opening morn forbore
 To breathe my silent plaints, &c. POTTER.

EPISTLES OF JULIAN.

in silence. But when you became a man, and joined the army, you did, by Jove, just what you say of truth; it gave you offence, and you deserted it. By how many witnesses can I prove this, and those not of the vulgar and abandoned, but some by whom you yourself were repulsed, who came to us from that neighbourhood?] To depart from princes in enmity, most sagacious Dionysius, is no proof either of courage or wisdom. Much more would it become you to conciliate, by your intercourse with mankind, their affections to us. But such, by the Gods, will never be your conduct, nor that of thousands more who are like-minded.

If rocks dash against rocks, and stones against stones, instead of being serviceable to each other, the strongest easily breaks the weakest. I say not this with Laconic brevity; for I think on your subject I seem more loquacious than the Attic grasshoppers *. For your drunken abuse † of me, with the leave of the Gods, and powerful Nemesis, I will inflict upon you a deserved punishment. "To what purpose?" you say. [To restrain as much as possible your mind and tongue, and] to

---

* This is said of a man immoderately talkative, or very musical; because this insect, living only on dew, chiefly delights in singing. And Socrates, in the Phædron of Plato, relates that some who were so absorbed by music that, neglecting their food, they were famished, were changed by the Gods into grasshoppers. ERASMUS.

† See the Fragment (from Suidas) on Musonius.

prevent your offending [in the leaft] either by words or deeds; in fhort, to diveft your fcurrilous tongue of fo much flander. I well know that the fandal even of Venus is faid to have been ridiculed by Momus *. But you fee that Momus, though envious of all her beauties, could find nothing but her fandal to depreciate. May you grow old, fretted, in like manner, with envy, more decrepid than Tithonus, more wealthy than Cinyras, and more effeminate than Sardanapalus, fo as to verify the proverb, " Old men are twice children ! †"

[But why does the divine Alexander feem to you fo renowned? Why do you profefs yourfelf his imitator and rival? Is it for that with which the youth Hermolaus ‡ reproached him? Of that no one is fo filly as to fufpect you; but of the contrary, for which Hermolaus, grievoufly complaining, fuffered ftripes, and, it is faid, would have killed Alexander, there is no one who is not per-

---

* Viz. The creaking of it. See Philoftrati Epift. XXI.

† On the word Καταγηρασαι, Suidas has the above paragraph (not mentioned as a quotation from Julian) with this addition, " which is faid of thofe who live long. For " Tithonus, being fuperannuated, was, at his own defire, " changed into a grafshopper. Cinyras, a defcendant of " Pharnaces, king of Cyprus, was famous for his riches. " And Sardanapalus, the laft king of Affyria, fell a victim " to intemperance and luxurious delights."

‡ " We confpired to kill you," faid Hermolaus, " be" caufe you have begun not to govern us as free-men, but " to tyrannife over us as flaves."   Q. CURTIUS.

fuaded

suaded that you are guilty *. From many, by the
Gods, who said they had a great regard for you,
I have heard several things advanced by way of
extenuating this offence; and one there was who
disbelieved it. But he was a single swallow, who
does not make a spring †. Perhaps Alexander
appears great to you, because he cruelly slew
Callisthenes ‡; or because Clitus ‡ fell a sacrifice
to his intemperance; and also Philotas ‡, and
Parmenio ‡; whose son Hector was afterwards
smothered in the whirlpools of the Ægyptian Nile,
or of the Euphrates, for both have been mentioned §. I omit his other follies, that I may not
seem to revile a man, who, though by no means
distinguished for virtue, was a most valiant and excellent commander. Of both which, virtue and

---

* Hermolaus, a noble youth, of the royal guards, for killing a boar, which the king had destined for his own spear, was by his command scourged; a disgrace which he so bitterly resented that he wept, and formed the abovementioned conspiracy. Q. CURTIUS.

† See Erasmi Chiliad. xciv.

‡ The cruel deaths of this philosopher and these generals are well known, and are related at large by Quintus Curtius. " One," said Hermolaus, [Clitus] " sprinkled " your table with his blood; another [Philotas] suffered " more than one kind of death. Parmenio was massacred " unheard, &c."

§ According to Curtius, as this youth, one of the few dear to Alexander, was attempting to follow him down the Nile, the small vessel in which he had embarked, being overloaded, sunk. Hector, after long struggling with the stream, at length reached the bank, but there, for want of assistance, perished. Of this, however, Alexander seems to have been innocent. Philotas was also a son of Parmenio.

valour,

valour, you have a less portion than fish have of hair. Now hear with calmness what I advise:

Not these, O daughter, are thy proper cares!
Thee milder arts befit, and softer wars *.

What follows, by the Gods, I am ashamed to transcribe. I would have you, however, attend to it, since it is highly reasonable that deeds should follow words, and that one who has been remiss in his deeds should never start at words. But you, who revere the shades of Magnentius and Constans, wage war with the living, and, in some way or other, asperse the best characters. Are the living less able to revenge affronts? This you will by no means think proper to affirm, be the confidence which you mention, whatever ᛰ may. Rejecting that plea, will you admit this, that you deride them because they are insensible? Nor is this, I presume, the true reason. For who among the living is so stupid, or pusillanimous, as to think your good opinion of the least importance, and would not prefer being totally unknown to you, or, if that were impossible, would not rather choose to be reviled by you, as I am now, than honoured? I would by no means err so egregiously in my judgement as not to think your praises better than your reproaches. But even this, perhaps, that I am now writing to you, proves that I am hurt. By no means, I call the preserving Gods to witness; I only wish to check the intolerable arrogance

* Il. V. 428. Pope, 519.

of this reviler, the petulance and prurience of his tongue, the frenzy of his mind, and his fury on all occasions. If I were injured by you, I might by deeds, not words, have a legal remedy, as you, being a citizen, and of the senatorial rank, have disobeyed the command of the Emperor. But for this there was no occasion, nothing but the last extremity requiring it. I did not think proper therefore to subject you to any punishment, but rather chose first at least to write to you, hoping that a short epistle might effect your cure. But as you persevere in these crimes, or rather exhibit to the public the frenzy which was before concealed, let no one, for the future, think you a man, who are not a man, or mistake the fury, which transports you, for courage, or suppose you to be learned who are an utter stranger to literature, as may easily be proved from your epistles.]

None of the ancients, for instance, ever used τὸ φρȣδον, to signify " manifest," * as you have, besides many other blunders, in your letter. No one, in the longest discourse, could express your loose and indecent behaviour, your self-prostitution. For you

---

* Φρȣδον is rather αφανις, ικπεδων, αφανιον. (" Far distant, obscure.") See Hesychius and Harpocratio.   FABRICIUS.

† Among the flagrant crimes of which he accuses Dionysius, Julian here condescends to arraign his phraseology, and, like a former Dionysius, exchanges his sceptre for a rod. Thus a mistake in the meaning of a word, or in the graces of style, is put on a level with treachery and treason, and seems as unpardonable to this Imperial critic, as an offence against the graces of behaviour was to a late British peer.

you seduce, not only such as are willing and forward, * * * * nor those who hunt after public employments, but those who, in consequence of a sound judgement, act right, [and therefore have been selected by us for their prompt obedience.

You make fair promises, though not by way of intreaty, or submission, if we will again employ you in some place of trust. But so far is that from my intention, that when others have been admitted, I never sent for you, as I have for many, known and unknown to me, of the inhabitants of that heaven-beloved city, Rome. Such value I set on your friendship; of such attention I thought you worthy! I shall therefore act in the same manner probably for the future. And this epistle, which I am now writing, I intend, not only for your perusal, but think it necessary to be communicated to many more. I will give it indeed to all, for all, I am persuaded, will readily receive it; such a general indignation your insolence and arrogance have excited.

You have here a complete reply, so that you can desire from us nothing farther. Nor do we wish any return from you. Make what use you please of our letters; for you have sold our friendship. Farewell; amidst your banquets abusing me!]

peer. The above criticism is perfectly in the spirit of Bentley *versus* Barnes. But Julian should have recollected that this Roman wrote Greek in compliment to him.

Epistle LX. To Jamblichus.

YOU came, and acted. For you came, though absent, by your letter. But, by the ardour of the friendship which I feel for you, I do not decline your love †, * * * nor in any respect desert you, but, as if you were present, I view you with my mind, and am with you, though absent, nor can any thing else give me complete satisfaction. You are never weary of obliging the present, and not only delighting, but preserving the absent by your writings. For being told that a friend was arrived with a letter from you, though I had been three days ill of a pain in my stomach, and was much indisposed with a fever, yet hearing, as I said, that a letter from you was at the gate, like one not master of himself and divinely inspired, I sprung up and rushed out to him before he could enter. But as soon as I had taken the letter into my hands, I swear by the Gods themselves and that regard for you which inflames me, my pain at once abated, and the fever instantly fled, abashed, as it were, at the evident presence of some tutelar deity. And when I had opened and read it, what, think you, were my sensations, or how great was my satisfaction, praising immoderately, and loving

† Imperfect.

the moſt friendly, as you ſtyle him, * * * * †, who is really deſerving of love, and the miniſter of good, for being inſtrumental in forwarding to me your letter, and conſigning it to me, like a bird, by a favourable and proſperous gale, which not only gave me the delight of hearing that your affairs were in a proper ſtate, but alſo recovered me from illneſs! As to other things, how ſhall I expreſs what I felt when I firſt read that epiſtle, or how can I ſufficiently demonſtrate my affection? How often did I turn back from the middle to the beginning! How much did I fear, leſt, when I had finiſhed it, I ſhould forget it! How often, as in the circuit and compaſs of a ſtanza, did I carry back the concluſion to the beginning, repeating at the cloſe, as in a muſical compoſition, that meaſure with which the ſong began! And what followed? How often did I apply the letter to my lips, as mothers kiſs their infants! How cloſely did I preſs it to my mouth, as if I had been embracing my deareſt miſtreſs! How frequently did I accoſt and kiſs even the ſuperſcription, which, as a well-known ſignature, you had written with your own hand; and then fixed my eyes upon it, rivetted, as it were, by the fingers of that ſacred hand on the traces of the letters?

† Imperfect. The name of the friend who forwarded the letter ſeems all that is wanting.

"Much

"Much falutation from us attend you!" as fays the fair Sappho *; and, not only during our feparation, but fare you well always, not failing to write, and, as is fitting, to remember us! As to ourfelves, there will never be a time, there can never be an occafion, there will never be a difcourfe, in which we fhall not remember you * * * *. And if Jupiter fhall ever allow me to revifit my native country, and again to enter your facred manfion, fpare not the fugitive; but, as a deferter from the Mufes, brought back from flight, bind him, if you pleafe, to your delightful benches, and, when properly chaftifed, reprimand him. I will by no means decline the punifhment, but will fubmit to it voluntarily and chearfully; as to the provident and falutary correction of an indulgent father. But if you will permit me to pronounce my own fentence, I will with pleafure acquiefce in this; the being faftened, my noble friend, to your veft, fo as never to be feparated from you, but clofely to adhere to you, and every where to be carried about with you, as fables feign of double men: unlefs they ludicroufly mean it as an allufon to the excellence of friendfhip, expreffing the congenial agreement of each foul in the bond of communion.

* Χαιρε δη και αυτος ημιν πολλα. This muft be in fome poem that is loft.

Epistle LXI. To the same.

I HAVE suffered, I confess, sufficient punishment for my absence from you, partly in the fatigues which I endured in my journey, but chiefly on account of my long separation from you. Though I have every where met with a variety of accidents, so as to have left none unexperienced; though I have sustained the tumults of battles, the distress of sieges, the wanderings of flight, with terrors of every kind, and also the severities of winter, the dangers of diseases, and many and various other calamities from Upper Pannonia to the passage of the Chalcedonian strait, I can truly say, that nothing has happened to me so grievous and perplexing, since my leaving the East, as my not having seen, for such a length of time, you, the general blessing of the Greeks. Wonder not therefore, if I say, a kind of darkness and thick clouds hang over my eyes. For, in truth, the sky will be serene, the light of the sun more splendid, and a most beautiful spring of life will, as it were, be renewed to me, when I can embrace you, the great ornament of the world. Then, like a darling son, escaped from war, or returned from a long voyage, and restored unexpectedly to an excellent father, relating to you all my sufferings, and the dangers that I have surmounted, and resting, as on a sacred anchor,

anchor, I shall find a sufficient solace for my sorrows. For calamities are consoled, and sufferings alleviated, by communication, and by the knowledge of our friends participated. Mean while I tender you my best services, nor will I ever fail to write to you, and during the whole time of my absence to send you such epistolary tokens. If I can obtain the same from you, the perusal of your letters, like an auspicious omen, will abate my grief. Receive mine with complacence, and be more favourably disposed to make a return. For whatever good you shall express or communicate, I shall prefer to the eloquent voice of Mercury, and the skilful hand of Æsculapius.

Epistle LXII. †. To **** (Imperfect.)

* * * * * * * *
SHOULD not the same indulgence, which is given to wooden blocks, be allowed to men ‡ ? For suppose that one invested with the priesthood be unworthy, should he not be spared, till, having ascer-

† The Gentiles, who peaceably followed the customs of their ancestors, were rather surprised than pleased with the introduction of foreign manners; and in the short period of his reign, Julian had frequent occasions to complain of the want of fervour of his own party. See Epistles LXII. and LXIII.
GIBBON.

Many of the Epistles of Julian are the effusions of private friendship; some are public Edicts; while others are justly

ascertained the enormity of his offence, he can be removed from the ministerial function, and deprived of the name of priest, injudiciously perhaps conferred upon him, and may be subjected also to censure, fine, and other punishments? If you understand not this, you cannot have even a superficial knowledge of any thing; for how ignorant must you be of what is just and right, not to know the difference between a priest and a private man! And what must have been your temper, if you have beaten one to whom you ought to have risen from your seat! Nothing can be more shameful, in you it is particularly unbecoming, in the sight both of Gods and men. The bishops and presbyters of the Galileans perhaps associate with you; and if not publickly, through fear of me, yet by stealth and

---

justly styled by Mr. Gibbon " pastoral letters," and are dictated by the Emperor as Sovereign Pontiff. In this pontifical character he addresses the Epistle, of which this fragment only is preserved, to a Gentile priest, who, forgetting the nature of his spiritual warfare, had violently assaulted and beaten one of his brethren. As a Christian Pontiff would have quoted St. Paul to Titus, *A bishop must be no striker*, this Gentile apostle appeals to the Didymæan oracle, and then pronounces a sentence of suspension.

‡ This paragraph is unintelligible, for want of that which precedes it. Julian perhaps had been speaking of such images of the Gods as were worn out and decayed, which he has mentioned also in his long Fragment. " If " any one," says he, " thinks, that, because they have " been once called the images of the Gods, they can " never decay, he seems to me to have lost his senses. " For then they could not have been the workmanship of " men," &c.

at

at home with your concurrence. But the priest has been beaten. Otherwise your pontiff would not have preferred such a complaint against you. Passages from Homer you think fabulous; hear therefore the oracle of the Didymæan lord, and consider whether he rightly admonished the Greeks of old, and afterwards, in his discourses, taught men to be wise and virtuous:

>They, whom depravity and folly lead
>To scorn the priests of heaven's immortal powers,
>And to the wise intentions of the Gods
>Their own vain thoughts contemptuously oppose;
>In safety live not half their days, condemn'd
>To perish by th' eternal Gods, who deem
>Their servants honour sacred as their own *.

Not only those, you see, who beat or insult priests, but such as deny them honour are [declared †] to be enemies to the Gods; so that he who beats them is guilty of sacrilege. I therefore, as the Sovereign Pontiff of the religion of my country, having now obtained the præfecture of the Didymæan oracle, forbid you to interfere in any thing that relates to the priesthood for three whole months. If, within that time, you should appear deserving, on my hearing from the chief-priest of your city, I will consult the Gods whether you shall be reinstated. To this punishment, which I inflict upon

* This passage has been quoted before, in the Duties of a Priest, p. 127.
† Some such word is wanting in the original.

you for your rashness, the ancients used formerly to add, by words and in writing, the curses of the Gods. But of this I do not approve, as it never seems practised by the Gods. And in other respects, knowing that the priests are the ministers of our prayers, I join my hopes and prayers to yours, that by many and earnest intreaties you may obtain the pardon of the Gods.

Epistle LXIII. To the High-Priest THEODORE *.

A. D. 361.

THE Epistle that I have addressed to you differs from that which I have transmitted to others †, as I think your friendship for me superior to theirs. It is no inconsiderable circumstance, that we have

* This High-Priest Theodore was, as may be inferred from this Epistle, a zealous Pagan, the disciple of Maximus, who, like Julian, had been initiated by Maximus, and instructed, like that prince, in the principles of theurgy. This letter is inserted in the edition of F. Petau, but only in Greek. It had been copied from a MS. so defective, that it was not possible to translate it. M. Spanheim, from a MS. less imperfect, has given it, with a Latin version, which is not answerable to the reputation of that learned writer. LA BLETERIE.

† Julian had sent, without doubt, a circular letter to the Pagan pontiffs as soon as he was in peaceable possession of the empire. As this seems to have been written at the same time, I assign it to the year 361. *Ibid.*
Julian must then have been at Constantinople.

one

one common master, and you well remember *....
In a conversation that passed between us, a few
evenings ago, it gave me great pleasure to hear
him express the highest regard for you. In my
friendships I am usually very cautious. As for you,
I had never seen you. Before we can love, we must
know; and before we can know, we should try.
But a certain reason determined me †. I have therefore thought proper to rank you among my friends.
And now I entrust to you an affair very interesting
to me, and highly advantageous to all men. You
will transact it, I doubt not, with propriety, which
will afford me much joy here, and better hopes
hereafter ‡. For I differ in opinion from those
who

---

* He intimates by half a word, and a mysterious air, what they saw, or thought they saw, when they were initiated by Maximus.   LA BLETERIE.

† It is impossible to guess this reason; but we may partly discover, that, in the initiation of Theodore, something happened which induced Julian to conclude that a man so agreeable to the Gods deserved to be the minister and the assistant of the apostle of Paganism.   *Ibid.*

‡ As this Epistle was not written to be shewn, it proves to what a degree Julian was fanatical and convinced of his false religion. It shews, at the same time, that he believed a providence, another life, and the immortality of the soul. He detested the materialists. In one of his works he speaks with horror of Pyrrhonism, and of the doctrine of Epicurus. He thanks the Gods for having extinguished those sects, and caused most of the books which contained their pernicious tenets to be destroyed. [See the Duties of a Priest, p. 134.] Probably the free-thinkers would not have triumphed in his reign. Why then

who think that the soul perishes before or with the body *. We rely, however, on no man, but only on the Gods, as they only can be well acquainted with these things, or rather they alone necessarily know them. Men may form conjectures, but knowledge belongs to the Gods. The commission that I now give you is the superintendence of all the priests in Asia, both in the cities and in the country, with full powers to treat every one according to his deserts.

In a high-priest the principal requisite is moderation, together with kindness and benevolence to the deserving. As to those who are unjust or insolent to men, and irreligious to the Gods, let them be rebuked with boldness, or punished with severity. Whatever is necessary to be regulated in common, in order to render divine worship as perfect as possible, I will soon direct, with many other particulars. Some of them, in the mean time, I will here mention, in which it is right for you to

---

then should they defend him? But some common interests often serve to unite in appearance irreconcileable enemies. *And the same day they were made friends together; for before they were at enmity between themselves.* Of this the affection which Julian testified for the Jews is a remarkable instance. *Ibid.*

* Those who believed the soul to be immortal, and even the materialists, distinguished in the soul the intellectual part, νες, and the sensitive part, ψυχη. There were some who imagined, no doubt, that the intellectual part was withdrawn, and others that it was destroyed, when they saw the body reduced to a mere animal life. *Ibid.*

be

be advised by me. For on many of these subjects I speak, as all the Gods know, with much premeditation. In circumspection no one exceeds me, and I am an enemy, and have been so styled, to all innovation, especially in matters of religion, thinking it highly proper to adhere to our ancient paternal laws *, which were certainly given us by the Gods. They could not be so excellent, if they proceeded from men. But by the prevalence of riches and pleasures they have been so neglected and corrupted, that they require, I think, a new foundation. Seeing therefore so great an indifference among us towards the Gods, and all sense of religion banished by debauched and luxurious manners, I have continually lamented in private.

* Paganism, in general, had no religious code, unless it were some pretended oracles, apparently very modern, as to the ceremonies which ought to be observed in sacrifices, and the victims which were suitable to every kind of Gods. Eusebius quotes some passages of these oracles in the fourth book of his Evangelical Preparation. I imagine that the laws which Julian here mentions are principally the ancient rites of every nation, city, and temple. These rites had in time suffered various alterations, and in the decline of Paganism some were abolished.

Julian, deeply versed in antiquity, was desirous of restoring things to their former state. As to the wisdom quite divine which he admires in these rites, that is the work of his imagination. He considers them as symbolical. Being an ingenious and fruitful allegorist, by the force of arbitrary explanations he discovered some wonderful things in the worship, as well as in the history, of his Gods. To be convinced that he every where found all that he chose, we need only read his discourse " on the Mother of the Gods."

LA BLETERIE.

For those who are distinguished in the school of impiety * are so zealous as to suffer want and famine rather than taste swine's flesh †, or that of any thing strangled, or even killed by accident; while we are so regardless of the Gods as to forget the laws of our ancestors, and not even to know whether any such exist. But these men are in part only religious, as the God whom they worship is really most powerful, and most benevolent, and governs the visible world ‡.

They therefore who do not transgress the laws seem to me to act right. I blame them only for

---

* Δυσσιβιας σχολη προσχοιιας, "Those who are attached to the school of impiety." I think that we should read περιχοιιας, "the chiefs, the principal teachers." The sequel shews that this refers to the Jews. LA BLETERIE.

† This would only prove that Julian speaks of the Jews. Indeed the Christians, through respect for the Council of Jerusalem, abstained from blood and things strangled longer than the reasons subsisted on which the prohibition was founded; and the Oriental Christians continue to abstain from them still. But after God had revealed to St. Peter (Acts xv.) that the distinction of meats was abrogated, no Christian scrupled eating swine's flesh, except the Judaising Christians, who were not tolerated till the second destruction of the Jews, which happened under the Emperor Hadrian. *Ibid.*

‡ In the books of Julian against the Christian religion, of which St. Cyril, in refuting them, has preserved a considerable part, this prince says, in direct terms, that "he worships the God of Abraham, of Isaac, and of Jacob:" Αν προσκυνω τον Θεον Αβρααμ, και Ισαακ, και Ιακωβ. But it appears, in the same books, that he means, by this God, the *Demiurgus*; in which he is mistaken if he makes the *Demiurgus*, or *Logos*, of a different nature from the BEING, το ον, τ'αγαθον. *Ibid.*

worship-

worshipping God alone, and despising the worship of other Gods. Hurried into this frenzy by the pride of Barbarians *, they think that he is hidden from us Gentiles only. But from the Galilean impiety, like a pestilential distemper † * * * *.

[*The remainder is wanting in the original.*]

* Whatever incense Julian gave the Jews in the Epistle which he wrote to them, this text, and many others, shew that he despised them. In general, what most prejudiced the Pagans against both the Christian and Jewish religions, was their being exclusive and admitting no community with any other. But they endured the Jews with less impatience, and contented themselves with despising them, because the latter gained few proselytes. The barrenness, with which the synagogue was struck, made it find grace in the sight of our common enemies; but the fertility of the church alarmed and enraged them. They foresaw that she would at length destroy their altars. Julian, in particular, kept good terms with the Jews, because they entered into his plan, 1. By their implacable hatred to the Christians; 2. from the design which he had formed to restore the nation and the temple, in order to falsify the scriptures. Besides, the religion of the Jews ordained sacrifices, and in this point of view was agreeable to Julian, who, as may be seen in his life and his works, had a taste for bloody sacrifices more worthy of a butcher than a philosopher. La Bleterie.

† It is evident that Julian here launched forth against Christianity and the Christians; perhaps in a manner so atrocious as to shock the transcribers. *Ibid.*

Epistle LXIV. *. To the People †, clamorously applauding in the Tychæum, or Temple of Fortune.

A. D. 361.

WHEN I enter the theatre, even privately, you may applaud; but in the temples be silent, and transfer your applauses to the Gods. Praises are much more properly due to them.

* This Epistle was first published by Muratori, in his *Anecdota Græca*, from a MS. 700 years old, in the Ambrosian library, and is copied by Fabricius, in his *Bibliotheca Græca*.

In the edition of Wolfius, is the MCCXXth Epistle of Libanius. And the editor subjoins in a note, "I neither understand what Libanius here means, nor the occasion on which he wrote this Epistle." Yet as Muratori and Fabricius had previously given it to Julian, I cannot account for its being there ascribed to Libanius. Surely it seems much more characteristic of a prince than of a sophist; and is besides a subject, which Julian has discussed in the Misopogon, Vol. I. p. 241, &c.

† Probably "of Constantinople." Fabricius inscribes it *Byzantinis*, like Epistle XI. But see a note on that Epistle, p. 24.

EPISTLES OF JULIAN.

Epistle LXV. To a Painter*.

* Not being able to satisfy myself as to the meaning of the first part of this short Epistle, I will add the original, with the Latin translation of Muratori, by whom this also is preserved:

Πϱος ζωγϱαφον.	Ad Pictorem.
Ει μεν μη ειχον, και εχϱησα μοι, γνωμης ουα αξιος. Ει δε ειχον μεν, εκ' εχϱησαμην τι, τες Θεες εφεϱον, μαλλον δε υπο Θεων εφεϱομην. Συ με αλλοιον σχημα πως ιδιδως, εταιϱε; Οιον με ειδες, τοιουτον και γϱαψον.	Siquidem non haberem, et mihi fuisses gratificatus, venia dignus esses. Sin autem haberem, neque uterer, Deos ferrem: imo potius, Dii me ferrent. Tu vero quare alienum mihi habitum dedisti, O amice? Qualem me vidisti, talem etiam pingito.

The meaning of the two last paragraphs is sufficiently clear. "But why, my friend, have you given me a foreign "dress? Paint me as you see me." The painter perhaps had drawn him, like a Roman Emperor, with a small beard, and not like a Grecian Philosopher, with a large one.

Epistle

Epistle LXVI. To Arsaces, Satrap of Armenia *.

A. D. 363.

ARM, arm, Arsaces, against the furious Persians, and hasten to join my forces, swift as thought. My martial preparations and determined resolution have one of these ends in view; either

* The feeble Arsaces Tiranus, king of Armenia, had degenerated, still more shamefully than his father Chosroes, from the many virtues of the great Tiridates; and as the pusillanimous monarch was averse to any enterprise of danger and glory, he could disguise his timid indolence by the more decent excuses of religion and gratitude. He expressed a pious attachment to the memory of Constantius, from whose hands he had received in marriage Olympias, the daughter of the præfect Ablavius; and the alliance of a female, who had been educated as the destined wife of the emperor Constans, exalted the dignity of a Barbarian king. Tiranus professed the Christian religion; he reigned over a nation of Christians; and he was refrained by every principle of conscience and interest from contributing to the victory which would consummate the ruin of the church. The alienated mind of Tiranus was exasperated by the indiscretion of Julian, who treated the king of Armenia as his slave, and as the enemy of the Gods. The haughty and threatening style of the Imperial mandates awakened the secret indignation of a prince, who, in the humiliating state of dependence, was still conscious of his royal descent from the Arsacides, the lords of the East, and the rivals of the Roman power. GIBBON.

This Epistle, printed, for the first time, in the *Anecdota Græca* of M. Muratori, is inserted in the *Bibliotheca Græca*, [*tom.* VII. *p*. 86.] of Fabricius. It is in very bad Greek. vulgar, brutal, meanly vain-glorious, without genius, contrary

either to pay the debt of nature, bravely fighting, and exerting my utmost efforts, if success should attend the Parthians; or, if the Gods should assist me, to return triumphant, and to erect trophies

trary to policy; and, what is still more remarkable, it contains expressions that could not proceed from the pen of a superstitious Pagan, at the eve of a great enterprise, and in circumstances where the least word of bad omen was scrupulously avoided, as capable of being fatal. Can it be supposed that Julian would have ventured to say, even by way of circumlocution, that " he was resolved to perish?" Would he have communicated the prediction that we find at the end of the Epistle? Whatever the illustrious M. Muratori may say of it, I can scarce believe that it is the same which Sozomen has mentioned; especially as this does not contain all that the Ecclesiastical historian relates. I do not insist on this last reason, because it may be answered, that we have not the whole Epistle. But, after all, it is so strange a piece, that, instead of ascribing it to Julian, I would rather say, which is not necessary, that Sozomen was deceived by a spurious piece.

LA BLETERIE.

Muratori has published an Epistle from Julian to the Satrap Arsaces, fierce, vulgar, and (though it might deceive Sozomen) most probably spurious. La Bleterie translates and rejects it. GIBBON.

And so does the present translator.

The passage of Sozomen, to which M. de la Bleterie refers, is as follows: " He wrote also to Arsaces, king of
" the Armenians, an ally of the Romans, to join him in
" the field. In this Epistle, after boasting immoderately,
" and extolling himself as fit to reign, and dear to the Gods
" whom he worshipped, and stigmatising Constantius as
" pusillanimous and impious, he threatened Arsaces most
" contumeliously. And as he had heard that he was a
" Christian, in order to aggravate his reproaches, he ut-
" tered some wicked blasphemies against Christ, with great
" pride and ostentation, signifying, that the God whom
" he worshipped would by no means defend him, if he
" neglected his commands." *Hist. Eccl. l.* VI. *c.* 1.

taken

taken from the enemy. Shake off therefore your inactivity, forego all evasions, and thinking no longer of that Constantine of happy memory *, or of the wealth of the nobles, which was lavished on you and other Barbarians, by the effeminate and too aged † Constantius, now cultivate the friendship of Julian, Sovereign Pontiff, Cæsar, Augustus, the servant of Mars and the Gods, the destroyer of the Franks and Barbarians, but the deliverer of the Gauls and Italians. If you have any other design, for I hear that you are very crafty, a bad soldier, a boaster, I shall not be surprised, as you now secrete a public enemy, trusting to the chance of war. To destroy the enemy, we need only the assistance of the Gods; but if Fate, whose decree is their will, should determine otherwise, I shall submit with fortitude and complacence. Know, however, that you, in consequence, will be subjected to the Persian power, your house and your whole family will be destroyed by fire, and the kingdom of

---

* Μακαριτην εκεινον Κωνςαντινον, "That blessed Constantine." Julian would hardly have spoken so favourably of his uncle, the constant object of his hatred and ridicule. It appears by the conclusion of the Cæsars, p. 220, that he rather thought him cursed than "blessed."

† Πολυετης Κωνςαντιος, *annosi Constantii*. Constantius lived only 44 or 45 years.   La Bleterie.

In like manner, Julian, in his 1st oration, styles Licinius "an old man," (γεροντος), at the Battle of Cibalis in 314, though he was then not 50. M. de la Bleterie translates παλυτης; "qui n'a vecu que trop long tems" ("who had lived too long.")

Armenia

EPISTLES OF JULIAN.

Armenia subverted. The city of * Nisibis will also share your misfortunes. This the Gods revealed to us long ago.

Epistle LXVII.   To the People [of Antioch †.]

SOME are so audacious as to prophane the sepulchres and consecrated graves of the dead, though to remove from them even a stone, or to dig the earth, and pull the turf, was always deemed by

12 Feb. 363.

---

* The bulwark of the East, given up to the Persians by Jovian; now reduced to 150 houses. See *Voyages de Niebuhr*, tome ii. p. 300—309.

Be this letter genuine, or not, "Arsaces," as M. de la Bleterie expresses it, "attentive only to his own interest, "and dissatisfied with Julian, would not leave his own "frontiers." This prince, in the reign of Valens, was treacherously seized, imprisoned, and put to death, by Sapor, king of Persia, as Ammianus relates, xxvii. 12.

† I take this law from the Theodosian Code, ix. xvii. 3. tit. *De sepulchris violatis*. It is the only piece of any length that is left of the Latinity of Julian. It is forcible and elaborate, but much less pure than his Greek. The reader perhaps will not dislike being enabled to judge for himself. The following is the whole Epistle.

IMP. JULIANUS A. AD POPULUM.

Pergit audacia ad busta diem functorum et aggeres consecratos; cùm et lapidem hinc movere, terram solicitare, et cespitem vellere, proximum sacrilegio majores semper habuerint. Sed ornamenta quidam tricliniis, aut porticibus, auferunt de sepulchris. Quibus primis consulentes, ne in piaculum incidant contaminatâ religione bustorum, hoc fieri prohibemus pœnâ Manium vindice cohibentes.

Secundum

by our ancestors next to sacrilege. Some take away the ornaments of tombs to adorn their porticoes or parlours. To prevent, in the first place, the criminal impiety of polluting sepulchres, we prohibit it under pain of the punishment that is due to those who offend the Manes *.

Secundum illud est, quod efferri cognovimus cadavera mortuorum per confertam populi frequentiam et per maximam insistentium densitatem, quod quidem oculos hominum infaustis incestat aspectibus. Qui enim dies est benè auspicatus à funere? Aut quomodo ad Deos et templa venietur? Ideóque, quoniam et dolor in exequiis secretum amat, et diem functis nihil interest, utrùm per noctes, an per dies, efferantur, liberari convenit populi totius aspectus; ut dolor esse in funeribus, non pompa exequiarum, nec ostentatio, videatur.
Datum prid. id. Feb. Antiochiæ, Juliano Aug. IV. et Sallustio, Coss. LA BLETERIE.

* The profanation of sepulchres was considered in all times among the Romans as a kind of sacrilege. Those who dug up the body, or the bones, of a dead person were punished with death, if they were of mean condition. They were confined in an island, if they were of genteel rank. Those who destroyed a sepulchre, or took any thing away from it, were condemned to the mines, or banished. Constantine, in a law, whose object was to render divorces less frequent, and to make the Roman jurisprudence as to marriage again somewhat like the gospel, by restraining divorce to certain cases, specifies, among the crimes which gave a woman a right to repudiate her husband, murder, poisoning, and the violation of tombs. *Si homicidam, vel medicamentarium vel sepulchrorum dissolutorem maritum suum esse probaverit.* III *Cod. Theod. tit.* XVI. *De repudiis.* But the respect for the dead, and their tombs, which nature herself seems to inspire, was carried to an excess among the Pagans. They honoured the souls of the dead as divinities, and sepulchres as temples.

The Christian religion, which enlightened the world as to the fate of those wretched divinities, and the impiety of the worship that was paid them, no sooner became the religion

religion of the empire, than many individuals fell into an excess opposite to that of Paganism. A zeal ill understood, and, under the mask of zeal, avarice, always ready to draw from the truest principles false conclusions which favour it, destroyed tombs, applied the stones and ornaments to other uses, and dispersed the ashes of the dead, in order to find some valuable stuffs, or trinkets, which superstition might have interred with them.

M. Muratori, in his *Anecdota Græca*, has inserted near eighty short copies of verses composed by St. Gregory Nazianzen, against the violators of sepulchres. As several of them seem made in order to be engraved on the tombs of his friends, of whom the majority at least professed Christianity, we may infer that the tombs of the Christians were not spared, were it only by the Pagans, who, without doubt, used reprisals. The law, above quoted, shews what the Emperor Constantine, long after his conversion, thought of these disorders, which not only outraged nature, but also might render Christianity odious, on whose account they had become more common, though it had always condemned them. However, in the reign of Constantine, the laws were not executed with rigour. It appears by a law of Constans, that some individuals, and even some of the magistrates, had violated them with impunity. He caused a search to be made for the guilty: but he moderated the severity of the ancient laws, and reduced it to pecuniary penalties. Constantius renewed and even augmented it, as he suffered the pecuniary penalties to remain, when he re-established the punishment of death. Other christian princes, particularly Valentinian III. exerted themselves, in like manner, against this crime.

Julian, who considered the worship of the Manes as an essential part of Hellenism, here condemns from superstition what those princes condemned from a principle of humanity and Christianity, though some Pagan expressions have crept into their ordinances, which, without doubt, must be ascribed to their secretaries. The first part of the law of Julian is in the Code of Justinian, with some alteration. That which favoured too much of Paganism has been reformed. La Bleterie.

If an ancient were to revisit the world, with what astonishment would he be struck in the amphitheatre of the Academy Royal, which no law authorises to have dead bodies!

Secondly, we have heard that dead corpses are carried to interment through large crowds of people and numerous spectators, a sight, that defiles the eyes of men by its inauspicious appearance. For what day is well-omened by a funeral? And how can we afterwards approach the Gods and the temples?

For these reasons, and because funereal grief loves privacy, and as it is of no consequence to the deceased, whether they are interred by day or by night, it is proper that funerals should be secreted from the public view, so as to be expressive of sorrow, rather than of pomp and ostentation *.

bodies! A corpse was esteemed by the ancients a sacred object, which was respectfully placed under a funeral pile; and he who dared to lay hands on it was declared impure. What would he say on seeing that corpse horribly cut and mangled; and all the young surgeons, with their arms stripped and bloody, joking and laughing amidst those dreadful operations! *Tableau de Paris.*

* Whatever respect the Pagans had for the dead, by a contradiction, of which I will not here trace the origin, they considered a human corpse as the impurest thing in the world. They thought they ought not to enter into a temple on a day when they had attended a funeral. But, delivered from a vain superstition, the Christians, and perhaps some Pagans, after their example, paid the last duties to the dead in open day. Julian was desirous of reviving the ancient practice, and even endeavoured to support, by philosophical ideas, the Pagan notions on which that practice was founded. This second part of his law is in the Theodosian Code, though it does not appear to have been observed after his death. La Bletérie.

Of the laws which Julian enacted in a short reign of sixteen months [Dec. 361—June 363.] fifty-four have been admitted into the Codes of Theodosius and Justinian. (*Gothofred. Chron. Legum. pp.* 64—67.) Gibbon.

Given at Antioch, on the day preceding the ides of February, Julian Aug. (for the IVth *time), and Sallust being Consuls.*

Epistle LXVIII.   To Libanius *.

YOU have made a proper return to Aristophanes † for his piety to the Gods, and his
affection for you, by making what was formerly
a disgrace to him redound to his glory, not only

A. D.
362.

---

* This Epistle was copied by the illustrious Rostgaard
from the Modenese MS. D. collated with the two Medicean
E. and F. and is not to be found among those which have
been published, except, with many more, in the *Salutaris Lux
Evangelii* of our Fabricius, p. 323. But it is here more enlarged.   It is thus inscribed: Ιουλιανος Αυτοκρατωρ Λιβανιω τω Σο-
φιστη χαιρειν.   WOLFIUS.

Libanius answers this Epistle (occasioned by his oration
in defence of Aristophanes) in his DCLXXth, which see
Vol I. p. 317. The original of it is inserted by Wolfius, in
his notes on that Epistle.

Muratori observes that in one of the Ambrosian MSS. [at
Milan] there was a short Epistle of Julian, not yet published;
" but," he adds, " the evanescent letters made me totally de-
" spair of reading it. I hope, however, that it will some time
" or other be published, together with some other remains
" of the Apostate, by Frederick Rostgaard, a noble Dane.
" For when he was travelling through Italy, and collecting
" the Epistles of Libanius from various MSS. in order to
" give them to the public, he thought he had sagacity
" enough to decypher also this Ambrosian MS."
See the first note on the next Epistle.

† Meaning Aristophanes, a Corinthian, the son of Me-
nander, for whom there is an oration of Libanius, in Vol.
II. of Morell's edition, p. 210.   FABRICIUS.

VOL. II.   O   as

at present, but in future times; as the calumny of Paul *, and the sentence of that judge †, can by no means be compared with your orations. For such fiery proceedings were instantly detested, and, together with their authors, are now extinct; while your orations delight the true Greeks of the present age, and, unless I am much mistaken, will also delight their posterity.

Be assured, in short, that you have convinced me, [or rather that you have induced me to retract my opinion of Aristophanes, and that I think him superior to all the allurements both of profit and pleasure. Can I refuse to concur with the most philosophical of orators, the greatest partisan of truth? After this, perhaps you may ask, why we have not placed his affairs in a more prosperous

---

* This Paul, who pleaded for the informers against Aristophanes, before the Emperor Constantius, is mentioned in the same oration of Libanius, p. 222.   FABRICIUS.

Julian has stigmatised Paul as a "notorious slanderer," in his Epistle to the Athenians, Vol. I. p. 92. See also Ammianus, xix. and xxii. He was burnt alive, by the order of that prince, soon after his accession to the empire; a fate to which he seems to allude above by αιθυλα, ("fiery") and συναπισθη, ("extinguished together.") In Fabricius it is αθυλα, ("at their first appearance.")

Libanius, in the oration above mentioned, says, in one place, "Aristophanes received many severe stripes from "balls of lead" [tied, probably, to strings], "which "Paul thought fit instruments of death;" and in another, that "he had irritated Paul by some expressions suitable "indeed to him, but which it would have been better to "have suppressed."

† The Emperor Constantius.   FABRICIUS.

EPISTLES OF JULIAN.

state, and removed every inconvenience attending his disgrace.

When two their efforts join, &c. *.
You and I will confer together. For you are worthy to be consulted, not only as to the propriety of assisting a man who devoutly honours the Gods, but also in what manner, of which indeed you have given some hints. But of these matters it will be better perhaps to discourse than to write. Farewell, my most dear and beloved brother †.]

---

* Συν τι δυ' ερχομενω, κ. τ. λ. Iliad X. 224.
An expression of Diomed, enforcing the propriety of an assistant in his nightly expedition. The same meaning is conveyed by our English proverb, "Two heads are better "than one."

† This was immediately followed by Αννγνων δε χθες τον λογον, κ. τ. λ. ("Reading yesterday your oration, &c.") which is the XIVth Epistle of Julian [see p. 28.] published by Ezech. Spanheim, among his works, as a single Epistle, and (as is very probable) totally unconnected with the former.   WOLFIUS.

The concluding farewell is exactly the same with that of Epistle III. to Libanius also.

All that is between [ ] is only in the copy published by Wolfius.

Epistle LXIX *. To Sosipater †.

WHEN an opportunity offers of writing to our friends by a domestic, the pleasure it affords is much augmented. For thus your letters convey to them something more than a mere image of your mind. So fortunate am I at present. And therefore, as I was sending to you Antiochus, the tutor of my sons ‡, I could not omit this opportunity of informing you, that if you wish to have any intelligence concerning us, you may learn it particularly from him. And if you have a regard for your friends, and that you have some I am certain, when you have a similar opportunity of writing, you will by no means neglect it.

* This, and the seven following Epistles (and also great part of the LIXth and LXVIIIth, as has been observed in the notes on each) were first published by Fabricius, in his *Lux Evangelii*, 1731, with a Latin translation. He was indebted for them, he says, to Count Christian Danneshiold de Samsoa (then lately deceased), who purchased them in 1726, together with many hundreds of unpublished epistles of Libanius, at the public auction of the library of the " most " noble and learned Frederick Rostgaard," having been transcribed by him in Italy, from the Vatican, Medicean, and Ambrosian libraries. See p. 193, note *.

† Or was it " to Sopater," the son-in-law of Jamblichus, who is frequently mentioned in the XXVIIth, XLth, and LIIId Epistles of Julian?   FABRICIUS.
See p. 70, note †.

‡ This probably must be the person mentioned by the same appellation (Τροφευς των παιδων παιδιων) in Epistle XL. See p. 102. note †.

Epistle LXX. To Philip *.

WHILE I was Cæsar, the Gods can witness, I wrote to you, and, I think, more than once. Great certainly was the impulse I felt, but many and various were my avocations; and, besides, as the friendship between me and the blessed † Constantius, in consequence of my advancement, was that of wolves, I was extremely cautious of writing to any one beyond the Alps, lest I should involve him in the greatest difficulties. Consider my writing to you now as a proof of my friendship, for frequently the tongue refuses to correspond with the heart. And subjects perhaps have reason to exult and glory in being able to shew the letters of princes, displaying them to the unexperienced, like rings to persons unacquainted with

A. P.
362.

---

* This seems to be the same to whom there are several Epistles of Libanius, in [one of] which he says, that the letters which he received from Philip were written "not with ink, but with a Pegasean liquor." FABRICIUS.
Libanius had two correspondents of this name, one a præfect, whom he mentions in his Life, p. 25, and the other a poet.
It must have been written in the spring of 362, probably at Constantinople, when Julian was preparing to remove to Antioch.

† So Julian used to style Constantius, now dead, as he calls him μακαρίης in his XXXIst and LVIIIth Epistles, and in his XXIIId, ικεινω μεν ων, επειδη μακαριης εγενετο, κωφη γη.

Ibid.

such

such trinkets. True friendship is generally found between equals; but there is a second kind, when one has a real, not a pretended, esteem for the other, and though superior in rank and genius, is loved for his good-nature, affability, and discretion. But such epistles are apt to be filled with vanity and trifles. And I often reproach myself for making them too prolix, and being too loquacious, when I should teach my tongue a Pythagorean silence.

I have received your presents, a silver cup, a pound in weight, and a piece of gold coin. I am indeed desirous, as you say in your letter, of having your company here. But now the spring approaches, the trees begin to blossom, and the swallows, though not yet expected, when they arrive, will expell us, engaged on a like expedition, from our houses, and bid us remove to a distant country. Therefore, as we shall pass near you, it will be better for you, if the Gods permit, to meet us in your own neighbourhood. This, I hope, will soon happen, unless something providential prevents; which may the Gods avert!

EPISTLES OF JULIAN.

Epiftle LXXI. To Eutherius *.

WE live, preferved by the Gods †. Offer fa-crifices therefore to them in acknowledgement of my fafety; but not for the fafety of one individual only, but of all the Greeks ‡ in general. If you have leifure to pafs over § to Conftantinople, I fhall think myfelf not a little honoured by your company.

A. D. 361.

---

* To this Eutherius I have three Epiftles of Libanius in MS.   Fabricius.
There are fix in the edition of Wolfius. Julian muft have written this foon after his arrival at Conftantinople in the winter of 361.

† Ζωμεν υπο των Θεων σωθεντες. On the fame occafion Julian ufes an expreffion very fimilar to this in his XIIIth Epiftle, to his uncle: Ζωμεν δια τους Θεους. In the Latin of Fabricius it is mifprinted *Vicimus*.

‡ Meaning the Gentile worfhippers of idols.
                  Fabricius.

§ This expreffion (διαβηναι) fhews, that Eutherius was then on the oppofite fide of the Bofphorus.

Epistle LXXII. To the Patriarch *.

THIS is the second letter that I have sent in favour of Amogila †, my former having been rendered ineffectual by the powerful influence of her oppressors. Lamenting therefore the fate of my former Epistle, pay due regard to this, and make it not necessary for us to write a third.

---

* Mention is made of Julus, the Patriarch of the Jews, whom he calls " most venerable," in the XXVth Epistle of Julian.   FABRICIUS.

See p. 50.
This, as has been observed of the LXIVth Epistle, p. 184. has also, by mistake, been ascribed to Libanius, being printed in the edition of Wolfius, as the DCCCXXXVth of his Epistles. There are six more so inscribed. But a MS. of one of them in the Vatican library has the addition of Ἀντιοχεων. This therefore, and all of them, were probably addressed, not to the Jewish Patriarch, as Fabricius supposes, but to the Christian Patriarch of Antioch, who in the year 361 was Meletius.

† Ἀμωγιλης. In the copy (above mentioned) ascribed to Libanius, the name is Ἀμμωνιλλης, (" Ammonilla.")

This is followed in Fabricius, by

" To Ætius. (See p. 78.)

" Κοινως μεν απασι, &c. This, in the editions of Petau and
" Ez. Spanheim, is the XXXIst Epistle, p. 405, but instead
" of Κοινως, (" in general,") we there read Λοιποις, (" the
" rest,") and then instead of the words μεχρι τε στρατοπεδε
" τε εμε, (" as far as [my] camp,") there is only in the
" Medicean MS. μεχρι τε στρατοπεδε. This Epistle, by which
" we find the bishops, whom Constantius had banished,
" recalled by Julian, is mentioned by Sozomen, *l.* v. *c.* 5."

Epistle LXXIII. To Diogenes.[*]

AFTER your departure, Diogenes, your son came to me, and said, you were angry with him, and as much enraged as a father could be with a son: he begged me therefore to intercede for him, and to reconcile you to him. If his offence be flight, and such as may easily be forgiven, yield to nature, and, recollecting that you are a parent, restore your son to favour. But if it be such as cannot be pardoned, you yourself are the best judge which is most expedient, to act generously on this occasion, and to conquer the disposition of your son by the best advice, or to trust his amendment, and the reparation of his fault, to length of time.

---

[*] An Athenian philosopher, to whom there are some Epistles of Libanius. FABRICIUS.
In one of them he acquaints Diogenes with the death and burial of his wife. He is also mentioned by Julian in his XXXVth Epistle. See p. 60. He was the uncle of Aristophanes, the Corinthian, mentioned p. 193.

Epistle LXXIV. To Priscus*.

A. D. 362.

ON receiving your letter, I immediately dispatched Archelaus †, and gave him some epistles for you, with a passport, as you desired, for a longer time. If you are inclined to speculate the ocean, every thing, under God, will prosper to your wish, unless you dread the inelegance of the Galatians, or a storm. But this will be as God shall think fit. I swear to you by him, who is to me the giver and preserver of all good, that I wish to live only for the sake of being useful to you. By you, I mean the true philosophers; of whom convinced that you are one, you well know how much I have loved, and love you, and wish to see you. May divine Providence preserve you in health many years, my most esteemed and friendly brother! The excellent Hippia, and your children, I salute.

* The father of the præfect Anatolius. FABRICIUS.
Anatolius was master of the offices, and was killed in the same skirmish in which Julian himself was mortally wounded. He would otherwise perhaps have succeeded that prince, as he himself is said to have wished. For an account of Priscus, see p. 6. note †.

† To this Archelaus, as I suppose, Libanius has four Epistles, in one of which he expostulates with him for enviously burning some of his declamations.

EPISTLES OF JULIAN.

Epistle LXXV. To LIBANIUS, Sophist and Quæstor *.

HOW fortunate was our disappointment of a public carriage! For instead of the terror and apprehension attendant on such a vehicle, where we meet with drunken muleteers, and mules, like those in Homer, "pampered with barley †," such are their idleness and repletion, and are annoyed with clouds of dust and the intolerable dissonance of clamorous drivers and smacking whips ‡, I now travel at my leisure on a pleasant shady road, abounding with fountains, and having many commodious inns, and when the hour of refreshment arrives, I rest wherever I please, beneath the spacious, fragrant boughs of the plane or cypress, with the Myrrhinusian § Phædrus ||, or some other work of Plato, in my hands. As I thus enjoy an unembarrassed journey, did I not communicate this pleasure to you, my dearest friend, I should think myself inexcusable.

---

* So styled also in Epistle XXVIIth. But here, for a reason given below, I suspect it to be an anachronism.

† Ακοστησαντι. Iliad. VI. 506. XV. 263.

‡ The inconveniences of the public vehicles in those days seem by this account very similar to those experienced in our times. Had Julian then been Emperor, or even Cæsar, all the public carriages, with their motions, would have been at his command.

§ Of Myrrhinus in Attica. FABRICIUS.

|| The book of Plato so inscribed, from his scholar of that name.

Epistle

Epistle LXXVI. To the Philosopher Euclid*.

WHEN did you leave us, that we must write to you? or when do we not view you, as if you were still present, with the eyes of our mind, seeming not only to be constantly enjoying your company and conversation, but also taking the same care of your affairs as when you were here? If, however, you would have me write to you as to one who is absent, consider whether this request does not prove that you are really absent. Be that as it may, if it gratifies you, even in this we readily obey you. Indeed, according to the proverb, you will spur to the field a free horse. See then that you make a similar return, and fail not to be punctual in your replies. Though I am unwilling to interrupt your labours for the pnblic good, yet, as I observe that you pursue what is excellent, far from offending I shall seem to render an essential service to all Greece by dismissing you unmolested, like a generous hound, to track learning through all her paths, through every footstep †. If you have such alacrity as neither to neglect your friends, nor to discontinue these pursuits, haste, and exert yourself in both those courses.

---

* I do not recollect that this philosopher is elsewhere mentioned, either by Julian or Libanius. An Eucladius occurs in the DCLXXIIId Epistle of the latter.

† Βημαίι, otherwise Ανμμαίι, ("argument.") FABRICIUS.

Epistola

Epistola LXXVII *. Ad Photinum †.

TU quidem, O Photine, verisimilis videris et proximus salvare, benefaciens nequaquam in utero inducere quem credidisti Deum. Diodorus ‡ autem Nazaræi magus ejus pigmentalibus mangoneis acuens irrationabilitatem acutus apparuit sophista religionis agrestis. * * * * Quod si nobis opitulati fuerint dii, et deæ, et musæ omnes, et fortuna, ostendemus infirmum et corruptorem le-

---

* This Epistle, mentioned by Fabricius, in his *Lux Evangelii*, p. 310. is preserved by Facundus, bishop of Hermania in Africa, in his book dedicated to the Emperor Justinian, in defence of the "three chapters," as they were called, which were the writings of Theodore of Mopsuestia, Theodoret of Cyprus, and Ibas of Edessa, against all which Justinian had published an edict, A. D. 544. See Mosheim, I. 299. It was printed by Sirmond, at Paris, 1629, 8vo; and from that edition, p. 163, this letter is extracted.

This letter of Julian, if not written originally in Latin, seems to have been translated in a very bombast style. He here threatens his work against the Christians. I will not give it in English.

† Photinus, bishop of Sirmium, published, in the year 343, his opinions concerning the deity, which were equally repugnant to the orthodox and Arian systems. His temerity was chastised, not only by the orthodox in the councils of Antioch and Milan, held in the years 345 and 347, and in that of Sirmium, whose date is uncertain, but also by the Arians, in one of their assemblies held at Sirmium, in the year 351. In consequence of all this, Photinus was degraded from the episcopal dignity, and died in exile in the year 372. Mosheim.

For his extravagant notions see vol. I. of this historian, 223.

‡ Of Antioch, bishop of Tarsus, an orthodox prelate. See Mosheim, I. 188, and Moreri, article *Diodore d' Antioche*.

gum, et rationum, et mysteriorum paganorum, et deorum infernorum, et illum novum ejus deum Galilæum quem æternum fabulose prædicat indignâ morte et sepulturâ denudatum confictæ a Diodoro deitatis! Iste enim malo communis utilitatis Athenas navigans, et philosophans, imprudenter musicorum participatus est rationem, et rhetoricis confectionibus odibilem adarmavit linguam adversus cælestes deos usque adeo ignorans paganorum mysteria omnemque miserabiliter imbibens, ut aiunt, degenerum et imperitorum ejus theologorum piscatorum errorem. Propter quod jam diu est quod ab ipsis punitur diis. Jam enim per multos annos in periculum conversus, et in corruptionem thoracis incidens, ad summum pervenit supplicium. Omne ejus corpus consumptum est: nam malæ ejus conciderunt, rugæ vero in altitudinem corporis descenderunt, quod non est philosophicæ conversationis indicio, sicut videri vult a se deceptis, sed justitiæ pro certo deorumque pœnæ quâ percutitur competenti ratione usque ad novissimum vitæ suæ finem asperam et amaram vitam vivens et faciem pallore confectum.

FRAG-

FRAGMENTS

OF

EPISTLES OF JULIAN,

Translated from SUIDAS.

Article AMPHION.

....FOR you have leisure, you have excellent natural endowments, and, if any one ever had, a love for philosophy. These three united were sufficient to render Amphion the inventor of ancient music *; namely, time, divine inspiration, and the love of harmony. The want of instruments cannot be any impediment to these; and he who is possessed of these three will easily find those. Have we not heard that Amphion not only invented music, but also the harp, either by the wonderful powers of his genius, or some divine assistance, or some unusual co-operation? And most of the ancients, by principally attending to these three, seem to have philosophised without disguise, and to have required nothing else.

---

* The lute, on which Amphion played so harmoniously as to bring together the stones with which the tower of Thebes was built, is said by others to have been presented to him by Mercury. Some suppose that there were two Amphions, and that the younger, called the Dircæan, from the river Dirce, in Bœotia, was the musician and the inventor of music.

Article

Article HERODOTUS.

WHO is ignorant of what the Æthiopians said of the most nourishing food we have? On tasting some of our bread, "they wondered", they said, "how we could live upon dung," if we may credit the Thurian historian *. Those who have treated on the various climates of the earth also relate that there are nations of men who feed on fish and flesh, and never, even in a dream, saw such diet as ours. If any one of them should attempt to adopt our mode of living, he would fare no better than those who swallow hellebore or hemlock.

---

* Herodotus, so called from Thurium in Magna Græcia, where he lived and died. Julian gives him the same appellation in Epistle XXII. The passage to which he here alludes is in the IIId book of that historian, and is part of the enquiry which the Æthiopians made of the *Ichthyophagi*, or "fish-eaters," whom Cambyses sent to explore that country. Their king, they said, lived upon bread, explaining the nature of wheat, and that eighty years was the longest period proposed by a Persian. The Æthiopian answered, " I do not wonder, as you live upon dung, that " you are so short-lived; and, were it not for this " beverage (wine), you would not live so long."

This extraordinary person was born at Halicarnassus, a Grecian colony in the lesser Asia, not long before the invasion of Greece by the armies of Xerxes. In his youth he retired from his native city to Samos, in order to avoid the arbitrary proceedings of Lygdamis, the grandson of the famous Artemisia, who acquitted herself with much honour in the naval engagement of Salamis. There he formed himself upon the dialect of Ionia, and compiled his

history

history, which begins with Candaules and Cyrus, and comes down to the battle of Mycale, towards the latter end of the reign of Xerxes, a period of 120 years. In the mean time he spared no pains to inform himself of all that was necessary, in the best manner which he could. To this end he travelled into Ægypt, surveyed its chief towns, conversed with the priests of Thebes and Memphis, and penetrated into the principles of their religion and learning, as far as his own sagacity could carry him, and their recluseness would permit him. He travelled through the several districts and republics of Greece, saw the principal cities of Asia, and visited the borders of Thrace, Scythia, and Arabia. Returning, however, after a long voluntary exile, into his own country, he bore a considerable share in the expulsion of the tyrant; but meeting with envy from his fellow-citizens, instead of that gratitude which he expected as the just reward of his services, he went to Athens, and after about a twelvemonth's stay there, departed into Italy with a colony of Athenians, to build a city called Thurium (hence the above appellation) near the ruins of the ancient Sybaris. As soon as he had drawn up his history from the materials he had collected with such infinite diligence and industry, he determined to expose it to the judgement of all Greece. It happened, that during his residence at Athens, besides the feast of Panathenæa where he read his work aloud, the Olympian exercises were performed, to which the Grecians resorted in general from each state, and thus he had a very favourable opportunity of putting his design into execution. Many of his auditors had, no doubt, been personally engaged in some of the battles against Xerxes and Mardonius, and not one of them could be unacquainted with the principal facts of a war, so honourable to Greece, and so inglorious to Persia. In the midst of this assembly he declared, that "he appeared before them not so much a spectator of their games, as a competitor for the prize of reputation;" and recited his work publickly a second time with universal applause. Of this nothing can be a greater testimony than that the names of the nine Muses have been given to the nine books of his history, as if the composition were above the standard of humanity, and the joint labour of those celebrated divinities.

Article MUSONIUS *.

THE drunken abuse, with which the commander in Greece † has loaded me, you have borne with serenity, thinking that it did not in the least concern you. As to your earnest desire to be serviceable to the city in which you reside, that is a certain proof of a philosophical mind. The first seems to me suitable to Socrates, the second to Musonius. He said that it was wrong for a good man to suffer himself to be injured by the wicked ‡. For he had the superintendence of the towers when he was banished by Nero.

* For an account of Musonius, see the Epistle to Themistius, Vol. I. p. 25. note ‖.

† This possibly might be Dionysius, whose " drunken " abuse" Julian mentions in Epistle LIX. p. 165. The words in the original are similar, παροινιαν and πεπαρωνηκας.

‡ Though I have literally translated this passage, I do not clearly apprehend its meaning, or its connection with what follows.

Article XPHMA.

...OUR journey lay through the Hercynian forest *. There I saw a most wonderful sight (χρημα, εξαισιον). I can confidently assure you, that you have never seen the like, though I know that there are many of the kind in the Roman dominions. But let any one think of the inaccessible Thessalian Tempe, or of Thermopylæ †, or of steep and extensive Taurus ‡; and all these will seem insignificant when compared in ruggedness with the Hercynian forest.

A. D. 357.

* This seems also to be styled the Hercynian forest by Zosimus, *l.* III. It is at present called *der Spessard*, formerly a part of the Hercynian forest, and is on the left bank of the Mayne, not far from the confluence of the Rhine and Moselle, as Cluverius says, *l.* III. *c.* 7.
          VALOIS.

In Cæsar's time this forest extended from the country of the Rauraci (Basil) into the boundless regions of the North. Julian mentions his being "sent into the Hercynian forest when he had scarce arrived at manhood," in the Misopogon, p. 275; and Ammianus, XVII. 1. where it is styled *sylvam squalore tenebrarum horrendam.*

† Straits between the mountains of Thessaly and Phocis, which divide Greece, famous for the defence of Leonidas against the Persians.

‡ The highest and most extensive mountains in Asia.

INDEX to the EPISTLES.

Epistle I. (37)	To * * * *	page 3
II. (11)	To Prohæresius.	5
III. (31)	To Libanius.	6
IV. (17)	To Aristomenes.	7
V. (44)	To the most honoured Theodora.	10
VI. (30)	To Ecdicius, Præfect of Ægypt.	11
VII. (6)	To Artabius.	13
VIII.	To George.	14
IX. (23)	To Ecdicius.	17
X. (22)	To the People of Alexandria.	19
XI. (40)	To the Byzantines.	24
XII. (13)	To Basil.	26
XIII. (5)	To his Uncle Julian.	27
XIV. (43)	To Libanius.	28
XV. (9)	To the Philosopher Maximus.	29
XVI. (41)	To the same.	31
XVII. (3)	To Oribasius.	33
XVIII.	To the Philosopher Eugenius.	38
XIX. (38)	To Ecebolus.	39
XX.	To Eustochius.	41
XXI. (18)	To Callixene, Priestess of Ceres.	43
XXII.	To Leontius.	45
		XXIII.

INDEX TO THE EPISTLES.

Epistle		Page
XXIII. (7)	To Hermogenes, formerly Præfect of Ægypt.	46
XXIV.	To the most excellent Serapion.	47
XXV. (14)	To the Community of the Jews.	57
(19)	To the principal Physicians. An Edict.	63
XXVI. (27)	To the Alexandrians. An Edict.	64
XXVII. (35)	To Libanius, Sophist and Qnæstor.	65
XXVIII. (47)	To Duke Gregory.	73
XXIX. (12)	To Alypius, Brother of Cæsarius.	ib.
XXX.	To the same.	76
XXXI. (10)	To Bishop Ætius.	78
XXXII. (46)	To the Sophist Lucian.	79
XXXIII. (45)	To Dositheus.	ib.
XXXIV.	To the Philosopher Jamblichus.	80
XXXV.	For the Argives.	83
XXXVI. (24)	To Porphyry, Treasurer of Ægypt.	92
XXXVII. (39)	To Amerius.	93
XXXVIII. (4)	To Maximus.	96
XXXIX. (16)	To the same.	100
XL.	To Jamblichus.	101

INDEX TO THE EPISTLES.

Epistle		Page
XLI.	To Jamblichus.	107
	(20) An Edict relating to Professors.	110
XLII. (20)	—— forbidding the Christians to teach polite literature.	112
XLIII.	To Ecebolus.	118
XLIV.	To Libanius.	120
XLV. (25)	To Zeno.	121
XLVI. (36)	To Evagrius.	122
XLVII. (42)	To the Thracians.	125
XLVIII.	To * * * *	127
XLIX. (32)	To Arsacius, High Priest of Galatia.	ib.
L. (28)	To Ecdicius.	134
LI. (29)	To the Alexandrians.	136
LII. (26)	To the Bostrenians.	142
LIII.	To Jamblichus.	148
LIV.	To George.	151
LV.	To Eumenius and Pharianus.	152
LVI.	To Ecdicius.	153
LVII.	To the Philosopher Elpidius.	154
LVIII. (15)	To the Alexandrians.	155
LIX.	To Dionysius.	158
LX.	To Jamblichus.	171
LXI.	To the same.	174
LXII.	To * * * * (Imperfect.)	175
LXIII. (8)	To the High-Priest Theodore.	178

LXIV.

INDEX to the EPISTLES.

Epistle			Page
LXIV.		To the People, clamorously applauding in the Tychæum.	184
LXV.		To a Painter.	185
LXVI.	(34)	To Arsaces, Satrap of Armenia.	186
LXVII.	(33)	To the People [of Antioch.]	189
LXVIII.		To Libanius.	195
LXIX.		To Sosipater.	196
LXX.		To Philip.	197
LXXI.		To Eutherius.	199
LXXII.		To the Patriarch.	200
LXXIII.		To Diogenes.	201
LXXIV.		To Priscus.	202
LXXV.		To Libanius.	203
LXXVI.		To the Philosopher Euclid.	204
LXXVII.		Ad Photinum.	205

Fragments of Epistles. 207—211

N. B. Those translated by M. de la Bleterie are marked with Arabic figures, which shew the chronological order in which he has endeavoured (as far as he could) to arrange them. Gallus to Julian, and Julian to Themistius, are his two first. And those to the Athenians and Constantius he has omitted.

THE LIFE

OF

LIBANIUS, the SOPHIST.

From the Latin

Of JOHN ALBERT FABRICIUS, D. D. *

LIBANIUS was born of an ancient and noble family at Antioch, on the Orontes, in the year of our Lord 314. Suidas calls his father "Phasganius;" but this was the name of one of his uncles †; the other, who was the elder, was named Panolbius. His great grandfather, who excelled in the art of divination, had published some pieces in Latin, which occasioned his being supposed by some, but falsly, to be an Italian. His maternal and paternal grandfathers were eminent in rank and in eloquence; the latter, with his brother Brasidas, was put to death, by the order of Diocletian,

---

* In his Bibliotheca Græca, vol. VII. p. 378.

† Libanius, in his Life (which he says, p. 19, he wrote when he was sixty), vol. II. p. 6. and 40, and *Orat.* XXIV. p. 534. He mentions, p. 46. that he attained his fiftieth year under Jovian; and, p. 48, his fifty-seventh under Valens.   FABRICIUS.

LIFE OF LIBANIUS.

Diocletian, in the year 303, after the tumult of the tyrant Eugenius. Libanius, of his father's three sons the second, in the fifteenth year of his age, wishing to devote himself entirely to literature, complains that he met with some " shadows " of sophists." Then, assisted by a proper master *, he began to read the ancient writers at Antioch, and from thence, with Jasion, a Cappadocian, went to Athens, and residing there for more than four years became intimately acquainted with Crispinus of Heraclea, who, he says, enriched him afterwards with books at Nicomedia, and went, but seldom, to the schools of Diophantus. At Constantinople he ingratiated himself with Nicocles of Lacedæmon (a grammarian, who was master to the Emperor Julian), and the sophist Bemarchius. Returning to Athens, and soliciting the office of a professor, which the proconsul had before intended for him when he was twenty-five years of age, a certain Cappadocian happened to be preferred to him. But being encouraged by Dionysius, a Sicilian, who had been præfect of Syria, some specimens of his eloquence, that were published at Constantinople, made him so generally known and applauded, that he collected more than eighty disciples, the two sophists, who then filled the chair there, raging in vain, and Bemarchius ineffectually opposing him in rival orations, and when he could not excell him, having recourse to

---

* This was probably the same whom Libanius freed from the resentment of the Emperor Constantius, as he relates, p. 34. FABRICIUS.

the frigid calumny of magic. At length, about the year 346, being expelled the city by his competitors *, the præfect Limenius concurring, he repaired to Nice, and soon after to Nicomedia, the Athens of Bithynia, where his excellence in speaking began to be more and more approved by all, and Julian, if not a hearer, was a reader and admirer of his orations. In the same city, he says, he was particularly delighted with the friendship of Aristænetus †, and the five years, which he passed there, he styles " the spring, or any thing else that " can be conceived pleasanter than spring, of his " whole life." Being invited again to Constantinople, and afterwards returning to Nicomedia, being also tired of Constantinople, where he found Phœnix and Zenobius, rival sophists, though he was patronised by Strategius, who succeeded Domitian as præfect of the East, not daring, on account of his rivals, to occupy the Athenian chair, he obtained permission from Gallus Cæsar to visit, for four months, his native city Antioch, where, after Gallus was killed in 354, he fixed his residence for the remainder of his life, and initiated many

---

* The jealousy of his rivals, who persecuted him from one city to another, confirmed the favourable opinion which Libanius ostentatiously displayed of his superior merit.

GIBBON.

† The death of this Aristænetus, præfect of Bithynia, who was overwhelmed at Nicomedia by an earthquake in 358, he laments, p. 40, and in his XXIXth and XXXIst Epistles. See also the following Monody.

in the sacred rites of eloquence. He was also much beloved by the Emperor Julian, who heard his discourses with pleasure *, received him with kindness, and imitated him in his writings. Honoured by that prince with the rank of quæstor †, and with several Epistles [of which six only are extant ‡], the last § written by the Emperor during his fatal expedition against the Persians, he the more lamented his death in the flower of his age, as from him he had promised himself a certain and lasting support both in the worship of idols and in his own studies. There was afterwards a report that Libanius, with the younger Jamblichus, the master of Proclus, enquired by divination who would be the successor of Valens ||, and in consequence with difficulty

* Fabricius corrects this mistake in his *Lux Evangelii*.
† See p. 65.
‡ Viz. the iiid, xivth, xxviith, xlivth, lxviiith, and lxxvth.
§ The xxviith.
|| In the year 373, or 374, whilst Valens was at Antioch, a discovery was made of a consultation which some Gentiles had together for finding out the name of the person who should succeed the Emperor. There are accounts of it in several of our Ecclesiastical historians, and in divers Heathen authors, particularly Ammianus Marcellinus, who is the fullest of all, and was then in the East, and possibly at Antioch. The confessions made by Patricius and Hilary, both skilful diviners, he thus particularly relates:

" A tripod made of laurel was artificially prepared, and
" consecrated with certain prescribed secret charms and
" invocations. It was then placed in the middle of a
" room, perfumed with Arabian spices. The charger, on
" which it was set, had on its utmost brim the four and
" twenty letters of the alphabet, neatly engraved, and set
" at due distances from each other. Then a person, clad
" in

"in linen vestments, with linen socks upon his feet, and
"a suitable covering upon his head, came in with laurel
"branches in his hands, and, after some mystic charms
"performed, shook a ring, hanging at a curtain, about
"the edge of the charger; which jumping up and down,
"fell upon some letters of the alphabet, where it seemed
"to stay; the priest also then composing certain heroic
"verses in answer to the questions that had been proposed.
"The letters, which the ring pointed out in this case, were
"four, Θ, E, O, Δ, which being put together, one that
"was present immediately exclaimed, that the oracle
"plainly intended Theodorus" [then second in the secretaries office], " nor did we make any farther enquiries,
"being all well satisfied that he was the person intended,
"though himself was totally ignorant of this proceeding."

Cave's Translation.

Zonaras gives a different account of the method of divination then made use of. He says, " that the four and
"twenty letters of the alphabet were written upon the
"ground, and at each one was placed a grain of wheat or
"barley. Then, after some mystic forms, a cock * was let
"out, which picked up such grains as lay at those four
"letters." But it is much more reasonable to rely upon Ammianus, who was contemporary, and likely to be well informed. His account also is agreeable to that in Sozomen and Zosimus, who have both mentioned the tripod.

When Libanius says, that " Valens hoped to have had
" him also accused as one of the conspirators," I take it to be a mere flourish. He was willing to make a merit of some danger with the rest of his friends, though really he was safe enough. LARDNER.

For this consultation and divination many were put to death, viz. Simonides and Maximus, philosophers, the latter the friend and perverter of Julian, Diogenes, who had been præfect of Bithynia, and Theodorus, the person named, perhaps with many more who owned the fatal syllables. Theodosius succeeded. Alypius too (see p. 73.) who had been vice-prefect of Britain, was condemned, but only banished; and his son Hierocles, when he was leading to execution, was happily saved, it is supposed, by a tumult of the people.

* To this method Fabricius plainly alludes by the word *alectryomania*.

The

LIFE OF LIBANIUS.

difficulty escaped his cruelty *, Irenæus attesting the innocence of Libanius. In like manner he happily escaped another calumny, by the favour of Duke Lupicinus, when he was accused by his enemy Fidelis, or Fidustius, of having written an elogium on the tyrant Procopius †. He was not, however, totally neglected by Valens, whom he not only celebrated in an oration, but ob-

---

The inquisition into the crime of magic, which, under the reign of the two brothers, was so rigorously prosecuted both at Rome and Antioch, was interpreted as the fatal symptom, either of the displeasure of heaven, or of the depravity of mankind. Lardner has copiously and fairly examined this dark transaction. GIBBON.

* That future events may be conjectured by the motions of the stars Libanius does not deny, in an Epistle [the xivth of Zambicari, *l.* I.] to Eustolius. That he also studied the interpretation of dreams may be deduced from Vol. II. of his works, p. 74. FABRICIUS.

† Procopius, a relation of the Emperor Julian, who had hastily promoted him, from the obscure station of a tribune and a notary, to the joint command of the army of Mesopotamia, retired, after the death of that prince, to his ample patrimony in Cappadocia. But being suspected and ordered to be apprehended by the new sovereigns Valentinian and Valens, A. D. 365, he escaped from his guards, passed over to the country of Bosphorus, and, after remaining many months in that sequestered region, embarked for Constantinople, and assumed the sovereignty. Being joined by some Gallic soldiers, whose numbers rapidly increased, he subdued the unarmed provinces of Bithynia and Asia, the city and island of Cyzicus, &c. but being at last deserted by his troops, in two engagements, after wandering some time among the woods and mountains of Phrygia, he was betrayed by his desponding followers, conducted to the imperial camp, and immediately beheaded.

Abridged from GIBBON.

tained

tained from him a confirmation of the law against entirely excluding illegitimate children from the inheritance of their paternal estates, which he solicited from the Emperor, no doubt, for a private reason, since, as Eunapius informs us, he kept a mistress *, and was never married. The remainder of his life he passed, as before-mentioned, at Antioch, to an advanced age, amidst various wrongs and oppressions from his rivals and the times, which he copiously relates in his Life, though, tired of the manners of that city, he had thoughts, in his old age, of changing his abode, as he tells Eusebius in his DLIVth Epistle [edit. Wolf.] He continued there, however, and on various occasions was very serviceable to the city, either by appeasing seditions, and calming the disturbed minds of the citizens, or by reconciling to them the Emperors Julian and Theodosius. That Libanius lived even to the reign of Arcadius, that is, beyond the seventieth year of his age, the learned collect from his oration on Lucian and the testimony of Cedrenus; and of the same opinion is Godfrey Olearius, a man not more respectable for his exquisite knowledge of sacred and polite literature, than for his judgement and probity, in his MS. prælections, in

---

* He laments her death, and mentions a son, whom he had by her, in his Life, p. 82. and in several of his Epistles. In others it appears that his name was Cimon; that his father sent him to study at Athens, and that he died before him.

which,

LIFE OF LIBANIUS.

which, when he was profeſſor of both languages in the univerſity of his own country, he has given an account of the life of this ſophiſt.

The writings of Libanius * are numerous, and he compoſed and delivered various orations, as well demonſtrative as deliberative, and alſo many fictitious declamations and diſputations. Of theſe Frederick Morell † publiſhed as many as he could collect in two volumes, folio, in Greek and Latin. In the 1ſt vol. Paris, 1606, are XIII. Exerciſes (*Pro-*

---

* The voluminous writings of Libanius ſtill exiſt; for the moſt part they are the vain and idle compoſitions of an orator, who cultivated the ſcience of words; the productions of a recluſe ſtudent, whoſe mind, regardleſs of his contemporaries, was inceſſantly fixed on the Trojan war, and the Athenian commonwealth.   GIBBON.

† The Latin tranſlation of Morell has been obſerved by many of the learned to be often obſcure, and in numberleſs places to have miſtaken the ſenſe of Libanius. Whoever therefore ſhall undertake another edition of this author, muſt new tranſlate many paſſages, eſpecially in the IId volume. It is ſaid, neverthelefs, that Morell applied to his verſion with ſuch intenſe application, as not to ſuffe himſelf to be interrupted by an account that his wife was at the point of death, if we credit Iſaac Voſſius, in Colomeſius, p. 99. of his works: "I have heard from M. "Voſſius, that while Frederick Morell was employed on "Libanius, ſome one came to inform him that his wife "was very ill:" to which he replied, "I have only three "or four ſentences more to tranſlate, and then I will go "and ſee her." Another coming to tell him that ſhe was dying; "I have only two words," ſaid he, "I will be "there as ſoon as you." At laſt, being informed that his wife was dead, "I was very happy," he anſwered coldly, "ſhe was an excellent woman."   FABRICIUS.

gymnaſmata)

gymnasmata) XLIV Declamations *, and III moral differtations, and in the IId vol. Paris, 1627, are the Life † of Libanius, and XXXVI other orations, moft of them long and on ferious fubjects.

Befides what are contained in thofe volumes, and his Epiftles, ten other works of this fophift have been feparately publifhed, moft of them orations ‡, and in the *Excerpta Rhetorum* of Leo Allatius,

---

* That his Declamations were "poffeffed, read, and "thought worthy of being imitated by many," appears from an Epiftle of Libanius to Archelaus [XLIVth of Zambicari, *l.* 1.], who, from envy, had committed fome of them to the flames. Erafmus (I. 550.) has tranflated the 1ft of them, the "oration of Menelaus," which Morell has adopted *verbatim*, without acknowledgment, (I. 189.) his name being prefixed as the tranflator of them all.

† Libanius has compofed the vain, prolix, but curious narrative of his own life, of which Eunapius (p. 130—135.) has left a concife and unfavourable account. Among the moderns, Tillemont, Fabricius, and Lardner have illuftrated the character and writings of this famous fophift.

GIBBON.

‡ Of thefe, as of all the others, Fabricius has given the titles and fubjects. The Vth of them, "an oration "for the Temples," that they may not be deftroyed, to Theodofius the Great, 390, firft publifhed by Godefroi, Geneva, 1634, 4to. is tranflated into Englifh by Dr. Lardner, in his Jewifh and Heathen Teftimonies, Vol. IV. p. 137—158, with Obfervations. The VIth, "On reveng- "ing the death of the Emperor Julian," addreffed to the fame Theodofius, 379, was firft publifhed, from the Bodleian MS. by Olearius above-mentioned, Leipfic, 1701, 8vo. to which he afterwards added a Latin tranflation, and learned notes, at the defire of Fabricius, which he publifhed, in Bibliotheca Græca, Vol. VII. p. 145—179, with the original, and alfo with the VIIth, "To thofe who "called him troublefome," 373; and the VIIIth, "To "the Antiochians, on appeafing the refentment of the "Emperor"

LIFE OF LIBANIUS.

Allatius, Greek and Latin, Rom. 1641, 8vo. are xxxix Narrations, vii Descriptions, and vii more Exercises of Libanius, with translations by Allatius. His unpublished works are,

1. Many hundred Epistles * yet concealed in various libraries, a mode of writing in which it appears he excelled by the testimony even of the ancients, particularly Eunapius and Photius; and of that the perusal of them will easily convince the intelligent reader; for they abound with Attic wit and humour, and every where recommend themselves by their pointed conciseness no less than by their elegance and learning †.

2. Several

"Emperor" [Julian], 363, both for the first time, and a correct copy of the "funeral oration on Julian," with translations of them all by the same Olearius.

* Eleven years after Fabricius printed the above, John Christopher Wolfius, his pupil, friend, and collegue, assisted by the collections of Frederick Rostgaard, a noble Dane, (see p. 196.) published at Hamburgh, in one volume, folio, 1738, with learned notes, MDCV Epistles of Libanius, in Greek and Latin, two-thirds of them collected from various MSS. to which he added DXXII Epistles of the same author, in Latin only (xc of them duplicates, being also in the Greek), translated from the originals, collected in Greece, and published at Cracow, about the middle of the XVth century, by Francis Zambicari of Bologna, and republished there by John Sommerfeld, M. A. 1504. See Vol. I. p. 330, note *.

† The critics may praise their subtle and elegant brevity; yet Dr. Bentley (Dissertation upon Phalaris, p. 487.) might justly, though quaintly, observe, that "you feel by "the emptiness and deadness of them, that you converse "with some dreaming pedant, with his elbow upon his "desk." GIBBON.

LIFE OF LIBANIUS.

2. Several Orations, as in a MS. of the Barberini library, of excellent character, most correctly written on vellum, from which Allatius asserts *, that all the published works of Libanius might also be given much more correct and perfect.

3. Various Declamations, in the above MS. and one in the Vatican library.

And that there are many MS Epistles, Orations, and Declamations of Libanius in the Imperial library [at Vienna], Nesselius has observed, affirming also that several Greek scholia are frequently inserted in the margin.

Though so many of the writings of this sophist are preserved, there is no doubt that many both of his Epistles and Orations have been lost †.

<hr/>

The MDLXXIVth Epistle of Libanius occurs among those of Phalaris, and is inscribed to Antimathius, n. XXVII.
It is thought at present by almost all the learned, Bentley, the prince of critics (*viro κριτικωτάτω*) at their head, that these Epistles of Phalaris may justly be ascribed to some sophist. It may be worth while to consider whether all of them perhaps were not fabricated by Libanius. I recollect, at least, that in my notes I have frequently compared the phrases and expressions of Phalaris with those of Libanius. See, for instance, the notes on Ep. MCXLI.   WOLFIUS.

* *Præf. ad Excerpta Rhetorum Græcorum.*

† Of XI of these, mentioned by Libanius himself in different parts of his works, Fabricius recapitulates the titles, besides various Counsels (συμβυλαι ‡) to the Emperor Theodosius, mentioned in the beginning of his oration for the temples of the Heathens. And many more, which Fabricius has omitted, might be specified from several of his epistles.

‡ Translated by Dr. Lardner, " Orations, and the counsel delivered in them."

A MONODY

A MONODY* by LIBANIUS,

On NICOMEDIA,

Destroyed by an Earthquake †.

HOMER never suffers even a tree to perish without commiseration; but, as if he himself had been the planter or gardener, when he sees it stretched on the ground, he sings a lamentation

A. D. 358.

---

* A mournful song, recited by one only on the stage, without a chorus, was called Μονωδια. And mention is made of a *Monodiaria*, or of a woman who sung a monody.
WOLFIUS.

Libanius, in his XXXIst Epistle, mentions two Monodies which he composed on this occasion; one (which is now before us) relating to the city, the other, no doubt, to Aristænetus, Præfect of Bithynia, who perished in it (see the next note); but the latter is lost. "I also," says he, (Ep. xxv.) "am one of those who are overwhelmed by "that great calamity. For Afistænetus, O Jupiter, has "perished; and, besides this, we have suffered another "stroke, as fate has not spared the head of Hierocles."

All the ancients speak of Nicomedia as a place of great note: Pliny calls it "a famous and beautiful city:" Ammianus, "the mother of all the cities of Bithynia." In this city the Roman emperors resided, when the affairs of the empire called them into the east. Constantine the Great chose Nicomedia for the place of his abode after he retired from Rome, and there remained till the buildings that he had begun at Byzantium were finished. This city, once so famous, is now but a small village, known to the Turks by the name of Schemith ‡. UNIVERSAL HISTORY.

‡ According to Pococke, Ismit.

† At break of day, on the 9th of the calends of September, the sky, which before was clear, was obscured by thick dark clouds; and the light of the sun being veiled, neither near nor contiguous objects were discernible. Then the Supreme Deity throwing, as it were, fatal thunder-bolts, and removing the winds from their very hinges ‡, the fury of the storm abated; and to these hurricanes and whirlwinds succeeded an horrible earthquake, which totally overthrew the city and suburbs. And on account of the declivity of the hills, some houses fell upon others, all resounding with the dreadful crash of the ruins. Mean time the lofty roofs re-echoed with various cries of those who were seeking their wives and children, or dearest friends. After the second hour, but long before the third, the sky, now fair and clear, discovered the funereal carnage. For some, crushed by the overwhelming force of falling rafters, perished under the weight of them: some, buried up to the neck, though they might have survived if they had had timely assistance, died for want of help; others hung fixed to the tops of standing beams; many men were killed a little before by one blow; then were seen promiscuous slaughtered bodies; some, the roofs of their houses falling in, were confined unhurt, victims to anguish and famine. Among whom Aristænetus, who governed the diocese lately desired with vicarial power, to which Constantius, in honour of his wife, had given the name of the Eusebian Piety ‖, by this calamity, long tortured, expired. Others, crushed by sudden bulky ruins, are still covered by the same heaps. Some, who had their sculls fractured, or had lost their arms or legs, between life and death, imploring with earnest intreaties those who were assisting others, were deserted. And the greater part of the inhabitants might have survived the sacred and private buildings, had not flames, widely dispersed, for fifty days and nights, consumed whatever was combustible.

AMMIANUS.

See also an Epistle on this subject from Libanius to Julian, Vol. I. p. 303.

‡ *Ventosque ab ipsis excitante cardinibus.*
Not unlike to this are Milton's " winds," that
─────── rush'd abroad
From the four hinges of the world.   *Par. Reg.* IV. 409.

‖ After the example of the Julian Piety, a name given to Po'a in Istria (of which see Plin. l. 111. c. 19.)   LANDENBROG.

over it [*]. And can I permit Nicomedia, where I increased my knowledge of the liberal arts, especially eloquence, and acquired, besides, a degree of reputation which I had not before, to be destroyed, can I see such a city, a city no longer, reduced to ashes, unmourned, unwept? This concern I share in common with the vulgar; let her also participate of the oratory which she cherished. As, if I had been a musician, and had gained many victories there in musical contests, should I have suffered others to lament without joining in the lamentation?

Let me now address the Gods, supposing them present, and thus endeavour to estimate our calamity.

When, sitting in the palace of Jupiter, with the other Gods, you, O Neptune, were enraged on account of the wall which the Grecians had built

---

[*] Homer deplores the destruction of plants in Iliad IX and XVIII.   MORELL.

——————— a monstrous boar,
That levell'd harvests, and whole forests tore.
POPE, IX. 659.

Much more expressive in the original.
In the XVIIIth I find a plant, or a tree, mentioned only thus,
Like some fair olive, by my careful hand
He grew, he flourish'd, and adorn'd the land.
POPE, 175 and 512.

If Libanius had been acquainted with the Psalmist, and unprejudiced by Paganism, he could not have overlooked that beautiful allusion of the "vine brought out of "Ægypt," and the complaint of its being "rooted up, "burnt, and cut down." Ps. LXXX. 8—16.

at Troy to cover their ships, was not their neglect of the Gods, when they laid the foundation, the principal subject of your complaint *? And therefore, when Troy was taken, you judged right in thinking it necessary to destroy that wall; which you easily accomplished by turning against it the rivers that rushed from Ida †. But in the foundation of this city what was the offence that induced you to treat it in the same manner? Did not its first founder ‡, designing to build a city on the shore

---

* Hom. Il. vii. 450.
See the long walls extending to the main,
No God consulted, and no victim slain, &c.   POPE, 535.

† Ibid. xii. 17.
Then Neptune and Apollo shook the shore,
Then Ida's summits pour'd their watery store;
Rhesus and Rhodius then unite their rills, &c.

These, turn'd by Phœbus from their wonted ways,
Delug'd the rampire nine continual days;
The weight of waters saps the yielding wall,
And to the sea the floating bulwarks fall.
Incessant cataracts the Thunderer pours,
And half the skies descend in sluicy showers, &c.
                                                POPE, 15.

This is a noble passage in the old bard; storm, inundation, and earthquake magnificently combined.   B.

Milton alludes to it in his vision of the Deluge, b. xi.
———————— Then shall this mount
Of Paradise, by might of waves, be mov'd
Out of his place, push'd by the horned flood,
With all his verdure spoil'd, and trees adrift,
Down the great river to the opening gulf,
And there take root, an island salt and bare,
The haunt of seals, and orcs, and sea-mews' clang. 829.

‡ Nicomedia is said to have been first built by Olbia, and had its first name from him. It was afterwards re-built by

shore opposite to that where it now stands, or rather where it once stood, begin his work from you? Were not the altars covered with victims, and surrounded by a crowd of worshippers? But by an eagle and a prodigious snake you diverted their attention to the hill; of these, the former with her talons snatched the head of the victim from the fire; and the latter, large and resembling those which are bred in India, issued from the earth. The one cleaving the sea, and the other the air, repaired to the brow of the hill. The people followed, led, as they thought, by the guidance of the Gods. These omens were all deceitful. The city was at first overwhelmed by the torrent of war *. Be it so. Your own Corinth † also, and the land of

by Nicomedes I. king of Bithynia, though Olbia seems rather to have been near it, and that the inhabitants of it were transplanted to this place. POCOCKE.

Nicomedia, Astacus, and Olbia are spoken of by Ptolemy as three neighbouring but distinct cities. Strabo writes that Nicomedes, the son and successor of Zipœtes, destroyed Astacus, and transferred its inhabitants to Nicomedia.
UNIVERSAL HISTORY.

* This must probably have been in the reign of Nicomedes III. who was twice driven from his throne by Mithridates the Great, king of Pontus.

† Among other names which Corinth anciently had we find that of Heliopolis, or city of the sun, for which this reason is commonly given; that the poets feign Apollo and Neptune to have contended for it, and that Jupiter having appointed Briareus, the Cyclop, their umpire, he adjudged the Isthmus to the latter, and the Promontory, which commands the city, to the former. UNIVERSAL HISTORY.

Cecrops,

Cecrops *, your best beloved, have experienced the same fate †. Another founder came, who, making the Gods his principal leaders, and, by the superior magnitude of his offering, rendering your minds more propitious, restored the city. How then, like the land of Ætolia, for the offence of Œneus ‡, did she deserve to be punished with contempt? Is it right, has it been usual, for the Gods to destroy with their own hands works like these, in which they have co-operated with mortals, and to imitate the pastime of children, who are accustomed to pull down what they have erected §? Or did it become you, O Neptune, to enter into a contest with your niece for an Attic city not then in being, and to overflow a citadel so distant from

---

* An Ægyptian fugitive, who introduced religion into Greece, and founded the Athenian monarchy. See note * p 233.

† Corinth was surprised by Antigonus and Aratus, taken and burnt by the Romans, &c. Athens was destroyed by Mardonius, taken by the Lacedæmonians and Sylla, &c.

‡ Oeneus, king of Ætolia, or Calydon (its chief city) sacrificing to the rest of the deities, neglected his duty to Diana, who in consequence sent a wild boar to ravage and destroy the country, which was killed by his son Meleager, and his company. See Hom. Il. IX. 539.

§ Thus Tibullus, ——— *puer è virgis extruet arte casas.*
l. II. el. 1.
And Horace of a boy, ——— *amata relinquere pernix.*
MORELL.

Libanius had here, no doubt, in his view that passage in the Iliad to which Julian also refers in his XLth Epistle. See p. 106.

the sea *, yet to display no regard for such a great and important city as this, but even to subvert it from the foundations? What city was more beautiful? I will not say larger, for in size it was exceeded by four †, but contemned all that increase of extent, which would have wearied the feet of its citizens ‡. In beauty also it yielded to these, and was equalled, not excelled, by some others: for, stretching forth its promontories, with its arms

---

* Cecrops not knowing what name to give to his new-built city, an olive-tree, and a fountain of water (or, as others say, a horse) appeared. The oracle, being consulted, answered, that "Neptune and Minerva were contending "for the honour of naming it, that the olive was the gift "of Minerva, and the fountain (or horse) that of Neptune; and that that which they esteemed most bene-"ficial to mankind should adjudge the prize to the giver." The men and women being assembled to give their judgement, the former gave it for the God; but the women, who were more numerous, gave it for the Goddess; and the city was named from her *Athena*. Neptune, in revenge of the affront, overflowed their territories. APOLLODORUS.

Here we have an account of the Ροθιον mentioned by Libanius, which Morell has rendered *Procella*, though it signifies properly "the violence and force of water, a billow "of the sea:" as, in the poem on Hero and Leander, the poet says, he stood on the shore,

Μαινομενων ροθιων πολυηχεα βομβον ακουων·

where βομβον excellently expresses the heavy sound occasioned by the fall of the waves.   B.

† Rome, Byzantium, Antioch, and Alexandria.

‡ Τοσουτον αιμασασα τυ μεγεθος, οσον εμελλε λυπησειν των οικη-τορων τυς ποδας. This is an odd passage, and seems to me a puerile conceit. Morell's marginal reading, ισ. παιδας (for ποδας) is pleasant enough. I wonder he should think any alteration necessary, as he understood the true sense of the place; for men may be fatigued as well as children. I have no doubt that he was a great walker.   B.

it embraced the sea. It then ascended the hill by four colonnades extending the whole length. Its public buildings were splendid, its private contiguous, rising from the lowest parts to the citadel, like the branches of a cypress, one house above another, watered by rivulets, and surrounded with gardens *. Its council-chambers, its schools of oratory, the multitude of its temples, the magnificence of its baths, and the commodiousness of its harbour I have seen, but cannot describe. This only I can say, that, frequently travelling thither from Nice †, we used on the road to discourse on the trees, and the soil, abundant in all productions, and also of our families, our friends, and ancient wisdom. But after we had passed through the intricate windings of the hills, when the city appeared, at the distance of a hundred and fifty stadia ‡, on all other subjects a profound silence instantly ensued, and, no longer engaged either by the towering branches of the gardens, or by the fruitfulness of the soil, or by

---

* In like manner, Dr. Pococke describes the present town, as " situated at the foot of two hills, and all up the south " side of the western one, which is very high, and on part " of the other: it is near the N. E. corner of the bay. All " the houses have small gardens, or courts, to them, espe- " cially those on the hills. The gardens are planted with " trees §, and the vines, being carried along on frames built " like roofs, make the city appear exceedingly beautiful. " There are very few remains of the ancient Nicomedia."

† Thirty-two miles.   POCOCKE.

‡ About nineteen miles.

§ Κηποι αιωρεμενοι τοις κλαδοις are the words of Libanius.

the

ON NICOMEDIA.

the traffic of the sea, our whole conversation turned on Nicomedia. And yet mariners, or those who labour at the oar, and ensnare the fish with nets, or hooks, naturally attract the observation of travellers. But the form of the city, much more fascinating, by its beauty tyrannised over our eyes, and fixed their whole attention on itself. Similar were the sensations of him who had never seen it before, and of him who had grown old within its walls. One shewed to his companion the palace, glittering over the bay; another the theatre embellishing the whole city; others various other rays darted from various objects: which surpassed it was difficult to determine. Revering it as a sacred image, we proceeded; in our way to Chalcedon, it was necessary to turn, till the nature of the road deprived us of the sight *. This seemed like the cessation of a feast.

A city so great, so renowned, ought not the whole choir of the Gods to have surrounded and protected, exhorting each other to decree that it should never be subjected to any calamity? But now some of you have deceived, others have deserted, and none assisted her. And all these particulars, which I have mentioned, once were, but remain no longer. What a beautiful lock has For-

---

* He first mentions the pleasure arising from the prospect of the city, as they approached; and then their concern at losing sight of it, as they proceeded from it to Chalcedon. B.

tune

tune now severed from the world *! How has she blinded the other continent by thus bereaving it of its illustrious eye! What a deplorable deformity has she diffused over Asia; as if her most spacious grove had been felled, as if her most conspicuous feature † had been lopped off! O most injurious earthquake, why didst thou perpetrate this? O departed city! O name of it in vain remaining! O grief dispersed over land and sea! O dire intelligence, distressful to the hearts of all ranks, of all ages! for what heart is so stony, what heart is so adamantine, as not to be wounded by this relation? who is so destitute of tears as now to with-hold them? O dreadful misfortune, which has reduced the innumerable ornaments of the city to one ruinous heap! O unpropitious ray ‡, what a city didst

---

* Thus Pindar styles Ætna " the front," or forehead, " of the fruitful earth," ευκαρποιο γαιας μέτωπον, Pyth. I. and Nicomedia was a beautiful city " high-mounted on a " hill," as Sandys says of some other. I am afraid the hill of Nicomedia hardly deserved the name μέτωπον γαιας; but a panegyrist may make mountains of molehills. B.

† Βοστρυχος, οφθαλμος, what next? αλσος, ρις (" The lock, "'the eye, the *grove*, the nose.") In the name of propriety, what has αλσος to do here? Are we to understand it of the hair of the head? B.

This idea seems anticipated by βοστρυχος. The metaphor indeed seems here lost, " a grove," or " wood," being no feature, like the others. P. seemed in English to require a circumlocution.

‡ Ω δυστυχης ακτινος, οιαν μεν προσεβαλλε την πολιν ανασχουσα· οιαν δε αφεισα καθίω. Morell translates ακτινος *tridentis radius*. But why should it not mean (as usual) the " sun's ray?" Ανεχω and καταδυνω are used for the " rising and setting of the sun."

ON NICOMEDIA.

didst thou smite at thy rising, what a city sunk with thee! The day had almost advanced to noon *; the tutelar deities of the city abandoned the temples, and she was left like a ship deserted by its crew. The lord of the trident shook the earth, and convulsed the ocean; the foundations of the city were disunited; walls were thrown on walls, pillars on pillars, and roofs fell headlong. What was hidden was revealed, and what had appeared was hidden. Statues, perfect in beauty, and complete in every part, were blended by the concussion in one confused mass. Artificers, working at their trades, were dashed out of their shops and houses. In the harbour was much destruction, and also of many worthy chosen men collected about the Præfect †. The theatre involved in its ruins all who

---

sun." I do not recollect that ακλη is used absolutely, as here, for the "prong of the trident." The trident too is thrust under the foundation. See the beginning of the Phœnissæ of Euripides, where Jocasta, addressing the Sun, complains of his darting an "unpropitious ray" on Thebes. Ἡλιε, θοαις ιπποισιν, κ. τ. λ.

  O thou, that glorying in thy fiery steeds,
  Rollest the orient light, resplendent Sun,
  How inauspicious didst thou dart thy beams
  That day on Thebes, &c. POTTER. Possibly Libanius may allude to it.   B.

* Μικρον μεν απειχιν ημερα περι πληθουσαν αγοραν ειναι.
Literally, "it was near high market." But Ammianus says, that it happened at break of day; and George Cedrenus, in the night.

† Aristænetus, the great friend and patron of Libanius, who, in several of his epistles to him, celebrates his eloquence and sweetness of manners. See p. 227. note *. He was afterwards buried at Nice, of which he was a native.

were

were in it. Some buildings, which had long stood tottering, and others which had yet escaped, with all who were in them, shared at last the general fate. The sea, violently agitated, deluged the land. Fire, which abounded every where, seizing the rafters, added to the concussion a conflagration *; and some wind, it is said, fanned the flames. Much of the city, much of the ramparts, still remains. Of those who have escaped, a few still wander about wounded.

O all-seeing Sun, what were thy sensations on seeing this? Why didst not thou prevent such a city from leaving the earth? For the oxen profaned by the famished mariners † such was thy resentment as to threaten the celestial powers that thou wouldst give thyself up to Pluto ‡; but for the glory of the earth, for the labour of many kings, for the fruit of prodigious cost, destroyed in the day-time, thou hast no compassion.

O fairest of cities, on what a faithless and froward hill didst thou fix thy seat; which, like a vicious horse, has dismounted its excellent rider? Where are now thy winding walks? where are thy

---

* Thus at Lisbon, Messina, and in all great earthquakes, fire has been their constant attendant.

† Hom. Odyss. xii. Libanius has before taken Neptune to task; he here reprimands Apollo.

‡ Alluding to what Apollo says on that occasion in the same book of the Odyssey.
" Vengeance, ye Gods, or I the skies forego,
" And bear the lamp of heaven to shades below."
POPE, 450.

ON NICOMEDIA.

porticoes? where are thy courses, thy fountains, thy courts of judicature, thy libraries, thy temples? Where is all that profusion of wealth? Where are the young, the old? Where are the baths of the Graces and of the Nymphs? of which the largest, named after the prince, at whose expence it was built, was equal in value to the whole city *. Where is now the senate? Where are the people? where the women? the children? where is the palace? where is the circus †, stronger than the walls of Babylon ‡? Nothing is left standing; nothing has escaped; all are involved in one common ruin.

O numerous streams, where now do you flow? what mansions do you lave? from what springs do you issue? The various aqueducts and reservoirs are broken. The plentiful supply of the fountains runs to waste, either forming whirlpools, or stagnating in morasses; but drawn or quaffed by no one, neither by men nor birds. These are terrified

---

* As Diocletian, according to Lactantius, embellished Nicomedia with a great number of stately buildings, with a design of equalling it to Rome, possibly these baths might be part of them, and named after him, as we know his baths, now magnificent in ruins, were at Rome; which, says Ammianus, with no small exaggeration, "seemed rather a "province than a building."

† He [Diocletian] built there several basilics, a circus, a mint, an arsenal, a palace for his wife, and another for his son.   LACTANTIUS.

‡ The walls of Babylon were so celebrated among the ancients as to grow proverbial. Libanius mentions them in like manner in his cxcvith Epistle.

by the fire which rages every where below, and, where it has a vent, flames into the air. This city, once so populous, now in the day time is deserted and desolate, but at night is possessed by such a multitude of spectres, as I think must crowd the inhabitants of the infernal regions after they have passed Acheron.

Celebrated of old were the disasters of Lemnos [*], and the Iliad sings the woes of Troy. Their remembrance will be slighted, but the excess of our calamities any one may hence determine. Former earthquakes, though they destroyed some parts of the city, spared others; but this has overwhelmed the whole. Other cities have also perished, but never one of such a magnitude. If it had been deprived only of bodies infected with the plague, or of those persons who, contrary to the laws [†], were celebrating

---

[*] Great misfortunes were proverbially styled "Lemnian;" some say, from the slaughter of the Attic women, and the children which they had by them, by the Pelagians, who inhabited Lemnos; others, from the murder of their husbands, on account of their offensive breath, by the Lemnian women. See Ludolph Kuster on Suidas, tom. II. p. 441. Bayle's Dictionary, vol. II. p. 1780. and Erasmus, in his Chileades.   WOLFIUS.

Libanius, in his xxivth Epistle, thus alludes to this passage; "I said little when I expressed the ruin of Nicomedia by the misfortunes of Lemnos."

[†] Κατα νομον. It seems a little hard that people should be destroyed for sacrificing "according to law;" yet κατα νομον is certainly "according to law." Let us suppose an error of the press, and make it νομω. He alludes to some event, which I do not recollect. I suspect that he has taken a line from some Greek poet, and accommodated it to his purpose.   B.

Though

ON NICOMEDIA.

brating a general sacrifice without the city, and had not itself fallen, the stroke might have been supportable. The whole would not have been desolated; now both lie prostrate, and the form of the city is confused with the slaughter of the citizens.

Lament therefore, every island and every continent, peasants and mariners, cities, villages, cottages, every thing that is connected with human nature; and let tears prevail over all the world, as in Ægypt whenever Apis dies *. Even rocks should now be indulged with tears, and birds with reason, to join in an elegiac song. O harbour, which ships now carefully avoiding, rather steer into the ocean, their cables slipped, which formerly wert filled with loaded vessels, but now cannot boast even a pleasure-boat, and art more dreaded by mariners than even the mansion of Scylla! O disappointment to travellers, who no longer frequent the road, which, gloomy and in the form of a crescent, beautifully winded round the dykes of the haven, but embarking sail to-

---

Though Libanius, like Julian, was probably acquainted with the Mosaic history, I will not affirm that he here alludes to it; but certain it is, that this passage has no distant affinity to the earthquake that swallowed up Korah and his company, for offering unhallowed incense, and to the plague that destroyed their abettors. *Numbers* xvi.

* When Apis dies, they behave as if they had lost their dearest children, and bury him in the most sumptuous manner. Nor do the people cease from lamenting till the priests have found a calf with the same marks.

DIODORUS SICULUS.

wards the hill, to which they formerly haftened [by land], trembling as at Charybdis, and unable to conjecture in what part of the fea they ufed to ftand on the fhore! O deareft of cities! in your ruin you have involved your inhabitants; you have deftroyed them by your fall; fo that all mankind apply themfelves to fupplications, thinking the extinction of their whole race determined. After the lofs of this moft valuable poffeffion, nothing hereafter, they apprehend, will be fpared. Who will fupply me with wings to waft me thither? Who will place me on an eminence to view the diftrefsful fight? For a lover has fome confolation in being furrounded by the objects of his affection, though in ruins *.

* For the notes on this and the following Monody, marked B, I am obliged to a learned and amiable friend.

A MONODY by LIBANIUS,

ON THE

Daphnæan Temple of Apollo, destroyed by Fire, or, as it is said, by Lightning *.

FELLOW-citizens, whose eyes, like mine, are now involved in darkness †, this city we shall no longer style beautiful or great ‡.

A. D.
362.

---

* The Greek title of this Monody is more perfect in the Royal MS. which I have followed, than in the Bavarian; in which it is only styled, "A Monody on the Daphnæan "Temple of Apollo." But the corollary, which is added to the inscription here adopted, does not give the sentiments of Libanius, who had conceived an idea, that some incendiary by a small spark had kindled this great conflagration, as he says, in the beginning; and soon after, that he may obviate the opinion of thunder from heaven, he adds, that " it happened in a clear and cloudless sky;" which to the orthodox increases the miracle, of which St. John Chrysostom, the contemporary of our Libanius, in his 1st Discourse on the Martyr St. Babylas, p. 725. " As " soon as the bier was brought to the city, lightning " fell from heaven on the head of the image, and con- " sumed every thing." And the Emperor Julian too was well aware of this; " he knew that the blow came from " heaven;" though he asserts, in the Misopogon, that " the " temple was destroyed by the negligence of the keepers, " and the presumption of the impious." MORELL.

After the interment of St. Babylas, Apollo gave oracles as before; and Julian caused a superb colonnade to be built round his temple. But in the night of the 22d of October, 362, a fire consumed the wood work of that ancient edifice, and the statue itself; nor could Julian, who hastened

A MONODY BY LIBANIUS,

to the place, supply any remedy. That fire was ascribed by the Christians to the divine vengeance, and by Julian to the resentment and jealousy of the Christians. He suspected the sacrist, and the ministers who kept the temple, of being in a confederacy with them. But those idolaters, being put to the torture, accused no one. On the contrary, they constantly affirmed, that the fire began from above; and some peasants, who were that night on the road in their way to the city, said, they saw fire from heaven fall on the temple, though the weather was very calm, and there was no appearance of a storm. Julian, however, either by way of reprisal, or to prevent the Christians from triumphing, ordered the great church of Antioch to be shut, and its riches to be carried to the imperial treasury.
LA BLETERIE.

See also Vol. I. p. 247, 248.

† What darkness hangs over the eyes of the Antiochians? Is it the darkness of a cloud, which
With mists and films involves their mortal sight?
Such as the Pallas of Homer boasts to have removed from Diomed, and the Venus of Virgil from Æneas? Or is it the gloom of sorrow, which, hanging over the eyes of the mind, obscures the use of reason and thought? MORELL.

‡ On the beauty and extent of Antioch, see Philostratus on the Life of Apollonius, *l.* I. *c.* xii. *p.* 21. " Apollonius " came to Antioch the Great," &c. and our Libanius, in his oration to Theodosius the Great, on the sedition, in behalf of the Antiochians, where, in the conclusion on the misfortunes of that city, he adds, as here, " our city is be-" come different, or, to speak more truly, it is no longer " a city." Ausonius celebrates it among the famous cities,

Tertia Phœbeæ lauri domus Antiochia.

With the Phœbëan laurel grac'd, the third
Is Antioch.

After the first sentence, Chrysostom in the same place declares, that Libanius added something of the fable of Daphne, and perhaps it was the fable which Philostratus, in the above mentioned passage, calls " Arcadian," and explains as follows: " He entered the fane of Daph-" næan Apollo, to which the Assyrians ascribe the Ar-" cadian fable. For they say, that Daphne, the daugh-" ter of Ladon, was there transformed; and the river " Ladon flows among them, and the laurel-tree is ho-" noured by them, on account of that virgin." *Ibid.*

ON THE DAPHNÆAN TEMPLE.

··· [A king of Persia, one of the ancestors of him who is now at war with us, having by treachery taken and burnt the city, as he was preparing the same fate for Daphne, was so thoroughly diverted from his purpose by the Deity, that, throwing away the torch which he brandished, he prostrated himself, and adored Apollo: so appeased was his resentment, so checked was his fury *.] He, though he led an army against us, thought proper to preserve this temple, and the beauty of the image restrained his barbaric fury. But now, O heaven and earth, who and whence is that traitor, who wanting neither light † nor heavy-armed foot ‡, nor

---

* This I have not published in the Greek, because it was not in our Royal and Bavarian MS. And John Chrysostom himself, though he did not insert it in its proper place, hurried away by the eddy of his discourse, yet afterwards pays it as a debt, or brings it back as a fugitive, with this introduction, " You read this in the beginning of the " Monody, " A king of Persia," &c. [as above]. But who was this king of Persia, unless it were Sapor, the second king, who, according to Zosimus, succeeded Artaxerxes the first king?¡ The same took Antioch, and held it till the Emperor Gordian, having defeated the Persians in several battles, dispossessed king Sapor, and recovered Antioch, with Carrhæ and Nisibis, all which were under the Persian dominion, as Julius Capitolinus relates in his Gordian.

MORELL.

† The light-armed foot of the Greeks fought with arrows, darts, and slings; and were placed either in the van to begin an engagement, or on the flank of the wings to gall the enemies cavalry, and prevent their breaking in.

‡ The heavy-armed soldiers engaged with long spears, broad shields, and cutting swords. The Grecian cavalry was not very numerous.

horse, has consumed the whole with a small spark? Nor was our temple destroyed by a violent storm, but in a serene and cloudless sky. Hitherto, Apollo, your altars thirsting for blood, you have remained the constant and careful guardian of Daphne; and though neglected, and so far contemned as to be stripped of your outward ornaments, you acquiesced. But now, when many sheep, many oxen, have been offered to you; when the sacred lips of an Emperor * have impressed your feet; seen by him whom you have exalted, seeing him whom you have proclaimed, and delivered from the hateful neighbourhood of a certain dead body †, which disturbed you, you have withdrawn from the midst of your worship.

How can we now expect to be honoured, in future, by those who have a veneration for temples and images! When fatigued in our minds, of what a relief, O Jupiter, are we deprived! How pure, how free from all tumults, was the region of Daphne! how much still purer was the shrine! like a haven formed by nature within a haven; both being tranquil, but the inner affording the most tranquillity. Who did not there lose his diseases, his fears, his sorrows? Who there wished

---

* Julian. The Pagans used religiously to kiss the images of their Gods, if they could, and putting their hands to their mouths, they wafted kisses to them at a distance. From this custom some derive the word *adoro*. Thus Job, xxxi. 27. *If my mouth hath kissed my hand*, &c. WOLFIUS.

† The remains of Pabylas. See the Misopogon, Vol. I. p. 247.

for

for the island of the blessed? Ere long will be the Olympic games *; that annual festival will convene the cities; these cities too will come, bringing oxen as victims to Apollo. What then shall we do? Where shall we secrete ourselves? Which of the Gods will open the earth for us? What herald, what trumpet, but will excite tears? Who now will style the Olympic games a festival, as this late misfortune suggests so dire a lamentation?

Bring me my bow of horn †,

says the tragedy. I add, a little in the spirit of prophecy,

That thus I may attack, and thus destroy,

The vile incendiary,

O impious deed! O sacrilegious soul! O daring hand! Surely this was another Tityus ‡, or Idas §,

* Of Antioch. In the adjacent fields a stadium was built by a special privilege, which had been purchased from Elis; the Olympic games were regularly celebrated at the expence of the city; and a revenue of thirty thousand pounds sterling was annually applied to the public pleasures.

GIBBON.

In three of his Epistles Libanius urges three of his friends to supply these games with wrestlers; and in his Life, pp. 59 and 68, he mentions two orations which he composed on that solemnity, which are not now extant. A third is in his works, Vol. II. p. 538.

† Δος τοξα μοι κερουλκα. Euripides in Oreste, 268.

‡ Struck by Jupiter with a thunderbolt, for attempting to ravish Latona. See Odyss. xi. 575. and Æn. vi. 595.

§ — matchless Idas, more than man in war.
    The God of day ador'd the mother's charms,
    Against the God the father bent his arms.

POPE, Il. ix. 672.

Let us not imitate that daring Idas, who bent his bow, it is said, against the God; for this is waging war with Apollo.

LIBANIUS.

"A MONODY BY LIBANIUS,

the brother of Lynceus, not an archer, indeed, like the one, or a giant, like the other, but a proficient in nothing save frenzy towards the Gods. The sons of Aloëus *, while they meditated mischief against the Gods, you, Apollo, quieted by death; but him, bringing fire from afar, your arrow did not arrest, transfixing his heart. O wicked hand of Telchin †! O injurious fire! What did it first catch? Where did the evil begin? Seizing the roof, did it descend to the inferior parts, to the head, the face, the cup ‡, the tiara, or the flowing robe? Vulcan, the dif-

---

* Othus and Ephialtes, who being of a gigantic stature, and threatening to make war against the Gods, were transfixed and slain by the darts of Apollo and Diana. See Æn. vi. 582.

† The Telchines, who inhabited Rhodes, were the inventors of several arts and other things beneficial to mankind. They are also said first to have made images of the Gods, and some of the ancient statues were surnamed from them. Thus among the Lindians Apollo was called Telchinius. Juno was also styled Telchinia. . . They were called enchanters; and were said to produce, when they pleased, clouds and rain, and to generate hail, and to be invidious in teaching their arts.   DIODORUS SICULUS.

Thus it appears that the Telchinians were a people of great ingenuity, by which they got a bad name, like our Roger Bacon, and the German Faustus, who is supposed at this very day to have dealt with the Devil; so that this exclamation, Ω διξιας Τιλχινος, standing in immediate connection with the preceding sentence, Telchin here must be Apollo. And perhaps he means to give Apollo a rap here, as he did Neptune [and Apollo too] in the other Monody. B.

‡ The colossal figure of the deity almost filled the capacious sanctuary. He was represented in a bending attitude, with a golden cup in his hand, pouring out a libation on the earth; as if he supplicated the venerable mother to give to his arms the cold and beauteous Daphne. GIBBON.

On the DAPHNÆAN TEMPLE.

penser of fire, though indebted to the God for his former obliging discovery *, did not rebuke this wasting flame. Nor did Jupiter, who has the command of rain, pour water on it, though for the unfortunate king of Lydia he extinguished the funeral pile †.

What was the first suggestion of him who undertook this enterprise? whence this rashness? how could he retain his fury? how could he avoid abandoning his purpose through reverence for his beauty of the God? My fancy, O my countrymen, presents me with the form of the God, and sets before my eyes his image, the complacency of the aspect, the tenderness of the skin expressed in the marble, the sash over his breast confining the golden robe, so that some parts of it subsided, and others rose. What mind had such fervour that the whole appearance of the statue could not calm? For the God seemed in the act of singing; or as when he was once heard playing on his harp at noon. The song was in praise of the Earth, on whom, gaping to receive the virgin, and then contracting to con-

---

* Alluding to that passage of Homer, Odyssey VIII, where, in the loves of Mars and Venus, sung by Demodocus,

    Warn'd by the God who shed the golden day,
    Stern Vulcan homeward treads the starry way,
                                 BROOME.

† Crœsus, being placed by Cyrus on a funeral pile, praying to Apollo was saved by a shower of rain, which extinguished the flames, See Herodotus, I. 87. Julian ascribes this miracle to Jupiter.

ceal her, he seemed to pour a libation from the golden cup.

At the eruption of flames the traveller exclaimed; the guardian of Daphne, the domestic priestess of the God, was alarmed; the beating of bosoms, and shrill shrieks, echoing through the spacious groves, soon reached the city, diffusing universal grief and horror. The prince *, whose eye had scarce yet yielded to sleep, at the dreadful intelligence sprung from his bed. Transported with fury, and wishing for the wings of Mercury, he rushed forth to investigate the cause. Inwardly he burnt no less than the temple. The rafters now fell, scattering the fire below, which destroyed all that was within its reach; [the statue of] Apollo immediately, being near to the roof; then other ornaments of the temple, the Muses, the statues of the founders, the splendid marbles, the beautiful pillars. Crowds of spectators stood by lamenting, but unable to assist, like those, who from land beholding a shipwreck, can afford no relief but their tears. The Nymphs, leaving their fountains, loudly exclaimed; so did Jupiter, who sat not far distant, lamenting, as became him, the tarnished honours of his son; so did also an innumerable throng of Dæmons who inhabit the forest. Nor less was the lamentation of Calliope, in the middle of the

* Julian.

city,

ON THE DAPHNÆAN TEMPLE.

city *, when the high-priest of the Muses was injured by the flames * * * * †.

As propitious may'st thou now be to me, Apollo, as Chryses rendered thee, when he imprecated vengeance on the Greeks, full of indignation, and "dark as night ‡." Since while we were offering sacrifices to thee, and were restoring whatever had been purloined from thy temple, the object of our worship has been snatched away from us; like a bridegroom, who, while the garlands are weaving for his nuptials, dies.

---

* I have an idea that there was a statue of Calliope in the middle of Antioch, to which Libanius here alludes; and also in one of his Epistles. See Vol. I. p. 324. And from a passage in his DCCXXXVIIth Epistle, to Rufinus, it seems to have been erected to that chief of the Muses by the great-great-grandfather of that friend.

† Something here is wanting.

‡ Νυκτὶ ἐοικώς. Hom. Il. I. 47.
Breathing revenge, a sudden night he spread. POPE 65.

THE HISTORY OF THE EMPEROR JOVIAN.

From the French

Of the Abbé de la BLETERIE.

―― *Infelix brevitate regendi.*

THE AUTHOR's PREFACE.

AS the empire and religion are at the death of Julian in a kind of crisis which interests the curiosity of the reader, the Life of that prince would remain in some degree imperfect, if the History of Jovian were not annexed to it. Though he reigned only a few months, and though, in our age, when singularity alone may supply the place of merit, his character may be less interesting than that of his predecessor, I may venture to say, that his history presents some memorable facts, and suggests more reflections than the long reigns of many other sovereigns.

It is characterised by two remarkable events, one good, the other bad : I mean the re-establishment of Christianity, which is seen to re-ascend the throne of the Cæsars never again to leave it; and that fatal treaty of peace, which announces and begins the fall of the Roman greatness. It is thus that *he who dwelleth in the heavens laughs* at the designs of his enemies. Julian flattered himself with restoring his empire to its ancient splendor.

The AUTHOR's PREFACE.

He had, or seemed to have, most of the talents necessary for the execution of this plan; yet the imprudence of Julian must have been the cause, or, at least, the occasion, of the ruin of the empire. Julian made no doubt of suppressing the Christian religion: but Providence had decreed that he should be the last Pagan Emperor. The war which he waged with Sapor was preparatory to that which he meditated against us [the Gauls]. He thought that the conquest of Persia would give him sufficient leisure and authority to complete by force of arms the work which his cunning and his artifices had only sketched; yet it was really that war which preserved the Christians from the other which he was preparing against them; it was that war which took him out of the world, and gave the Romans an Emperor who was zealous enough to make Christianity triumph by means worthy of the true religion.

Hitherto the reign of Jovian has remained lost, as it were, in general history. I shall be thanked, perhaps, for snatching it from oblivion. I have treated it with all the care of which I am capable, and I dare not say how much it has cost me. History is not a compilation of facts collected at random, a brilliant collection of pretty thoughts, a tissue of learned dissertations. It is neither a panegyric, nor a satire; it ought to be an impartial and disinterested narration, simple and natural, though sentimental, always easy in its style, even when

when it offers the result of many researches and discussions. It ought, if I may so say, to render the reader contemporary with the events, to instruct without fatiguing him, to enlighten without dazzling him, to make him think, and to give him the pleasure of believing that he thinks for himself, not saying every thing, and leaving nothing to be wished, allowing neither too much nor too little to conjecture, and removing apparent contradictions by lucky discoveries; in a word, it should supply the place of original authors to those who have it not in their power to read them, and enable those, who can consult them, to read them with more pleasure and emolument. I have endeavoured to write in this manner the History of Jovian. I do not flatter myself with having succeeded; happy if connoisseurs find some marks of resemblance between the execution and the idea.

HISTORY

OF THE

EMPEROR JOVIAN.

A. D. 363.

IT may be seen, in the Life of Julian, that that prince, after passing the Tigris above Ctesiphon, by an extravagance which even success could not excuse, burned his fleet and provisions *. He was
desirous

---

* He destroyed, in a single hour, the whole navy, which had been transported above five hundred miles, at so great an expence of toil, of treasure, and of blood. Twelve, or, at the most, twenty-two small vessels were saved, to accompany on carriages the march of the army, and to form occasional bridges for the passage of the rivers. A supply of twenty days provisions was referved for the use of the soldiers; and the rest of the magazines, with a fleet of eleven hundred vessels, which rode at anchor in the Tigris, were abandoned to the flames, by the absolute command of the Emperor. The Christian bishops, Gregory and Augustin, insult the madness of the apostate, who executed, with his own hands, the sentence of divine justice. Their authority, of less weight perhaps in a military question, is confirmed by the cool judgement of an experienced soldier [Ammianus], who was himself spectator of the conflagration, and who could not disapprove the reluctant murmurs of the troops. Yet there are not wanting some specious, and perhaps solid, reasons, which might justify the resolution of Julian. The navigation of the Euphrates never ascended above Babylon, nor that of the Tigris above Opis. The distance of the last-mentioned city from the Roman camp was not very considerable; and Julian must soon have renounced the vain and impracticable attempt of
forcing

firous of penetrating into the heart of Assyria; but at the end of some days march, finding neither corn nor forage, because the Persians had laid all the country waste, he was obliged to approach the Tigris. Being unable to pass it for want of boats, he took for the model of his retreat that of the ten thousand *, and resolved to gain, like them, the country of the Carduci, called in his time

<blockquote>
forcing upwards a great fleet against the stream of a rapid river, which in several places was embarrassed by natural or artificial cataracts. The power of sails and oars was insufficient; it became necessary to tow the ships against the current of the river; the strength of 20,000 soldiers was exhausted in this tedious and servile labour; and if the Romans continued to march along the banks of the Tigris, they could only expect to return home without atchieving any enterprise worthy of the genius or fortune of their leader. If, on the contrary, it was adviseable to advance into the inland country, the destruction of the fleet and magazines was the only measure which could save that valuable prize from the hands of the numerous and active troops which might suddenly be poured from the gates of Ctesiphon. Had the arms of Julian been victorious, we should now admire the conduct, as well as the courage, of a hero, who, by depriving his soldiers of the hopes of a retreat, left them only the alternative of death or conquest. Recollect the successful and applauded rashness of Agathocles and Cortez, who burnt their ships on the coasts of Africa and Mexico.   GIBBON.
</blockquote>

<blockquote>
* ——————— the martial throng,
Up Tigris' banks who wound their march along;
O'er wilds and mountains held their toilsome way,
By hosts assaulted, and the solar ray;
By thirst, by famine, by eternal snows —
Whom heaven and earth united to oppose.
Unconquer'd still the Greeks each peril meet,
Regain their shores, and dignify retreat.   IRWIN.
</blockquote>

Corduenne, a name which is still found in that of Curdes and Curdistan. Corduenne, then subject to the Romans, is situated on the north of Assyria. Thus marching on that side, Julian had the Tigris on his left, and went up towards the source of that river.

Superior in every attack to the lieutenants of Sapor, whether they waited for him in line of battle, or contented themselves with insulting him on his march, he was still advancing, when on the 26th of June, 363, repulsing the enemy with too much ardour, he received a wound, of which he died the night following *.

At the death of Julian the Roman army was in a strange situation; victorious, but in want of every thing. Corduenne, its only resource, was still far distant. To reach this province it must traverse without provisions, beneath a burning sky, a ruined country, sustain in this march the continual at-

---

* The defection of this great man from the purest of all religions cannot be defended, though it may be accounted for; and his aversion and discountenance to Christians suit not the informed and liberal mind of Julian in other points. It will suffice to say, that his life seems to have belied the name of Apostate, which he brought upon himself by his deviation from the faith in which he was educated. If the paths of Virtue lead to the temple of Truth, he invariably trod them; and may charitably be supposed to have arrived, by an indirect course, at the divine goal. The circumstances of his death are so similar to those of Epaminondas, that we must be rejoiced to find their lives were equally dignified by pursuits that rendered their end immortal. IRWIN.

HISTORY OF JOVIAN.

tacks of the Persians, always formidable though vanquished, because they were as ready to rally as to fly, and, besides, as the death of Julian had raised the hopes of king Sapor.

It seemed difficult to remain without a chief; the moments were precious. On the 27th of June, therefore, at break of day, the officers met to choose a successor to Julian, who had just expired. The creatures of that prince *, and those who still remained of the old court †, having neither the same interests, nor the same views, all earnestly desired an Emperor of their own faction; but as neither of the two factions had had time to concert among themselves, all their suffrages, not one excepted, were united in favour of Sallust the second, Præfect of the Prætorium of the East. This illustrious Pagan, whose virtue cannot be sufficiently admired and lamented, completed the justification of that choice by the firmness with which he refused to load himself with a burthen too oppressive, he said, both for his age and infirmities. A subaltern officer ‡, then seeing the embarrassment into which the persevering refusal of Sallust had thrown the assembly, said to the generals, " What

---

* Nevitta, Dagalaiphus, and the Gallic officers.   B.
† Arintheus, Victor, &c.   B.
‡ Thus I translate that expression, *honoratior aliquis miles*. I suspect that Ammianus thus describes himself.   B.
The modest and judicious historian describes the scene of the election, at which he was undoubtedly present (xxv. 5.)
GIBBON.

" would

"would you do, if the prince, instead of marching in person, had given you the command of
the army? You would only think of extricating
yourselves from this dilemma. Act, as if he
were still living; and when we have once reached
Mesopotamia, in concert with the army of observation we will choose an Emperor, whose
election cannot be contested." This perhaps
would have been the best advice; but some on a
sudden exalted their voices in favour of Jovian, and
by their tumultuous clamours drew away all the
rest, without giving them time to consider.

Flavius Claudius Jovianus, aged about 33
years, was the first of the Emperor's guards *. He
had conducted the corpse of Constantius to the imperial city; and as, according to custom, sitting in
the funereal car, he received in some sort the
honours which were paid to that prince, it was
imagined, after the event, that this honourable, but
transient and mournful, employment had been the
prognostic and image of his future grandeur †.

The

---

* Jovian was not captain of the guards, as some have thought; but only what was called *domesticorum ordinis primus*. What rank this was we know not. *Domestici*, or *protectores domestici*, are certainly the body-guards. B.
The *primus*, or *primicerius*, enjoyed the dignity of a senator, and though only a tribune, he ranked with the military dukes. *Cod. Theodosian. l.* vi. *tit.* xxiv. These privileges are perhaps more recent than the time of Jovian. Gibbon.

† Wherever the Emperors passed, deputies were sent to them: they were harangued, samples of the provisions intended for the troops were presented to them, the horses were

The nobility of his family ascended no higher than count Varronian, his father, born in the territory of the city of Singidon in Mysia, and probably a soldier of fortune, who, for his merit, had been appointed to the command of the Jovians: Such was the appellation of a body of troops formed by Diocletian, who, it is known, had taken the surname of Jovius. It was owing perhaps to his regard for the troop of which he was chief, that Varronian made one of his children bear the name of Jovian. This officer, full of years and glory, still enjoyed his high reputation in retirement. Some even pretend that it constituted the principal merit of his son. But to refute them it is sufficient to say, that though Jovian had declared that he would rather quit the service than renounce the Christian religion, Julian did not cease to keep him near his person, and to take him with him, when he set out on his fatal expedition. Julian was well acquainted with his talents. A confessor of the faith, whom an apostate and intolerant monarch thought worthy to retain a place of confidence, was certainly no ordinary subject. The Pagans themselves do justice to his valour, and if

---

were shewn to them, &c. which the public maintained for the use of those who travelled by order of the court. The same ceremonial was observed with regard to the Emperors after their deaths. On that occasion he who attended the corpse acted and spoke, without doubt, in the name of the late Emperor. It was a kind of sovereignty which expired on the tomb of the prince. See Amm. *l.* xxi. *c. ult.* B.

they sometimes speak of him as a timid prince, this reproach falls rather on the politician than the warrior.

To finish his portrait, without copying the Christian authors, who might here perhaps seem less credible, I will chiefly confine myself to the testimony of Ammianus and Eutropius, both Pagans, who were in the Persian war, and of whom the former served in the guards with Jovian. With the sentiments of a generous and beneficent soul this prince united affable manners, a fund of gaiety which induced him to joke with those who approached him, sufficient application and activity, but too little experience. He had such a knowledge of mankind as promised discernment in the distribution of employments; some literature *, and great regard for men of learning; an extreme attachment to his religion, but a great respect to conscience, which he thought accountable only to God. Zealous without bitterness, and moderate without indifference, he professed orthodoxy; but he persecuted neither heretics, nor even Pagans. It is said, that these excellent qualities were accompanied with some faults. Ammianus accuses him of loving wine and the table, and some other pleasures still more unbecoming a Christian. Men are apt to be inconsistent, and their belief has not always a sufficient influence on their morals.

---

* This seems to me the sense of those words of Ammianus, *Mediocriter eruditus, magisque benevolus.*   B.

" But,"

" But," says the same author, " the respect which he owed to his purple would have corrected them *." Jovian was in stature much above the common standard, and large in proportion, so that it was difficult to find an imperial habit that would fit him. He was round-shouldered, as he appears also on his medals, and had a majestic air, but a heavy walk. The gaiety of his mind sparkled on his face and in his eyes. He is ranked among the good princes. Perhaps he would have been placed among the greatest, if he had ascended the throne at a juncture less fatal, and if he had reigned longer.

The army was still ignorant, it seems, of the death of Julian. It was beginning to leave the camp, in order to march, when the new Emperor appeared, and, invested with the marks of his dignity, repaired to the different quarters to shew himself to the soldiers. The name of *Jovian* resounded on all sides; but the resemblance of this name to that of *Julian* causing a mistake, some cried, JULIAN AUGUSTUS. Their cries, soon approaching by degrees to the vanguard already at a distance from the camp, were repeated with the most lively transports. It was imagined that the wound of Julian was not dangerous, and that he was leaving his tent, according to custom, in the

---

* These are the historian's own words, *Edax tamen et vino venerique indulgens; quæ vitia imperiali verecundiâ forsitan correxisset.* B.

midst of acclamations. But this transient joy was immediately succeeded by affliction and tears, as soon as the presence of Jovian announced what had just happened.

Such is the recital of an eye-witness, a Pagan indeed, but an impartial writer; I mean Ammianus Marcellinus. His testimony does not allow us to understand literally what Theodoret wrote about half a century after him, of the perfect unanimity with which all the army demanded Jovian for Emperor, while the officers were assembled for the election. Nothing, however, obliges us to reject what the same father adds: " Jovian," he says, " was placed on a tribunal prepared in haste; the " names of Augustus and Emperor were given " him. The prince then said to the soldiers, with " his usual frankness, that, being a Christian, he " could not command Pagans, and that he saw the " wrath of the living God ready to fall on an army of " idolaters." "You command Christians," exclaimed with one voice those who heard him. " The reign " of superstition has been too short to efface from " our minds and our hearts the instructions of the " great Constantine and his son Constantius. Im- " piety has not had time to take root in the souls " of those who have embraced it *."

While Jovian received the homage of the army,

---

* Ammianus, calmly pursuing his narrative, overthrows this legend by a single sentence: *Hostiis pro Joviano extisque inspectis, pronuntiatum est*, &c. xxv. 6. GIBBON.

an enfign of whom he had reafon to complain *; fearing his refentment, deferted to the enemy. He found Sapor, who had juft joined his troops, at the head of a confiderable reinforcement. This fugitive, admitted to an audience of the great king, told him, that " Julian was no more; and that the fervants " of the army had tumultuoufly fupplied his place " with the phantom of an Emperor, one only of " the body-guard, a man without vigour, without " courage, without capacity." At this unexpected news the monarch ftarted with joy. The valour of Julian, and the rapidity of his conquefts, had fo alarmed him, that he paid no attention to his hair, and ate on the ground as in the greateft calamities. The Perfians, even after the death of that formidable enemy, reprefented him, in their hieroglyphical paintings, under the emblem of thunder, or of a lion vomiting flames; fuch was the terror with which he had impreffed them. Sapor, who faw himfelf at the fummit of his wifhes at the very time when he thought himfelf on the brink of deftruction, flattered himfelf that the Romans would no longer ftand before him, and detached a body of cavalry † full fpeed to fall on their rear-guard, with the troops that had fought the preceding day.

Sapor had no doubt that the Romans were on their march; but the election of Jovian had fuf-

* He was an enemy of Varronian. By mangling the reputation of the father, he deferved the hatred of the fon. B.
† Perhaps the ten thoufand *Immortals*. GIBBON.

pended

HISTORY OF JOVIAN.

pended their departure; and this prince thought of deferring it till the next day. The Pagans, for all were not converted, having offered some sacrifices of thanksgiving for his election to the empire, the augurs found in the entrails of the victims that all would be lost, if they remained in the camp, but that they should gain some advantage, if they began their march. As the Emperor knew how much superstition can affect courage, he did not hesitate to pursue the latter. The Romans had scarce left their entrenchments when they saw themselves attacked. Their cavalry was at first put into disorder by the elephants which preceded that of the Persians; but the legionaries so vigorously sustained the shock of the hostile squadrons, that they forced them to retire. On the side of the Barbarians, besides some elephants, a great number of soldiers were left on the field. The Romans, however, paid too dearly for that advantage, as it cost them three of their bravest officers *.

After having paid them the last duties, as well as the time and place would permit, they encamped near a castle named Sumera †; and on the next day, for want of a better defence, they entrenched

---

* Tribunes.

† On the banks of the Tigris, about one hundred miles above Ctesiphon. In the ninth century, Sumere, or Samara, became, with a slight change of name, the royal residence of the Khalifs of the house of Abbas. The obscure villages of the inland country are irrecoverably lost; nor can we name the field of battle where Julian fell.

GIBBON.

themselves in a valley surrounded by eminences which left only one outlet. From the top of those hills, covered with trees, the Persians rained on the camp a shower of arrows, which they accompanied with the bitterest taunts, calling the Romans " traitors, and the murderers of their " Emperor." Those reproaches originated from the frivolous discourse of some deserters, and the endeavours which the great king ineffectually employed to discover who had delivered him from Julian. Sapor having offered a reward proportioned to the importance of the service without any one appearing to claim it, he concluded that Julian had been killed by one of his own subjects; as if it were impossible for that rash prince to have been struck either by a dart thrown at random *, or that the horseman, who wounded him, might himself have lost his life.

Libanius indeed has displayed all his rhetoric to give some colour to this accusation. This sophist absolutely insists that the fatal blow, which shortened the days of Julian, came from a Christian hand directed and employed by the chief of the Christians †. By this Libanius probably means

some

---

* Thus Ahab was killed by *a certain man* who *drew a bow at a venture*. 1 Kings xxii, 34.

† Εντολην πληρως του σφως αυτων αρχοντι. *Implens acceptum ab eo qui praeest illis mandatum.* Perhaps it should be translated *praeerat*; as the oration of Libanius was not composed till the reign of Theodosius. I have retained in the

French

some distinguished bishop, whom he makes the author of a conspiracy formed against the life of Julian. He pretends that he was privately acquainted with all the particulars of that dreadful tragedy, and that there needed only public authority to unravel and ascertain its horrors. Libanius, however, utters only conjectures that are easily confuted by other conjectures as probable as his; and as to the pretended conspiracy, the profound silence of all writers of the same religion is a proof either that they had not heard it mentioned, or at least that they considered it as a fable *. Those authors, and Zosimus himself, say expressly, or plainly suppose, that Julian was wounded by a soldier of Sapor. The malignity of Zosimus is well known: all the evil which he has not said of the Christians, and which others have said of them, has much the air of a calumny.

French the equivocal expression of the Greek. It is impossible to know what bishop Libanius had in view. It is surmised that it might have been either St. Basil or St. Gregory of Nazianzus. For my part, I think that in the time of Julian there was no bishop in the East who deserved the name of "chief of the Christians" better than St. Athanasius.   B.

* Above sixteen years after the death of Julian, the charge was solemnly and vehemently urged in a public oration, addressed by Libanius to the Emperor Theodosius. The suspicions are unsupported by fact or argument, and we can only esteem the generous zeal of the sophist of Antioch for the cold and neglected ashes of his friend.
GIBBON.

After

After all, that a rhetorician, like Libanius, a Pagan even to madness, should think the Christians capable of attempting the life of Julian, is not surprising. That it is possible for an ignorant and fanatical Christian to think that he shall immortalise himself both in this world and the next, by delivering the church from an implacable persecutor, history unhappily affords too many examples. But that an ecclesiastical historian, like Sozomen, should be tempted to canonise so detestable an action, might perhaps not be credited on my assertion. Let him speak for himself: "It is not "improbable," says that writer, "that one of "those who then served in the army might have "reflected, that the destroyers of tyrants were "highly extolled, not only by the ancient Greeks, "but by others even to our times, as men who for "the common liberty of all did not hesitate to die, "having chearfully assisted their countrymen, "friends, and relations. No one certainly," continues Sozomen, "can easily blame him, who, for "the sake of God and his religion, has acted such "a manly part *." Sozomen, it seems, had studied profane antiquity more than the morality of the gospel and the spirit of true Christianity. Let it be observed, that this historian was not a father

---

* *Sozom. Hist. Eccles. l.* VI. c. 2.

Sozomen applauds the Greek doctrine of *tyrannicide*; but the whole passage, which a Jesuit might have translated, is prudently suppressed by the president Cousin.

GIBBON.

of the church, that he has no authority in matters of doctrine, that his language is here contrary to all tradition, that he wrote towards the middle of the fifth century; and that he is the first in whom we perceive some marks of that anti-christian fanaticism. But it is time to resume the thread of the history.

While their enemies, posted on the heights, were insulting the army, a detachment of cavalry forced the gate of the camp, called the Prætorian gate; and were very near penetrating even to the imperial tent: but they were repulsed with loss. The Romans afterwards encamped at Carche; from whence on the succeeding day, July 1, they arrived near the city of Dura*, which must not be confounded with another of the same name, situated in Mesopotamia. Four days were there lost by the obstinacy of the Barbarians. As soon as the army was on the march, they harrassed it by continual skirmishes, sometimes in rear, sometimes in flank. If it faced about to receive them, by degrees they gave ground, being only desirous of retarding its march, and leaving to famine the care of fighting for them.

The fear of the worst misfortunes makes men credulous and ready to adopt the most hazardous expedients. On a sudden a report being spread that the

---

* Dura was a fortified place in the wars of Antiochus, against the rebels of Media and Persia. (Polybius, *l.* v. *c.* 48. 52.)   GIBBON.

frontiers of the empire are not far distant; on this false supposition the soldier will no longer coast the Tigris, but clamorously insists on being allowed to pass it. The Emperor, with the principal officers, opposes this rash project in vain. In vain, shewing this river always so rapid, and then swelled by the melting of the snows of Armenia, he represents that most of them cannot swim, that the enemy is master of the two banks, and that, if they gain the other side, it will only be to fall into his hands. These sage remonstrances are disregarded. The clamours increase, threats are added; every thing breathes sedition. It was necessary to allow a number of Gauls and Germans * to attempt the passage. Jovian flattered himself that if they perished, the rest would become more tractable, or, if they were so lucky as to succeed, he might reasonably make an attempt to transport the army.

By favour of the night, five hundred able swimmers cross the Tigris with more ease than could have been expected, and find the Persians, who guarded the opposite bank, buried in a profound sleep. They make a great slaughter, and as soon as the day begins to break, they raise their hands, and throw their cloaths into the air, to announce their success. The army, anxious to follow them, urges the engineers to construct a kind of [floating]

* The text of Ammianus gives *Sarmatis*; but it is probably faulty. Soon after, the same author calls them Germans. B.

bridge, which they propofed to make of fheep fkins faftened together *. They laboured on it two days; but it was impoffible to fix it on account of the violence and rapidity of the ftream. The foldiers, having confumed the provifions that they had left, became defperate, and rather chofe to perifh fword in hand than languifh under the horrors of a flow and cruel death.

Ths Perfians, on their fide, had alfo much to lament. The intoxication of Sapor was already difpelled; from the moft prefumptuous confidence, he relapfed into an extreme perplexity; he faw his country laid wafte, his towns taken by affault, his troops, always defeated when they dared to wait for the enemy, having no refource but in flight, and confiderably diminifhed by the lofs of an innumerable multitude of men, and almoft all the elephants. Every day fome new check made him perceive that the valour of the Romans was not buried † with Julian. Animated with the genius of that conqueror, they feemed to think as much, and perhaps more, of revenging him than of furviving him. Famine itfelf could not force from them the leaft propofal of peace. Was Sapor certain of avoiding a battle? And if he muft fight,

---

* Covered with a floor of earth and fafcines. A fimilar expedient was propofed to the leaders of the ten thoufand, and wifely rejected. It appears, from our modern travellers, that rafts floating on bladders perform the trade and navigation of the Tigris.   GIBBON.

† *Enfevelie.* A flight inaccuracy. Julian was not then "buried."

what

what had he not to fear from men resolved to determine their fate, either by gaining a complete victory, or at least by rendering their defeat fatal even to the conquerors? Could he flatter himself with annihilating the Roman army, he was not ignorant that Julian had left in Mesopotamia 40,000 men, under the command of his relation Procopius: at length the vast provinces of the empire might easily furnish other legions, who, by attacking Persia when exhausted and terrified, might overthrow the throne of the Artaxerxides already tottering.

Amidst these melancholy reflections, he was informed of the successful temerity of the Gauls and Germans. This exploit of a handful of determined men alarms him, and makes him sensible of what a whole army of desperadoes will be capable. Immediately he turns all his thoughts towards an accommodation with the Romans; he does not hesitate to make the first advances, proceeding to essentials, and desiring, at any rate, to commence a negociation, which, in the present circumstances, must infallibly terminate to his advantage. Thus, contrary to their expectations, the Romans saw the Surena (he was the general of the Persian cavalry), arrive in their camp, with another lord *. " The " Great King our master," said the deputies to

---

* Sextus Rufus (*de Provinciis, c.* 29.) embraces a poor subterfuge of national vanity. *Tanta reverentia nominis Romani fuit, ut à Persis primus de pace sermo haberetur.*
GIBBON.

Jovian and the principal officers, " is not dazzled
" by prosperity; he knows the situation to which
" fortune has reduced you; but he knows still
" better the uncertainty of human affairs. Sapor
" respects unsuccessful virtue, even in his enemies.
" He esteems you enough to seek your alliance,
" and to offer you peace on equitable terms."

As the Romans were supported only by despair, the hope of peace weakened them at once, and made, it may be said, their arms fall from their hands. Jovian, in particular, was eager to enjoy the empire, and to insure to himself its possession by repairing speedily to the capital. How did he know, but that, in his absence, some ambitious leader, Procopius for instance, then at the head of an army, might seize the diadem? At that time, those who assumed the purple did not even deign to seek pretexts to colour their enterprise; and Procopius, as he was related to Julian, might allege the rights of consanguinity. The proposals therefore of Sapor were embraced with eagerness. They were vague, embarrassed, equivocal, and liable to great discussions. At all events, this able politician designed to protract the negociation, in order to famish the Romans more and more.

The Emperor, on the contrary, impatient to conclude it, dispatched, without losing a moment, Sallust, with Arintheus*, to draw from Sapor himself

* Libanius puts the general Victor in the room of Arintheus. The latter was reckoned one of the greatest captains

himself something determinate. They had many conferences equally long and intricate by the management of the old monarch, who negociated peace as he waged war. The more the Romans advanced, the more he retreated. He formed suppositions upon suppositions, and raised difficulties upon difficulties. Now he required time, then he would no longer grant what he had promised, and promised what he had refused. Besides, he seemed to think it strange that the death of Julian was not revenged; for he still thought that that prince had been killed by a Roman *; and as the deputies probably did not allow the fact, " if one " of my generals †," added he, " had lost his

---

captains of his age. Prodigies are related of his valour. He was of an extraordinary stature, yet so well made, that, St. Basil says, he was considered as the model of a man. His strength was equal to his courage. His looks alone had made him gain some battles. He received baptism before his death. We have a consolatory letter written by St. Basil to the widow of Arintheus, who had been the protector of the churches, and the friend of St. Basil. We have also a letter from the same saint to this general, in which he praises him for his generosity and liberality, of which every one perceived the effects. See M. de Tillemont on the Emperor Valens, *Histoire des Empereurs*, tom. V. p. 100.   B.

* For the Persians also had heard this report, and, in consequence, before Jovian made peace with them, the common soldiers reviled the Romans as traitors and murderers of the greatest of princes, as we learn from Ammianus, xxv. 6.   OLEARIUS.

† Libanius heard these words of Sapor to the Roman ambassadors, no doubt, from Sallust himself, with whom he was extremely intimate, as four of his epistles to Sallust sufficiently attest.   *Ibid.*

"life in a battle, those, who, being near his
"person, had the cowardice not to die with him,
"should not escape my just resentment. I would
"instantly send their heads to the family of that
"officer." We here discern the ideas and language of an Eastern monarch. Sapor, by affecting to interest himself in revenging Julian, was also desirous perhaps of testifying his esteem for that prince, with a view to insinuate, that he had little regard for his successor, and that he no longer feared the Romans.

They became less formidable every moment. A devouring famine consumed them, while by chicanery and affected delays he trifled with their deputies. "We passed four days," says Ammianus, "in a state more cruel than the severest
"punishments. During that time, if the Emperor,
"discovering the artifices of Sapor, before he
"sent deputies to that prince, had continually
"gained ground, he would certainly have arrived
"at the strong places of Corduenne, which then
"belonged to us; and which would have supplied
"us with provisions in abundance. We were but
"a hundred miles distant *."

* About thirty leagues.   B.
It is presumptuous to controvert the opinion of Ammianus, a soldier and a spectator. Yet it is difficult to understand, how the mountains of Corduenne could extend over the plain of Assyria, as low as the conflux of the Tigris and the great Zab: or *how* an army of sixty thousand men could march one hundred miles in four days.
                GIBBON.

I wish

I wish Ammianus had clearly explained the possibility of this march. If I am not mistaken, this is his idea. Sapor himself had occasion for a peace, and only offered it to his enemies because he feared to encounter them. Jovian therefore should have opposed craft to craft, should have expressed less eagerness for peace, should, however, have given good words to the envoys of Sapor, should have pursued his route, should have sent deputies to that prince, and have treated on his march. Sapor, from the fear of being forced to a battle, or of thwarting the accommodation, would not have attacked the Romans, and would have been taken in his own snare. Ammianus was a soldier: he understood his profession, and knew the country. He saw things near, and he saw them with reflection; to be convinced of this we need only read him. The judgement of an historian like him must embarrass the defenders of Jovian.

When Sapor thought he had subdued the Romans by famine, he threw off the mask, and, speaking with authority, he declared, first, that he insisted on their restoring to him, for so he expressed himself, the five provinces beyond the Tigris *, formerly conquered by the Emperor

---

* Most of these provinces were on this side the Tigris with regard to the Romans. In calling them " beyond the " Tigris" they conformed to the language of the Persians, whom they were on the other side of that river As to the particular names of the provinces, they are not the same in all authors. B.

HISTORY OF JOVIAN.

Maximian-Galerius from King Narseus, his grandfather; viz. Arzanenia, Moxoënia, Zabdicenia, Rehimenia, and Corduenne. Secondly, that besides these, there should be ceded to him fifteen castles, the city of Nisibis, that of Singara in Mesopotamia, and another important place called the Castle of the Moors (*Castra Maurorum*). Thirdly, that they would engage to interfere no more in the affairs of Armenia, and even refuse king Arsaces the assistance which he might demand against the Persians.

"It would have been a thousand times better," says Ammianus, "to have tried the chance of arms than to have accepted any one of these conditions." In fact, under pretence of a restitution, which is not honourable but when it is voluntary, to cede five provinces, annexed to the empire for about seventy years, was to pay a ransom the more humiliating as there were added to it almost all Mesopotamia, and even Nisibis, which had been possessed by the Romans ever since the wars of Mithridates; Nisibis, the bulwark of the East, and the rock which wrecked the pride of Sapor *.

By

---

* He acquired, by a single article, the impregnable city of Nisibis, which had sustained, in three successive sieges, the effort of his arms.   GIBBON.

The treaty of Dura is recorded with grief, or indignation, by Ammianus (xxv. 7.); Libanius (*Orat. Parent.* c 142. p. 364.); Zosimus (l. III. p. 190, 191.); Gregory Nazianzen (*Orat.* IV. p. 117, 118. who imputes the distress

to

HISTORY OF JOVIAN.

By binding his hands with regard to Armenia, Jovian furrendered at difcretion, to a revengeful, perfidious, and cruel prince, Arfaces *, the faithful ally of the Romans, to whom he was connected by the nearest and most honourable ties, as Conftantius had made him efpoufe Olympias, daughter of the Præfect Ablavius, who had been contracted to his brother the Emperor Conftans. Sapor was the declared enemy of the Chriftians; and, what muft perfonally affect Jovian, Arfaces, by his attachment to Chriftianity, had merited, like Jovian himfelf, difgrace from Julian. King Arfaces had been effentially ferviceable to the empire. He had juft ravaged the provinces of Perfia bordering on Armenia. That was his crime in the fight of Sapor, and the fecret reafon, but eafy to be gueffed, for which he required them to refufe him affiftance.

Thefe confiderations could not efcape Jovian; but he was befieged by a crowd of flatterers, who

---

to Julian, the deliverance to Jovian); and Eutropius (x. 17.) The laft-mentioned writer, who was prefent in a military ftation, ftyles this peace *neceffariam quidem, fed ignobilem*.
Ibid.

* See p. 186. The unfufpicious Tiranus was perfuaded by the repeated affurances of infidious friendfhip to deliver his perfon into the hands of a faithlefs and cruel enemy. In the midft of a fplendid entertainment, he was bound in chains of filver, as an honour due to the blood of the Arfacides; and, after a fhort confinement in the Tower of oblivion at Ecbatana, he was releafed from the miferies of life, either by his own dagger, or by that of an affaffin. The kingdom of Armenia was reduced to the ftate of a Perfian province. *Ibid.*

inceffantly

incessantly represented to him Procopius as an enemy more dangerous than Sapor *... His fear of Procopius was well grounded; and it may be said that his revolt † justified it two years after, if, nevertheless, this fear itself did not occasion his revolt. Besides, there is the greatest probability, that the irreparable loss of four days, imprudently consumed in inactivity, had rendered the army utterly incapable of fighting, and reduced Jovian to the indispensible necessity of accepting the peace. Thus the treaty was perhaps less the work of his timid policy than of his inability.

Be that as it may, to the disgrace of the Roman name, this prince received the law from Sapor, and agreed to all the articles proposed. All that he obtained, and that with difficulty, was, that the garrisons of the places ceded as well as the inhabitants of Nisibis and Singara, should retire into the territories of the Romans. Arsaces was included in the treaty, of which he did not fail to be soon after made the victim. On both sides a peace, or rather a truce, of thirty years was sworn, and in the mean time hostages ‡ were given for the performance of the treaty.

---

* La Bleterie has expressed, in a long direct oration, these specious considerations of public and private interest.
GIBBON.

This harangue being imaginary, I have omitted it.

† For an account of his revolt and death, see p. 221. note

‡ Remora, Victor, and Bellovædius, tribunes, on the part of the Romans; and Binefes, with three other satraps, on that of the Persians. AMMIANUS.
Rufinus

Rufinus and Theodoret, deceived by probability, pretend that Sapor furnished the Romans with provisions *. Nothing was more natural; but without doubt, the Persians had no magazines, and subsisted themselves with difficulty in an exhausted country. At least, it is certain that the Romans gained by that disgraceful peace not even the permission to deviate from the banks of the Tigris †, where the roads were rough and craggy, in order to cross the country to the place where they intended to pass that river. Thither they proceeded by long marches, continually tormented by famine, to which was also added want of water. Many, collecting their expiring strength, withdrew from

* Such a fact is probable, but undoubtedly false. See Tillemont, *Hist. des Empereurs*, tom. iv. p. 702. GIBBON.

† In the neighbourhood of the same river, at no very considerable distance from the fatal station of Dura, the ten thousand Greeks, without generals, or guides, or provisions, were abandoned, above 1200 miles from their native country, to the resentment of a victorious monarch. The difference of their conduct and success depended much more on their character than on their situation. Instead of tamely resigning themselves to the secret deliberations and private views of a single person, the united councils of the Greeks were inspired by the generous enthusiasm of a popular assembly; where the mind of each citizen is filled with the love of glory, the pride of freedom, and the contempt of death. Conscious of their superiority over the Barbarians in arms and discipline, they disdained to yield, they refused to capitulate; every obstacle was surmounted by their patience, courage, and military skill; and the memorable retreat of the ten thousand exposed and insulted the weakness of the Persian monarchy. GIBBON. See p. 256. note *.

the

the body of the army, and endeavoured to swim crofs the Tigris. Moft of them perifhed; the reft fell into the hands of the Perfians and Saracens pofted on the other fhore. Thefe Barbarians, incenfed by the maffacre of their companions whom the Gauls and Germans had flaughtered, put to death all who efcaped the waters, or if they fpared fome of them, it was only to fell them, and fend them to fuch a diftance that the Romans could never reclaim them.

When the Emperor and the army were arrived at the place of paffage, which no author, not even Ammianus, has taken care to point out to us, after fome flight preparations, the trumpet gave the fignal. It is impoffible to exprefs with what precipitation every one, caring only for himfelf, haftened to outrun his companions, and braved danger, to efcape, as foon as poffible, from that fatal country. Some on bad hurdles, by way of rafts, drew after them their horfes fwimming; others were carried on bladders; all availed themfelves of what was offered them by chance, or of what neceffity, ever fruitful in expedients, made them contrive. Twelve fmall flat boats, the remains of the fleet of Julian, ferved to tranfport the Emperor, with the principal officers, and made, by his order, as many voyages were neceffary to complete the tranfportation. " Thus," fays Ammianus, " by the divine goodnefs, we all paffed
" fafely,

" safely, excepting some who had the misfortune
" to be drowned."

Immediately after, advice was received that the Persians, out of the sight of the Romans, were constructing a bridge, no doubt that they might intercept the stragglers and the baggage; but seeing themselves discovered, they did not dare to execute their perfidious design. Thus the Persians, it appears, had materials for a bridge. Why then did not Jovian insist, as a preliminary, that they should facilitate his passage? Sapor was too great a gainer by the treaty to have made a difficulty of a condition which he could with ease perform. This seems worth remarking, as another proof of the inability of Jovian.

The Roman army, continuing its march with extreme diligence, encamped some leagues from the Tigris, near the town of Hatra *, situated on a hill in the midst of a vast desert, formerly inhabited by the Scenites Arabians: it had been reckoned impregnable, but had now been long abandoned. Perhaps the Romans, when they saw Hatra, consoled themselves a little on their disgrace, by recollecting that which had befallen, under the ramparts of that place, the two greatest

* So called by Ammianus, by Dio, (*lib. ult.*) Τα Ἄτρα, and by M. de la Bleterie, *Atra*.

M. d'Anville (see his maps, and *l'Euphrate et le Tigre*, pp. 92, 93.) traces their march, and assigns the true position of Hatra, Ur, and Thilsaphata, which Ammianus has mentioned. GIBBON.

generals that had filled the throne of the Cæsars. Trajan had made the taking it a point of honour, but nature absolutely armed against him, in defence of the besieged; and what may be considered as a prodigy of another kind, Severus, who, after having raised the siege, attacked it a second time, called back his soldiers very unadvisedly, when they were just ready to storm the place, and when he ordered them to return to the assault, he could never make himself obeyed. This prince, as well as Trajan, thought he should have perished before that town with all his army. Artaxerxes, the founder of the second monarchy of the Persians, was not more successful, and Providence * seemed constantly to declare in favour of Hatra. However, the frequent attacks of the Romans, and the danger to which the town was exposed, especially in the last siege, might make the Scenites Arabians think, that the liberty, of which they were always so jealous, and which they still preserve, was less endangered in their tents than under the shelter of the strongest walls. They abandoned Hatra We no where read that it was taken, and yet it had been long deserted when Jovian arrived there. The Romans were now informed, that they had a plain

---

* In this Dr. Delany, a learned English divine, thinks he discovers the marks of the visible protection of God to the descendants of Ishmael, agreeably to the promises made to Hagar and Abraham, Gen. xvi. and xvii. See the work, entitled, *Revelation examined with Candour*, vol. II. dissert. IV. B.

of thirty leagues to traverse, where nothing was to be found but wormwood and such kind of herbs, with a little putrid and brackish water. They provided therefore some fresh water, and killed some of the camels and other beasts of burden, whose unwholesome flesh prolonged their lives at the expence of health.

In about six days march they met, near the castle of Ur, a place dependent on the Persians, a convoy of some provisions, which Jovian, immediately after his election, had sent the tribune Mauricius to seek in Mesopotamia. This weak supply, the fruit of the oeconomy of the two generals Procopius and Sebastian, enabled the Emperor to recover breath, and to take measures to make himself acknowledged through the whole empire. He might even consider this assistance as an act of obedience on the part of Procopius and his collegue, whose submission necessarily drew after it that of the Eastern provinces. But who could insure to him the West, till Illyricum and Gaul had acknowledged him? The troops of Illyricum and Gaul had often disposed of the purple, and occasioned great revolutions. They were indeed less formidable since the time of Constantine. That prince, more on his guard against civil wars than against the invasions of the Barbarians, had, by good or bad policy, weakened the authority of the generals by dividing it. He had also dispersed in the inner part of the provinces the legions long stationed on

the

HISTORY OF JOVIAN.

the frontiers, where the proximity of their quarters placed them within the reach of keeping up correspondences, of secretly forming and suddenly executing conspiracies. Nevertheless, in spite of these precautions, the recent examples of Vetranio * in Illyricum, and of Magnentius † and Julian in Gaul, did not allow a doubt that the legions might again make Emperors there; and the distance must increase the uneasiness of Jovian.

He dispatched therefore, with the necessary orders to secure to him those important provinces, two confidential men, Procopius, secretary of state, who must be distinguished from the relation of Julian, and Memoridus, a tribune. The whole family of Jovian was in Illyricum; his wife, his son yet in the cradle, Count Varronian his father, and his father-in-law Count Lucillian. Both, after having quitted the service, enjoyed the repose of a quiet life. But the infirmities of age without doubt rendered Varronian incapable of acting, as the orders of the Emperor were addressed to Count Lucillian. The messengers carried him the com-

---

* Vetranio, an aged general, beloved for the simplicity of his manners, who had long governed the martial countries of Illyricum, assumed the purple in 350. But Constantius, having seduced his troops, and undermined his throne, at an interview with the usurper, appointed at Sardica, by the defection of his followers, Vetranio was deposed and banished to Prusa, where he lived six years in the enjoyment of ease and affluence. *Abridged from* GIBBON.

† For an account of the usurpation of Magnentius, see Vol. I. p. 175. note *.

mission

mission of master-general of the horse and foot*. Thus invested with two employments which were usually separated, he was to take with him some officers of merit and known fidelity, whose names were mentioned in a private dispatch, and to repair immediately to Milan, from thence to watch over the remainder of the West, and to resort, in case of commotions, where-ever the exigence of affairs might require his presence. The Emperor took from Jovinus the command of the troops in Gaul, and conferred it on Malarich, by nation a Frank, long attached to the service of the Romans. Thus he freed himself of a man whose superior talents rendered his fidelity suspected, and put in his place a foreigner, who, not being able to have any pretensions to the empire, would always consider the good fortune of his benefactor as the foundation of his own, and would confine his ambition to serving him well. The messengers had also orders to announce on their journey the death of Julian and the election of his successor, to convey to the governors of the provinces the letters of Jovian, and to publish every where that he had terminated the war by an advantageous peace. They travelled night and day, without stopping; but, more expeditious and more sincere than they, Fame outstripped them, and declared the truth.

* In M. de la Bleterie, *le brevet de généralissime de l'infanterie et de la cavalerie:* in the original of Ammianus, *magisterii equitum et peditum codicillis.* For obvious reasons I prefer the latter.

HISTORY OF JOVIAN.

Jovian wrote, without doubt, at the same time to the senate of New Rome, and especially to that of the Old, which still retained some kind of pre-eminence, praying them, at least for form-sake, to confirm what the army had done in his favour. It was at that time probably, that he nominated himself consul for the ensuing year, with his father Count Varronian, who had learned, in a dream, if we credit Ammianus, that he should be appointed to the consulship, but who certainly knew not that death would prevent his taking possession of that high dignity *.

If the Pagans of the army had been sensibly affected by the loss of Julian, it was no less distressing to the others, of whom there were such numbers throughout the empire; and, without doubt, the latter, not being constrained by the presence of their new prince, abandoned themselves to their grief with more freedom. " This intelligence," says Libanius, " was a stroke that pierced me to
" the heart. I cast my eyes on a sword, and wished
" to rid myself of a life that would henceforth be
" more cruel to me than death. But I recollected
" the prohibition of Plato, and the punishments re-
" served in hell for those who dispose of themselves

---

* Count Varronian thus dying soon after he had heard of his son's good fortune, and before he had seen him, Jovian declared his infant-son Varronian consul with himself, in the room of his grandfather; " because," adds Ammianus, " the old man was foretold in his sleep that " the highest magistracy should be borne by that name."

" without

" without waiting for the command of God. Be-
" sides, I reflected that I owed that hero a funeral
" oration *."

Libanius acquitted himself of that duty by consecrating to the memory of Julian two discourses, which have been transmitted to us. The first †, which seems to have been composed immediately, is only a very short and yet sufficiently tedious lamentation, with more wit than sentiment, and more pedantry than wit. The second ‡ is an historical elogium, laboured at leisure, in which the orator follows Julian step by step, and always shews the bright side of him. This piece, perhaps the best of his works, and worthy, almost in every respect, of the purest antiquity, makes, on the whole, a remarkable contrast to the eloquent discourse of St. Gregory of Nazianzus §.

At Carrhæ in Mesopotamia, a city entirely devoted to Paganism, the messenger who brought the first account of the death of Julian, was near

---

* *De vitâ suâ.*

† Ιουλιανος, η Επιταφιος επι τω Ιουλιανω. (" A funeral oration on Julian.") This discourse was published imperfectly by Morell; but more correctly, with Latin translation of Olearius, by Fabricius, Bibl. Græc. Vol. VII. p. 223.

‡ Υπερ τω Ιουλιανω τιμωριας. (" On revenging Julian.") Spoken before the Emperor Theodosius, 379, first published by Olearius, 1701, and afterwards, with his translation and notes, by Fabricius. See p. 224. note ‡.

§ Though in the editions of this Father the work is divided into two, it is, however, only one and the same discourse, as is proved by the judicious writer who has given a French translation of it, printed at Lyons, in 1735, a translation much less known than it deserves to be.' B.

being stoned to death, and really was so, according to Zosimus. Such was the despair of the Pagans. They saw their reign vanish like a dream, the flattering hopes which they had conceived from the youth and zeal of Julian pass away in smoke, Hellenism ready to be buried in the tomb of its restorer, and the Christian religion again invested with the purple, and more strengthened than ever, at the very time when, thinking it arrived at its fatal period, they only waited the return of Julian to give the last blow. Many had persecuted it without discretion, and had been betrayed into the greatest excesses. What probability that the most moderate Christian prince would let crimes, at which Julian himself had been forced to blush, pass with impunity!

On the other side, the Church, in the transports of a sudden deliverance, blessed by its canticles the God ever faithful to his promises, whose arm had exterminated the new Sennacherib. But the Christians, it must be owned, did not all confine themselves to the legitimate sentiments which this kind of resurrection planted in their hearts. Instead of a Christian joy, pure in its motives, humble and modest in its effects, mixed with compassion for a perishing enemy, and with fear at the prospect of prosperity; many gave themselves up to the merely human emotions of a proud and outrageous joy, and seemed already to threaten the vengeance of a religion which teaches only patience and forgiveness.

giveness. Those of Antioch, personal enemies to Julian on so many accounts, insulted at once the memory of the Pagan, the philosopher, and the author. In this great city, so voluptuous, and which thought itself so Christian, there was nothing but public entertainments, nothing but sacred and profane festivals. In the churches and oratories of the martyrs were seen dances, and the tumult of public shews; and the theatres resounded with religious exclamations. There was published the victory of the cross; there was apostrophised, though absent, the philosopher Maximus, the oracle and the perverter of Julian. "Foolish "Maximus," they exclaimed, "what is become of "thy predictions? God and his Christ have con- "quered."

But if the Church triumphed, the empire was covered with disgrace, and had received a deep wound, of which it never recovered. Thus the transports with which the interest of religion, especially when joined with animosity, at first inspired the people, were no sooner abated, than the public rejoicings gave place to uneasiness and alarms. To inveigh against Julian, to impute the calamities of the state to his apostacy and senseless conduct, publickly to expose the shocking remains of the human victims which he was accused of having sacrificed in his abominable mysteries, this might be a kind of consolation, but it was not a resource. Jovian alone gained by it, because he had

had the advantage of succeeding a prince that was hated, and consequently responsible, in the opinion of the multitude at least, for the first faults of his successor.

By the cession of the provinces beyond the Tigris, and of Nisibis, Syria was going to become almost a frontier, and the city of Antioch remained exposed, with the rest of the East, to the incursions of the Barbarians. Whoever had still a Roman heart must consider, that for the space of about eleven centuries, neither the annals of the republic, nor those of the monarchy, furnished an example of an event so grievous, so ignominious, all things considered, as the treaty of Jovian; that if, in former times, some generals had subscribed to dishonourable conditions, the supreme authority, which then resided in the people, by declaring those treaties null, had made all their infamy fall on their authors; that the majesty of the empire, after it was concentered in a monarch, had been no doubt deeply humiliated by the captivity of Valerian, who had grown old in the chains of another Sapor; but that this majesty had degraded and annihilated itself in the person of Jovian, who had forsaken the fundamental principle of the policy of the Romans, who yielded nothing by force, nor were ever more haughty, or more intractable, than when they seemed crushed; that this precious maxim, escaped from the wreck of the republic and of ancient manners, had supported to the present day the empire which it had formed; but when that was once abandoned, the Emperors would in future be seen succeffively to cede the provinces, to difmember the state, under a pretence of faving it; in short, that it was easy to forefee the fall and total ruin of that vaft body.

Without extending their views fo far, the inhabitants of Nifibis, fufficiently occupied with their own calamity, trembled to fee themfelves at the mercy of Sapor, and of Sapor provoked. They retained, neverthelefs, fome hopes founded on the importance of their fortrefs, their paft fidelity, and their recent fervices. They could not believe that Jovian would deliver them to Barbarians; and they flattered themfelves, that if, from a regard to his oaths, he did not dare directly to infringe the treaty, fenfible at leaft of the juftice of their remonftrances, he would not deprive them of the liberty of defending themfelves againft an enemy, whom they had already fo often repulfed.

The army, however, after having confumed the little provifions that it had received, again endured fo ftrange a famine, that they were on the eve of eating human flefh. If a bufhel of corn was found by chance, " which happened," Ammianus fays, " but feldom," it was fold for at leaft thirteen pieces of gold. By degrees, as the horfes were killed, the arms and baggage were abandoned; fo that there is perhaps lefs exaggeration than malignity in the picture which Libanius draws of the state of the troops at their return: "Our soldiers," says he, "returned without arms, without cloaths. They asked alms, being as naked, for the most part, as people who escape from shipwreck. If any one retained half his buckler, a third part of his spear, or even one of his boots, which he carried on his shoulder, he considered himself as a hero. All thought themselves sufficiently justified, by saying, that Julian was dead, and that it was not surprising that the Romans should appear in the deplorable state in which the Persians would have been, if that conqueror had lived."

It is supposed, that the army re-entered the territories of the empire at a place named Thisalphata. It was there, at least, that Procopius and Sebastian, with the officers of the troops of Mesopotamia, came to pay their duty to the Emperor, who received them graciously. Jovian soon repaired to the gates of Nisibis, and encamped under the walls, without listening to the prayers of the inhabitants, who conjured him, with reiterated intreaties, to lodge in the palace, like his predecessors. He was afraid to shew himself, and was still more afraid, no doubt, to confine himself in a Roman colony, of which he had put the Barbarians in possession.

That very evening he committed an act of despotism more suitable to the suspicious character with which he is reproached, than to the delicacy

of

HISTORY OF JOVIAN.

of confcience on which he piqued himfelf. At the beginning of the night, on his rifing from table, an officer, who had diftinguifhed himfelf in the laft war at the taking of Maogamalcha *, was put to death. He was dragged out, and thrown into a dry well, where ftones were heaped over him. He was named *Jovianus*, like the Emperor, and had had fome votes to fucceed Julian. To remain a fubject, after having appeared worthy to reign, is a fituation fo delicate, that the greateft circumfpection is fcarce fufficient to ward its dangers. Of this Jovianus was not aware. Ambition or vanity made him utter fome expreffions the more fufpicious as he occafionally invited fome officers to his table; and "to this," fays Ammianus, "his deftruction was certainly owing." The tragical end of this unfortunate man, who feems to have been more imprudent than culpable, is related by none of the modern writers who mention Jovian †. I queftion whether they would have omitted a fimilar paffage in the hiftory of his predeceffor.

• On the next day Binefes, a lord of the Perfian court, who attended Jovian, to ferve as an hoftage, and at the fame time to urge the execution of the

---

* Whilft the Barbarians defended themfelves, finging, according to their cuftom, the praifes of their king, and braving the Emperor, faying, he might fooner fcale the walls of heaven than take Maogamalcha, the legions entering by the mouth of the mine, furprifed them, maffacred them, and threw down the ramparts. B.

† A fubfequent hiftorian, Mr. Gibbon, ironically ftyles it "a *royal* act."

treaty

treaty of peace, escorted, no doubt, by a guard which the Emperor gave him, entered Nisibis, and displayed on the citadel the standard of the Great King. The sight of this fatal flag, and the order which the inhabitants received to retire somewhere else, threw them into the utmost consternation. At first they had imagined, that Jovian had engaged to deliver up the city with all its inhabitants. One would think therefore that it must have been some abatement of their grief to learn that their persons would not fall into the hands of Sapor. But besides their not being able, as I have said, to persuade themselves entirely that this engagement would take place, the banishment, to which they saw themselves condemned, appeared to them as terrible as slavery. Several perhaps would even rather have chosen to live slaves in the bosom of their country, that is, subjects of the kings of Persia, than to preserve in exile, in poverty, in the miseries of a new establishment, a chimerical liberty under the Roman Emperors, princes as absolute in fact * as those who bore the sceptre of Arsaces and Artaxerxes pretended to be by right.

It is very usual with historians, when they relate the ruin of illustrious cities, to recount in few words their origin and the principal events which rendered them distinguished. May I therefore be allowed to say something here of the famous Nisibis,

---

* Witness the instance just related.

HISTORY OF JOVIAN.

as the Romans then loſt it for ever, and as it in a a manner even periſhed itſelf by the total tranſmigration of its citizens? Niſibis, if we may credit the oriental hiſtorians, is the ſiſter and contemporary of Babylon, Nimrod alſo being its founder. According to ſome, he gave it the name of *Chalya*; according to others, that of *Achad*; and it is, ſay theſe, the ſame city of Accad which is mentioned in Geneſis, among thoſe of which the ſon of Cuſh laid the firſt foundations in the land of Shinar. It took afterwards the name of Niſibis; and if we had a right to inſiſt on an uncertain etymology *, we might conjecture that it was already, or then became, a place of ſtrength. One of the kings of Syria who ſucceeded Alexander, gave it the name of Antioch of Mygdonia, and certainly it was ſo called, as may be ſeen in Polybius, (*l.* v.) in the reign of Antiochus, ſurnamed the Great. It was ſituated in the north part of Meſopotamia, two days journey from the Tigris, near mount Maſius, in a pleaſant and fruitful plain, watered by the river Mygdonius, which interſected the city. Notwithſtanding its antiquity, Niſibis does not begin to figure in hiſtory till towards the latter time of the Roman republic.

Tigranes, king of Armenia, having taken it from the Parthians, being himſelf attacked by

---

* נצב ſignifies, it is ſaid, in Phœnician, "columns, "heaps of ſtones." It means in Hebrew, "a monument, "a ſtatue," &c. but it alſo ſignifies in the Bible "a gar-"riſon, ſtationary ſoldiers." 1 Sam. xiii. 12.   B.

Lucullus,

Lucullus, there lodged his treasures. He thought them safe in a city surrounded by two walls all of brick *, of a prodigious thickness, which a broad and deep ditch secured from being undermined, and also put out of the reach of machines. Thus it despised Lucullus, when he ventured to appear before Nisibis in the depth of winter. But by the favour of this contempt, and of a tempestuous night, he carried the place by scaling, sixty-eight years before the Christian æra. After the defeat of Crassus, it again became subject to the kings of Armenia. Occupied by their civil wars, the Romans did not think of retaking it; and the policy of Augustus, who fixed the limits of the empire to the banks of the Euphrates, was a law to his successors till Trajan. Thus for more than a hundred and fifty years the Romans saw without jealousy Nisibis and its territory in the hands of the kings of Armenia, their vassals, or of the kings of Adiabena, vassals of the Parthians. Trajan, the most warlike of the Emperors after Julius Cæsar, exploded the state-maxim introduced by Augustus, and carried his victorious arms far beyond the Euphrates. The taking of Nisibis was one of the first exploits on that side; but Hadrian soon abandoned it, with the

* Nisibis is now reduced to one hundred and fifty houses; the marshy lands produce rice, and the fertile meadows, as far as Mosul and the Tigris, are covered with the ruins of towns and villages. See Niebuhr, Voyages, tom. ii. p. 300—309. GIBBON.

HISTORY OF JOVIAN.

new provinces which Trajan had conquered in the East.

Lucius Verus, the brother and collegue of Marcus Aurelius, retook it; and in the time of Severus besieged twice, once by the people of Mesopotamia revolting against the Romans, and the other time by Volagesus king of Parthia, it defended itself with such vigour and success, that Severus, who first firmly established the Romans in Mesopotamia, not contented with fortifying Nisibis, and making it the capital of a particular province, raised it even to the dignity of a colony, and made it take the name of *Septimia*. In the time of Alexander the son of Mammea, Artaxerxes, who had just dethroned Artabanes, the last king of Parthia, and restored to the Persian nation the sceptre which she had lost for about 555 years, endeavoured, but ineffectually, to make himself master of Nisibis.

Under one of the succeeding Emperors it was taken either by the same Artaxerxes, or his son Sapor I.; but by taking it he only procured the younger Gordian the honour of re-conquering it. Julius-Philip, the murderer and successor of Gordian, deserved by some benefactions to be considered as a new founder of the colony, as on a medal which she caused to be struck in honour of Philip, she took the name of *Julia* with that of *Septimia*. The captivity of Valerian, and the effeminacy of Gallienus his unworthy son, ceded to Sapor I. most of the Asiatic provinces. It was

was necessary for another Barbarian, named Odenathus, the chief of some Saracens, more Roman than the Emperor himself, to take care of the interests of the empire; and he saved it in the East. Nisibis first submitted to that prince, whose services Gallienus rewarded with the title of Augustus. It seemed again separated from the empire in the reign of Zenobia, the widow of Odenathus; but it was re-united by Aurelian. The Persians having made themselves masters of it after the death of Carus, the terror of the arms of Diocletian forced them to abandon it.

In short, the æra of the glory of Nisibis, and the most brilliant parts of its history, must be sought in the IVth century after Jesus Christ. In the reign of Constantius, Sapor II. as has been said, was thrice foiled before its ramparts. Of those three sieges, the most memorable is that of the year 350 *, described by Julian with no less elegance than energy, in his two first orations, which the orator has found the secret to render interesting in a certain degree, though they are panegyrics, and the panygyrics of Constantius. To give an idea of that siege, I will add, that Sapor having learned that the revolt of Magnentius, and the progress of that usurper, called Constantius into the West, desirous of availing himself of that juncture, invaded Mesopotamia at the head of an

---

* The other two sieges were in 337, and 359, according to Spanheim. Mr. Gibbon, though he refers to this author, has (in his margin) by some mistake, placed the three sieges in 338, 346, and 350.

innumerable army, and that, after having taken some castles, he on a sudden invested Nisibis. At first he besieged it in form; but neither the ram, nor the mine, nor the tortoise, having any effect, he turned the course of the river Mydonius, hoping to reduce the inhabitants by drought. From this, happily, the springs and the wells preserved them. The Great King then conceived a design worthy of Darius and Xerxes. He surrounded the place with a high and strong mound, and stopped the river below it. The waters ebbing filled a bason that was prepared for them, and rose almost as high as the rampart, which was not more above their level than was necessary to prevent the city from being overflowed. Sapor then equipped on this lake a fleet of barks filled with machines to batter and scour the walls, and with soldiers to assault them. This new mode of attack continued several days with an amazing loss on the side of the Barbarians, and with prodigies of intrepidity on the side of the Romans, till a weak part of the bank breaking, buried in the waters great numbers of the besiegers.

Sapor, seeing his reputation endangered, stopped the Mygdonius above the city, and discharged the river against the walls, of which it threw down a hundred cubits, 152 feet. Though he played incessantly on the breach, the inhabitants raised a new wall some paces from the old one, with such expedition, and defended it with such vigour, that they repulsed all the assaults. The king, in the violence
of

of his passion, shot an arrow into the sky to revenge himself, as far he could, of the deity himself. But he made that impious prince still more sensible of his power by an army of gnats, whose stings so enraged the horses and elephants, that they crushed in pieces several thousand soldiers. At length, after losing 20,000 men, he burnt his machines, and raised the siege, which had lasted more than four months. Count Lucillian, who commanded in the city, and St. James, its bishop *, divided the honour of having saved it; the former by his courage and military talents, the latter by his fervent prayers, which he interrupted only to animate his people to fight for their liberty and religion; for they all professed Christianity, of which Sapor was the persecutor.

Such was the city of Nisibis, which the son-in-law of Lucillian ceded to the same Sapor. Those, whom he ordered to leave it and give place to Barbarians, were in general the same, who, thirteen years before, had so well defended it. The senate, in a mournful silence, and the people uttering lamentable cries, repaired to the camp of the Emperor, and, prostrate at his feet, said to him every thing that grief and the love of their country sug-

---

* The miracles which Theodoret (*l.* 11. *c.* 30.) ascribes to St. James, bishop of Edessa, were at least performed in a worthy cause, the defence of his country. He appeared on the walls under the figure of the Roman Emperor, and sent an army of gnats to sting the trunks of the elephants, and to discomfit the host of this new Sennacherib. GIBBON.

gested

gested to them most affecting. As the whole answer that he opposed to their supplications, to their arguments, to their sighs, was the sanctity of an oath; "Sire," said they, "if necessity constrains
"you to cede your rights to Nisibis, do not forbid
"us, at least, to support ours, sword in hand.
"We ask of you neither stores, nor troops, nor
"money. By conquering Sapor we are all be-
"come soldiers. Consider us as foreigners. Aban-
"don us to ourselves, or rather to Heaven, the
"protector of justice and innocence. That will
"continue to render invincible such Romans as
"shall fight for their altars, for their hearths, for
"those walls which they have cemented with their
"own blood. After we have repulsed Sapor, the
"only use that we wish to make of our liberty is
"to give ourselves back to you."

Jovian answered, that he had expresly sworn to deliver up the city, and that he was incapable of eluding an oath by vain subtleties. Then Sabinus, to whom his birth and riches gave a distinguished rank among his fellow-citizens, said to him with equal spirit and boldness: "Constantius,
"always at war with the Persians, was almost al-
"ways unfortunate; he shivered at the name of
"Sapor, and this terror embittered all the mo-
"ments of his life. Constantius, however, over-
"whelmed with misfortunes, Constantius, reduced
"to the necessity of escaping almost alone, and of
"eating a morsel of bread in the cottage of a
"poor

"poor woman, still preserved Nisibis. What do
"I say? He never ceded to the enemy an inch
"of ground; but Jovian no sooner comes to the
"empire than he surrenders the bulwark of the
"East." Jovian heard these reproaches unmoved,
still intrenching himself in arguments drawn from
a point of honour and conscience.

It was customary for every city to offer new princes a crown of gold. In the critical situation to which the inhabitants of Nisibis were reduced, they were particularly careful to perform that duty. The Emperor, who did himself justice, being very sensible that he did not deserve the crown, especially from them, refused that which they presented to him. But the inhabitants, with a perseverance proof against all refusals, conjured him to receive it, thinking, without doubt, that he would allow himself to be affected by that mark of attachment and respect, and that, if he accepted their homage, he would contract a kind of engagement with them. Jovian, in order to extricate himself from their importunity, seemed at length to accept it; and instantly a lawyer, named Silvanus, exclaimed, with a loud voice, " In like manner, great Emperor, " may you be crowned by the other cities!" At this speech he was so exasperated, that he immediately ordered the inhabitants to evacuate the city in three days, and sent some troops to hasten them, with orders to put any to death who should remain there after the time prescribed.

This terrible decree filled Nisibis with consternation. Instantly nothing was heard but groans, cries, imprecations against the government, and frightful howlings. To see some women of rank forced by their sovereign to banish themselves from the scenes of their birth, from the places where they had happily passed their days in the bosom of opulence, forced, I say, to abandon all their possessions, and, what was more distressful, to remove for ever from the tombs of their husbands, their parents, their children, whose ashes remained at the discretion of the Barbarians, was a sight capable of moving Sapor, if he had been present. Sometimes they tore their hair and their faces, sometimes they clasped in their arms the doors of their houses, bathing them with tears, and bidding them a last farewell. In a word, there was seen the image of a city taken by assault, and all the symptoms of grief and despair which great calamities produce among the orientals, whose passions were always more expressive than ours. But who could describe the anguish of heart which must be felt by those brave men who had sustained three sieges, and who would have thought themselves happy to shed the remainder of their blood for a country, which they considered not only as the place of their birth, but also as the theatre of their glory, and the monument of their valour! Every one seized in his haste, and as if he had stolen it, any thing, that he could carry away, of his own effects;

for,

for, to complete their misfortunes, beasts of burden were wanting, so that a large quantity of valuable furniture was obliged to be left.

The roads were soon covered with these poor fugitives, who, groaning under their burdens, and still more oppressed by the weight of their affliction, were going to seek the first asylum that providence should be pleased to offer them. Most of them retired under the walls of Amida, where Jovian ordered a walled suburb to be built for them, which was called the town of Nisibis. Amida, founded by Constantius, and almost ruined by Sapor, thus increased by the ruins of this ancient city, and repaired its losses with so much advantage, that it became the capital of what the Romans retained in Mesopotamia. As soon as the inhabitants of Nisibis were departed, Jovian dispatched the tribune Constantius to expell those of Singara, another Roman colony, and to deliver the five provinces to the officers of Sapor. Thus this famous treaty was literally executed, a treaty, which may be regarded as the epocha of the fall of the empire, and whose execution exposed Jovian, more than the treaty itself, to the reproaches not only of Pagan, but of some Christian authors. Are their reproaches well founded? This is a problem, whose discussion will be more properly placed at the end of this history *.

After

---

* The Abbè de la Bleterie, though a severe casuist, has pronounced, that Jovian was not bound to execute his promise;

After having fulfilled his engagements with the Persians, the Emperor ordered Procopius to convey to Tarsus in Cilicia the corpse of Julian, agreeably to the last will of that prince. In the funeral procession, which must have been a fortnight at least on the road, the customs of the Pagans were observed, of which the most fantastic was, to enliven the funeral pomp of the great, and even of the Emperors, at the expence of those whom they pretended to honour. They added humour and satire to the demonstrations of grief. Here were heard mournful songs and lamentations, and tears were seen to flow: there drolls and buffoons danced and acted some jocose scenes, or one of the troop, in a mask which represented to the life him whose obsequies were celebrated, imitated his gesture and his voice *, and made him utter, in a ludicrous strain, the language most proper to characterise him. The inferior personages loaded

---

promise; since he *could not* dismember the empire, nor alienate, without their consent, the allegiance of his people. I have never found much delight or instruction in such political metaphysics. GIBBON.

Not being convinced or edified by the Abbè's reasoning, I have not translated his dissertation.

* Of this we are informed by Suetonius in the following remarkable passage: "At the funeral of Vespasian, Favo, the chief of the comedians, who played his part, and imitated, as is customary, his words and actions while alive, asked the managers of the solemnity aloud, "What would be the expence of the funeral pomp?" and they answering, 'a hundred millions of sesterces,' the pretended Vespasian exclaimed, "if they would give him but a hundred sesterces, they might throw him into the river." B.

this principal performer with railleries and affronts. The pretended Julian must have been highly ridiculous, as the copy was always more extravagant than the original. Neither the faults of that unfortunate prince, nor perhaps his good qualities, were spared. He was reproached in the bitterest terms for his apostacy, his temerity, his defeat, his death. To conceive how far the licentiousness was carried, it must be remembered that the actors revenged themselves on the enemy of the stage, and that they were sure of the applause of the Christians.

As soon as Procopius had acquitted himself of this commission, alarmed at the fate of Jovianus, and at the false report that was spread, that Julian, his relation, had wished, at the point of death, to have him for his successor, he thought that his life was in danger. He therefore secreted himself, and had the art to elude the searches of Jovian, and afterwards those of Valens. About two years after the death of Julian, he appeared again in order to ascend the throne, from which he fell almost the same instant *.

From Nisibis Jovian took the road to Antioch, and came to Edessa, which should have been dear to him for the same reason † that had made it odious to his predecessor. He was in that city on the 27th of September, according to the date of a

* See p. 221. note †.
† Julian would not pass through Edessa, because that city was strongly attached to Christianity.   B.

law,

law *, which excuses the soldiers from going to forage more than twenty miles, or one day's journey, from the camp. Julian, the restorer of military discipline, had obliged them to go in search of it to that distance; but perhaps some officers sent them still farther. Jovian, interested in conciliating the affection of the troops, delivered or preserved them from that fatigue, to which there was no right to oblige them; and the spirit of his law agrees exactly with that of Julian.

The Emperor continuing his march by long stages, and received very sorrowfully on his route, entered Antioch in the month of October, and could not dispense with making some stay there, notwithstanding his impatience to go and shew himself at Constantinople, and afterwards, no doubt, in the provinces of the West. His troops were in extreme want of repose. Antioch, the abode of plenty, and the centre of all the conveniences of life, was the properest place in the world to recover them; and prudence did not yet allow Jovian to separate himself from an army, whose suffrages were the only right that he had to the empire.

During six weeks, more or less, that he passed in the capital of the East, he applied himself chiefly to regulate what concerned religion. That

---

* This law is dated in the consulship of Jovian and Varronian, and consequently the date is false, at least in that respect. It is well known, that the dates marked in the Theodosian code are so faulty, that scarce any stress can be laid on them. B.

portion of public affairs, so essential and always so delicate, then required extreme discretion. Julian, with his pretended toleration, which had been no more in fact than a persecution aukwardly disguised, in which the injustice of oppression was aggravated by the insolence of dishonesty, had in a manner set all the subjects of the empire at variance. The people were incensed against the people; cities were divided; families were disunited; the ferment of minds was so violent, that it seemed as if it could not be calmed but by the extinction of one of the parties. The unexpected revolution, which again gave the Christians a prince of their religion, was not sufficient to restore tranquillity. There was room to fear, that, under the appearance of zeal, the animosity of some ill-informed Christians, indulging itself in some unworthy reprisals, might drive the Pagans, with whom patience was founded on no religious principle, to extremities. Already the temples were every where * shut; the blood of victims flowed no longer; the priests of the idols absconded; the philosophers trimmed their beards, and quitted the cloak, to resume the common dress. This was not a panic fear: they had unworthily abused their credit. St. Gregory of Nazianzus, at the conclusion of his discourse against Julian, exhorts to the for-

---

* Τα ιερα των Ελληνων παντα απεκλειθο. Supposing that Socrates is not mistaken in saying that the temples were every where shut, this could not have happened before the law which we shall presently mention. B.

givenefs

HISTORY OF JOVIAN.

giveness of injuries in a manner that would induce a belief, that, on that occasion, he considered obedience to the precept as a great effort of virtue. One would be apt to think, that, though he inveighs with such warmth against the Pagans, and against the memory of Julian, it is a stroke of Christian policy; and that by taking, as it were, in the name of the church, and by public authority, a lawful vengeance, he means to prevent and disarm that of individuals.

The war kindled between the Christians and Pagans was not the only one of which religion was either the pretext or the cause. Not to mention some sects that were obscure or of little account *, every thing that bore the Christian name was divided between the faith of Nice and the heresy of Arius. The most vehement controversies are often no more than disputes on words. Here, under the appearance of disputes on words †, and even on letters, there were real divisions as to fundamental tenets; and the disputes were managed with as much animosity, as if incomprehensible truths had been in question. The Arians, whom the favour of Constantius had put in possession of the churches of Constantinople, and of the principal

---

* Such as the Valentinians, the Marcionites, the Montanists, the Manicheans.   B.

† The terms ὁμοούσιος, "consubstantial," "of the same substance," consecrated by the council of Nice, and ὁμοιούσιος, "like in substance," which most of the Arians admitted, only differ an iota more or less.   B.

fees of the East, subdivided into pure Arians and demi-Arians, agreed only against the Catholics. In less than fifty years they had made sixteen formularies of faith *, and it was doubted whether they had made the last. Arianism was a cruel sect, and even by that, according to St. Athanasius †, bore on its front a mark of reprobation. To cruelty it knew how to add cunning and artifice. Deceived by its equivocal forms ‡, under Constantius the whole world was surprised to find itself Arian without thinking of it; but error did not long enjoy this imaginary triumph. A reunion founded on duplicity had only produced a more cruel division.

On the other side, those who acknowledged the divinity of the Word, did not all agree as to the rest. Some, by an excess of delicacy, rejected the term " consubstantial," as not being in scripture; and though they admitted the tenet meant by that word, all had not, like Athanasius §, equity enough to compassionate their weakness, and to reckon them among the orthodox.

An obstinate schism, formed by mistake, and perpetuated by imprudence, rent the city of

---

* The enumeration of them may be seen in the Ecclesiastical History of M. Fleury, l. xiv. 23.   B.

† *Ath. Hist. Arian. ad Monachos*, t. 1. p. 382. Edit. Bened.   B.

‡ At the Council of Rimini.   B.

§ *Athan. de Synodis*, l. 11. p. 755.   B.

Antioch.

Antioch *. There were seen two Catholic bishops, besides one Arian. At Constantinople, and elsewhere,

> * In the year 330, under the reign of Constantine, having succeeded in deposing and banishing St. Eustathius, bishop of Antioch, the most zealous of the Catholics began to hold their separate assemblies. As they still acknowledged Eustathius, the name of Eustathians was given them. The see was successively filled by several bishops, more or less attached to the Arian cabal, with whom the great number of Catholics of Antioch, either through love of peace, or from weakness, did not fail to communicate. Things remained in this state during the reign of Constantius. But in 361 (the last year of that prince) Anianus, the Arian bishop, having been banished, and, besides, Eustathius having died in his exile, they were desirous to elect a bishop who might re-unite the church of Antioch. The Arians and the moderate Catholics cast their eyes on Meletius, the most amiable and most peaceable of men. Every one thought him of his own party. But in that the Arians were mistaken. Meletius was no sooner elected than he declared for the Catholic faith. The Eustathians, however, obstinately resolved not to acknowledge him, because the Arians had had great share in his election. On the other side, the Arians, enraged at being deceived in him, caused him to be banished a month after, to the great regret of the moderate Catholics, who, retaining an inviolable attachment to the holy bishop, would no more assemble, as they had hitherto done in the churches of the Arians, and offered to unite themselves with the Eustathians, or zealous Catholics. But these refused to admit them to their communion. There were then at Antioch therefore three parties; the Arians, the Eustathians, and the Meletians. After the death of Constantius, in 362, Lucifer, of Cagliari in Sardinia, whom that prince had banished into Syria, a man celebrated for his courage, and his sufferings in the good cause, but whose views were too confined, ordained as bishop the priest Paulinus, whom the Eustathians already considered as their head. Lucifer thought that the Meletians, more pacific than the others, would accept Paulinus, who, besides, was very worthy of the prelacy; but

where, the Macedonians *, orthodox, at least in appearance, as to the consubstantiality of the Son, denied that of the Holy Ghost. The Donatists, thinking that there was no church, or even sacraments, out of their society, carried fanaticism in Africa to a degree of madness. The Novatians †, whose heresy was to erect a desperate rigour into an article of faith, kept up some good understanding with the Catholics, who distinguished them extremely from the other sectaries; and it may be said, that they merited that distinction by the purity of their manners, and by their attachment to the ancient doctrine as to the divinity of Jesus Christ. They had supported with heroic courage the Arian persecutions: but some had shewn ‡, that for the defence of their faith they knew how to employ other arms than those of true Christians.

As the most natural effect of a foreign war is to suspend civil dissentions; in spite of the artifices of

---

but this imprudent step only served to put an end to the schism. Thus there were seen in the same city three bishops, Euzoius the Arian, Meletius, returned from his exile, and Paulinus, both Catholics. This division did not terminate till long after, under bishop Alexander, to whom the Eustathians re-united themselves in 415. B.

* So named from Macedonius, archbishop of Constantinople. B.

† The Novatians did not admit to penitence those who had fallen after baptism. B.

‡ Under Constantius the Novatian peasants of Mantinium in Paphlagonia, armed with scythes and axes, cut in pieces four companies of soldiers, who had been sent to oblige them to embrace Arianism. B.

Julian to foment the flame of difcord, there appeared in his reign between the moſt oppoſite communions a kind of truce refembling peace. Excepting only the Donatifts, who committed exceſſes againſt the Catholics, for which the magiſtrates thought it their duty to account to the Emperor; excepting, I fay, thofe madmen, the Chriſtians had feemed to forget their domeſtic diviſions, and to employ themfelves in concert in offering up prayers for their common deliverance. But as foon as the election of a Chriſtian prince was known, the flumbering difputes began to awaken, and the chiefs of the different communions were eagerly defirous of going to meet the Emperor as foon as he was in the Roman territories; either to engage him, or at leaft to render him favourable to their party.

Amidft fuch a diverfity of opinions, Jovian, as I have already faid, had the happineſs to know the truth. He had preferred Chriſtianity to his fortune, and openly profeſſed the Catholic doctrine. If the purity of his manners did not perhaps anfwer to that of his faith, at leaft he ardently wifhed, it cannot be doubted, to fee all his fubjects re-united in the bofom of the true religion. But Jovian was too well inſtructed in the nature of religion itſelf to offer violence to any one. A confeſſor of the faith become a perfecutor would have been a kind of prodigy. Who fhould be better acquainted with the rights of confcience than he who himself had been obliged to claim them? He was convinced that faith perfuades, but does not command; that to employ fire and fword, in the progrefs of the gofpel, is to combat at once the fpirit of the gofpel, and the principles of reafon; that fear only makes hypocrites; that God rejects forced homage, and that if he difapproves error, he detefts perjury; that the excellence of the end propofed cannot fanctify unlawful means; that, befides, in order to fucceed, the means muft be fuited to the end, and thus that confciences can no more be carried by force of arms than ramparts by arguments *.

But, befides, if Jovian had thought it lawful and poffible to convert men by the dread of punifhments and death, it would have been rifking too much at the beginning of a new reign to irritate the Arians, who ftill retained, among the Chriftian communions, that air of fuperiority which had been given them by the protection and favour of Conftantius. It would have been ftill more dangerous to attack Paganifm in front, which, under Julian, had recovered ftrength, and had even become again the religion of the ftate. It muft be fuppofed, that the Pagans, feeing themfelves at the

* Thefe truly Proteftant doctrines flow from the pen of a nominal Papift, but are as different from thofe of the murderers of Cranmer in former times, and of thofe of Calas in the prefent, as light from darknefs. Such liberal fentiments in fome ages and countries would have configned the author to the Inquifition.

difcretion

discretion of a prince who was a zealous enemy to idolatry, were extremely alarmed, and that many expressed so much uneasiness as to occasion some to that weakly established prince. With a view therefore to confirm them, and also to confirm himself, he hastened to make a law, by which he maintained them in the free exercise of their religion, and permitted them to re-open the temples, where, by forcible means, and without the authority of the prince, they had been shut since the death of Julian.

" You understand," says Themistius, a Pagan philosopher and senator of Constantinople *, in a panegyric on Jovian, which he pronounced before him, " that there are some things which a so-
" vereign cannot restrain. Among these are the
" virtues, and especially religion. A prince,
" who should make an edict to enjoin his subjects
" to love him, would not be obeyed. Could he
" flatter himself with being so for commanding
" them to have such or such a religious persuasion?
" Fear, without doubt, will effect transient meta-
" morphoses. But shall we consider as men con-
" vinced, those men more changeable than Eu-
" ripus †, persuaded by their variations to be the
" adorers of the purple, and not of the divinity,
" those ridiculous Proteuses who dishonour human
" kind, and who are sometimes seen in the temples

---

* See the Epistle to him, Vol. I. p. 4.
† This narrow sea, between Bœotia and Euboea, ebbed and flowed seven times in 24 hours, or oftener, or seldomer, as the wind sat.

" at

"at the feet of the statues and altars, and some-
"times at the holy table in the churches of the
"Christians? Thus, instead of using violence, you
"have made a law which allows every one to pay
"to the Deity the worship which he shall think
"the best. As the image of the Supreme Being,
"you imitate his conduct. He has placed in the
"heart of man a natural inclination which leads
"him to religion; but he does not force him in
"the choice. Thus the coërcive laws, which
"tended to deprive man of a liberty which God
"leaves him, have lasted at most during the lives
"of their authors; instead of which, your law,
"or rather that of God himself, subsists in all
"ages. Neither confiscations, nor exiles, nor
"punishments can annull it. The body may be
"imprisoned, tormented, destroyed; but the soul
"takes her flight: she escapes from violence, bear-
"ing in herself this indelible law, this liberty of
"thinking, of which it is impossible to deprive
"her, though the tongue should be forced
"to articulate some words. . . . . . The wisdom
"of your edict allays our cruel divisions. This,
"Emperor, beloved by God, you know better
"than any one: The Persians were less formidable
"to the Romans than the Romans themselves; the
"incursions of those Barbarians less dangerous than
"the accusations suggested by the spirit of party
"to destroy citizens. Continue to hold the ba-
"lance even. Allow all mouths to address prayers
"to heaven for the prosperity of your empire...

"A law

" A law so just must penetrate all the subjects of
" our divine monarch with respect and love, those,
" among others, to whom not contented to restore
" liberty, he explains the tenets of their religion
" as well as the ablest of their teachers."

Thus, in the presence of Jovian himself, spoke Themistius, one of the most illustrious magistrates of his age, and deputed by the body to harangue the Emperor. His authority sufficiently authenticates the law of Jovian, though it no longer exists, and though other writers seem to have been ignorant of it. The panegyrics of princes sometimes praise them for virtues which they do not possess, but never for laws which they have not made. It cannot be denied that Themistius, in the discourse, part of which I have just quoted, lays down, on occasion of that law, some very philosophical and even very Christian maxims. But as truth is very seldom found in the mouths of Pagans without any mixture of error, to the solid arguments which condemn cruelty and violence he adds the pretended impossibility of knowing how the Deity would be adored, and the imaginary honour which redounds to the Supreme Being from the variety of worships which divide the world. This philosopher confounds political toleration with indifference, while Jovian, by the light of the gospel, perfectly distinguishes them.

The same edict, which permitted the temples to be re-opened, ordered the abominable sanctuaries of impostures and witchcraft to be shut. It suffered the public sacrifices, and the worship formerly authorised, to remain; but it forbade enchantments, magic, and all worship visibly founded on imposture. Though the Roman laws had always condemned these practices, the foolish superstition and credulity of Julian had brought them extremely into fashion. The wisest among the Pagans must greatly praise his successor for the care which he took to proscribe what they deemed foreign to their religion, and likely to do it discredit. It seemed to them, no doubt, performing a legitimate act of the pontifical power, which they still ascribed to the Christian Emperors, and of which Constantine had usefully availed himself, to effect the destruction of idolatry.

Properly speaking, the Pagan religion had no dogmas; it consisted of a heap of practics, and the Sovereign Pontiff had a right to suppress such as he thought abusive *. Constantine therefore having formed the plan of dissolving it by little and little, and of destroying it by degrees, without shocking the Pagans, had confined it within very narrow bounds, by retrenching sometimes a worship contrary to good manners, sometimes a suspicious practice; here subverting a temple that was become the school of libertinism, there inter-

---

* See the Dissertation of the Baron de la Bastie, on the Sovereign Pontificate of the Roman Emperors (Part III.) in the *Memoirs of the Academy of Inscriptions and Belles Lettres*, t. XV. B.

dicting

dicting an oracle whose priests manifestly abused the public credulity. It appears that Jovian did not pretend to tolerate Paganism but in the state to which Constantine had reduced it. On that footing only it could in fact be suffered, and the moderate Pagans required nothing more.

The political toleration of Jovian was effective and sincere. Instead of seeking pretences to disturb the Pagans, he did not avail himself of the most natural occasions. He might, without injustice, have abandoned to the severity of the laws several priests of the idols, and the philosophers who had abused the confidence of Julian. Nevertheless, it is not to his reign that the rigours which, Libanius says *, were exercised against them, must be

---

* As Libanius did not pronounce his second funeral oration on Julian till eighteen months after the death of that prince, and consequently more than ten months after the death of Jovian, I know not why M. de Tillemont applies to the reign of the latter the bitter complaints of that orator. "At present," says that orator, (*Orat. Parent.* 148, *et seq.*) "those who declaim against the Gods are treated "with respect, while the priests, those who are only guilty "of serving the Gods, undergo unjust trials. That which "they have employed in divine worship, that which the "flame has consumed on the altars, they are forced to "surrender. Are they unable to pay? They languish in "fetters. The temples have been destroyed, or remain "half-built, to serve as a ridicule for Christians. The "philosophers are put to the torture. To have received "something from the Emperor is to have contracted a "debt. What do I say? It is to have committed a theft. "In the midst of summer, at noon-day, a man is exposed "quite naked to the heat of the sun. Besides what he "has

"has received, he is asked what every one sees he has not
"received. It is well known that this is to require an
"impossibility; but it is a pleasure to burn him; he must
"expire in this horrible torture. The professors of elo-
"quence, accustomed to live with the great, are driven
"from their doors, like infamous murderers. That nu-
"merous swarm of young disciples who always accom-
"pany them, seeing their masters thus treated, conceive
"that knowledge is good for nothing, and seek a better
"protection. In every city the members of the public
"council unjustly dispense with the service, which their
"country has a right to expect from them; and no one
"checks so outrageous a disorder. Nothing is every where
"seen but exactions, forced sales, confiscations, indigence,
"poverty, tears. The labourer chooses rather to beg than
"to cultivate the earth. He who to-day gives alms, to-
"morrow will be obliged to ask them. The Scythians, the
"Sarmatians, the Celts, in a word, all the Barbarians be-
"gin again to insult us on all sides," &c.

The odious strokes of this picture do not relate to Jovian. Indeed, during his reign, the bishops, and other Christian preachers, were in great esteem, and spoke against Paganism with full liberty. It is also very possible, that at the news of his election, in places where the Christians were the strongest, the populace might destroy some temples. Those which Julian was building remained unfinished, because Jovian would not furnish the expence, and the zeal of idolaters cooled. I also suppose that Libanius, and his fellows, did not find the same access to the great: some magistrate might have refused him admittance; a very sensible affront to that sophist, who treated Julian as an equal. But this is all that can reasonably be ascribed to the reign of Jovian. According to Libanius, it was "the height of "summer," ($\mu\iota\sigma\upsilon\ \theta\epsilon\rho\upsilon\varsigma$) when the philosophers were persecuted. Now Jovian did not enter on the territories of the empire till towards the beginning of autumn, and died before the end of winter. Besides, the philosopher tormented so cruelly is plainly the famous Maximus. But Priscus and he were brought to trial at the beginning of the reign of Valentinian and Valens.

As to what Libanius says of the venality of exemptions, and of the oppression of the people, no author reproaches Jovian with anything like it; on the contrary, the patrician

Petronius,

be afcribed. It is true, that, after the death of Julian, their protector and their dupe, some philosophers were called to a severe account for the immense sums, which, it was said, they had drawn from him; and this perhaps is the only time that the royal treasure has pursued men of letters. But those enquiries were not made till the reign of Valens. Eunapius, also a Pagan, and as plaintive as Libanius, affirms that Jovian continued to honour the philosophers * who were in the train of his predecessor. We may at least conclude, from that expression, that he had some regard for them. Themistius reckons as a merit in him his protecting philosophy at a time when almost every one else declared against it, and recalling it to court in a less disgraceful habit. Fear had at first driven the philosophers from it; but they soon recovered their courage; and Jovian allowed them to appear there again, but in the common dress. It may, however, be presumed, that they were not seen there with a very gracious eye, and that they must

---

Petronius, the father-in-law of Valens, a monster of avarice and cruelty, rendered immediately the government of his son-in-law highly odious, and ruined a multitude of families, by enquiring what was due to the treasury for near a century past. See Amm. xxvi. 6. In short, the two brothers reigned when the Barbarians, being no longer restrained by the fear of Julian, again took up arms. Those people had scarce had time to hear of his death, and to make some preparations, during the reign of Jovian. B.

* Τιμων τους ανδρας διδιλισιν. Illos viros honore prosequi non destitit.

suffer some mortifications, and perhaps insults, from the courtiers, which the Emperor did not take the trouble to avenge; and that, if I mistake not, is the meaning of what Themistius says, in a discourse addressed to Valens; that " it is a stain to " the glory of Jovian to have suffered insults to " be offered them, though, as to himself, he offered " them none."

Libanius continued incessantly to bewail Julian, and to praise him in his writings. Some would have made it a state crime, and Jovian was advised to send him to console himself with his hero. But he thought it beneath an Emperor to trouble himself with what a sophist might write. He was sensible also that by putting an author to death, his works, instead of being suppressed, are assured of immortality. As Jovian spared a Maximus and a Libanius, we may judge what tranquillity was enjoyed by such Pagans as could be reproached with nothing but their religion. It is certain, that at Constantinople sacrifices were publickly offered for the solemnity of the consulship of Jovian.

If this prince, in quality of common father and chief of the body politic, thought himself obliged not to restrain the consciences of his subjects, he did not forget that he owed a striking protection to the religious society of which he was a member. It appears by his medals that he replaced in the

Labarum

Labarum * the monogram of Jesus Christ. Not content with having thus declared that Christianity was the religion of the empire, he formally declared by a letter †, which he wrote to the governors

* The principal standard which displayed the triumph of the cross was styled the *Labarum*, or *Laborum*, an obscure though celebrated name, which has been vainly derived from almost all the languages of the world. It is described as a long pike intersected by a transversal beam. The silken veil, which hung down from the beam, was curiously enwrought with the images of the reigning monarch and his children. The summit of the pike supported a crown of gold, which inclosed the mysterious monogram, at once expressive of the figure of the cross, and the initial letters of the name of Christ. The safety of the Laborum was entrusted to fifty guards of approved valour and fidelity.   GIBBON.

Julian had replaced in the standards the antient Latin letters, S. P. Q. R.

† This letter, mentioned by Sozomen, is, I fancy, the very law of which Themistius gives the elogium. He says, plainly enough, that this law was the first of those of Jovian; and Sozomen asserts, that Jovian did not defer a moment (ὐδὲν μελλήσας) to write to the generals of the provinces. It is probable, that the law contained two heads. The Emperor there declared, first, that the Christian religion was that of the state, &c. Secondly, that he did not pretend to deprive any one of the liberty of following and exercising any other, &c. The Pagan philosopher dwells only on the second head, which was advantageous to the Pagans: the ecclesiastical historian mentions only the first, which favoured the Christians. Each of them comments in his own way on the article which interests him, and gives it too much latitude. In reading Themistius, one would think that Jovian had put all religions on the same level; but Sozomen, whose text I am far from understanding rigorously, says, that this prince declared Christianity the only religion of his subjects. M. de Tillemont did not know how to reconcile the law that Themistius mentions
with

nors of the provinces, all Pagans no doubt, as they had been put or left in place by Julian; enjoining them to act so that the Christians might assemble in the churches: for in several places they had either been destroyed or converted to profane uses. He recalled all who had been banished on account of religion, restored to the clergy, to virgins, and to widows the privileges granted by the Christian Emperors, and re-established the distribution of corn which the demesne allowed to every church for the subsistence of widows and orphans. The famine which then afflicted the empire obliged him to reduce to one-third that pious donation of Constantine; but he promised to give the remainder at the first return of plenty.

He made also a law, which we still have; addressed to Sallust the Second, Præfect of the prætorium of the East, denouncing capital punishment to those who should dare to steal away, or even solicit in marriage, the virgins consecrated to God *.

These

---

with that referred to by Sozomen. I flatter myself that this learned writer would have approved the method of agreement here proposed.   B.

 The Abbé de la Bleterie judiciously remarks, that Sozomen has forgot the general toleration, and Themistius the establishment of the Catholic religion. Each of them turned away from the object which he disliked, and wished to suppress the part of the edict the least honourable, in his opinion, to the Emperor Jovian.   GIBBON.

 * The following are the very terms of the law. *Imp. Jovianus A. ad secundum P. P. Si quis, non dicam rapere, sed vel atten-*

HISTORY OF JOVIAN.

These scandalous marriages had grown common under Julian. To accomplish them, some had employed violence, and others seduction. An officer, named Magnus, the same who was, under Valens, and perhaps from the time of Julian, treasurer of the Emperor's houshold *, had burned, by his private authority, the church of Beryta in Phoenicia. Ecclesiastical history represents Count Magnus † as unprin-

---

attentare, matrimonii jungendi causa, sacratas virgines vel invitas ausus fuerit, capitali sententiâ feriatur. Dat. XI. Kal. Mar. Antiochiæ, Joviano A. et Varroniano Coss. Instead of *invitas*, we should perhaps read *invitare*. Sozomen seems to have read *intueri*, as he translates the Latin word by these; ακολαςως προσβλιπσιλα, *impudicè aspicientem*. There is no probability that this was the sense. The date of this law is also false, like a number of others. Jovian did not take the consulship till a month at soonest after his leaving Antioch; and, besides, he was no longer in this world on the 19th of February, 364, as he died between the 16th and 17th of that month. B.

The new law which condemned the rape or marriage of nuns, is exaggerated by Sozomen; who supposes that an amorous glance, the adultery of the heart, was punished with death by the evangelic legislator. GIBBON.

* Thus, I think, *Comes largitionum comitatensium* should be translated. B.

† It was he who, in the time of Valens and of the governor Palladius, persecuted by an inferior order the Catholics of Alexandria, to oblige them to receive the bishop Lucius. Having caused nineteen, as well priests as deacons, to be apprehended and brought before his tribunal, some of whom were more than fourscore years of age, he said to them, "Embrace, wretches, embrace the opinion of "the Arians. If your religion be true, God will pardon "you for having yielded to necessity. You will please the "most clement, august Valens." After having put them

in

unprincipled, a slave to the court, ardent to distinguish himself in all persecutions, and committing with the baseness of a subaltern some crimes of supererogation. He was very near being beheaded by Jovian. Powerful intercessions obtained his pardon; but he was condemned to re-build the church of Beryta at his own expence.

Athanasius, the personal object of the hatred and persecution of Julian, hearing of the death of that prince, had on a sudden re-appeared in the midst of his people, who were agreeably surprised. As the orders of Julian had not then been revoked, a Pagan or an Arian might have made an attempt on the person of the holy prelate. How was it known whether the new Emperor would not be displeased that Athanasius should shew himself publickly in Alexandria, without the leave of the same authority which had banished him from all Ægypt? But his fears were immediately dispelled by a letter from Jovian, conceived in these terms:
" To the most religious friend of God, Athanasius,
" Jovian. As we admire beyond all expression the
" sanctity of your life, in which shine forth the

---

in prison, and caused them to be scourged and tormented, he banished them into an idolatrous country, made them set out immediately, urging them himself, sword in hand, without giving them time to take necessaries, without waiting till the sea became calm, without being moved by the cries and tears of the whole Catholic people. *Epistola Petri Alexandrini apud Theodoret.* l. iv. 22.   B.

" marks

HISTORY OF JOVIAN.

"marks of resemblance to the God of the uni-
"verse *, and your zeal for Jesus Christ our Sa-
"viour, we take you now under our protection,
"most respectable bishop. You deserve it by that
"courage which has made you reckon as nothing
"the most painful labours, and regard as an ob-
"ject of contempt the rage of persecutors and
"menacing swords. Holding in your hand the
"helm of faith, which is so dear to you, you cease
"not to combat for the truth, nor to edify the
"Christian people who find in you the perfect
"model of all virtues. For these causes, we re-
"call you immediately, and we order you to return,
"to teach the doctrine of salvation. Return there-
"fore to the holy churches; feed the people of his
"God. Let the pastor, at the head of the flock,
"offer up prayers for our person: for we are per-
"suaded that God will diffuse on us, and on those
"who are Christians like us, his most signal favours,
"if you grant us the assistance of your prayers."

It appears by the order contained in this letter, that the Emperor was ignorant, or chose to be ignorant, that Athanasius had resumed the public exercise of his functions †. Be that as it may,

---

* The word "celestial" faintly expresses the impious and extravagant flattery of the Emperor to the archbishop, της προς τον Θεον των ολων ομοιωσεως. GIBBON.

† He might be ignorant of it; for St. Gregory of Nazianus says, that the order for the recall of Athanasius was dispatched the first of all. *Greg. Naz. or.* XXI. B.

Jovian

Jovian wrote to him again, to afk inftruction of him as to the tenets which were then the fubject of difputes. Not that he was not a confirmed catholic. The letter juft quoted would alone prove it *; and, befides, thus to confult the great Athanafius, the man of the church and the bulwark of the faith, was loudly to declare himfelf for the doctrine of Nice. But not to mention the difpute which had been raifed concerning the divinity of the Holy Ghoft, the Arians, by their fophifms and captious formularies, fome of which were rather infufficient than erroneous, had introduced into a controverfy, fimple in itfelf, more difficulties than were neceffary to embarrafs a foldier like Jovian. Thinking himfelf then obliged by the ftate to labour on the great work of the re-union of Chriftians, and refolved to employ only perfuafion, he had need of fome palpable but decifive and keen arguments to convince the fectaries, without entering into thorny difcuffions, which would have been above his reach, and in one fenfe beneath his dignity.

Athanafius entered fully into his views; convened fome intelligent bifhops, and anfwered him

---

* Theodoret (l. iv. c. 2.) fays, that he ordered thofe, who had adhered to the faith of Nice in its purity, to be put in poffeffion of the churches. If that be true, the order was not rigoroufly executed. It appears, however, that Jovian gave a church new-built to the Catholics of Antioch (of the communion of St. Meletius); which feems to prove that under Julian the Chriftians might build churches. E.

HISTORY OF JOVIAN.

in the name of the whole patriarchate of Alexandria. After congratulating the Emperor on the care which he took to inform himself of the truth *, the holy teacher proves that he must attach himself to the faith of Nice. It is the faith of the Apostles and martyrs. They were in possession of that doctrine when Arius came to sow his errors. All the churches have received, and still receive, the decision of Nice; the small number of Arians that oppose it cannot form a prejudice against the rest †
of

---

* We have this letter in the History of Theodoret, and among the works of Athanasius. In the letter, as it is quoted by Theodoret, is a half phrase in which Athanasius seems to promise Jovian a long and tranquil reign, as the reward of his desire to be instructed in heavenly truths: Και την βασιλειαν μετ' ειρηνης πολλαις ἱων περιοδοις επιλεισις; " and " you will govern the empire many years in peace."

As Jovian reigned a very short time, Baronius imagines, that these words are an addition of some Arian, who was willing to make Athanasius pass for a false prophet; but in authors who are not inspired such sort of expressions ought to be regarded as wishes, and not as promises, much less as prophesies.   B.

Before his departure from Antioch ‡, he assured Jovian that his orthodox devotion would be rewarded with a long and peaceful reign. Athanasius had reason to hope, that he should be allowed either the merit of a successful prediction, or the excuse of a grateful, though ineffectual, prayer. In some MSS. this indiscreet promise is omitted; perhaps by the Catholics, jealous of the prophetic fame of their leader.   GIBBON.

† Συμψηφοι τυγχανουσιν αἱ κατα τοπον εκκλησιαι . . . παριξ ολιγων των τα Αρειου φρονουντων . . . και τινες αντιλεγωσιν ταυτη τη πιστει η δυνανται τεκμηρια ποιειν πασι τη οικουμενη. "All the churches " every where agree . . . a few excepted, who embrace

‡ This letter was rather previous to his coming to Antioch, and indeed occasioned it. See p. 334.

" the

of the world. At length Athanasius, willing to guard Jovian against the heresy of Macedonius, observes, that the same council of Nice has sufficiently established the consubstantiality of the Holy Ghost, by saying, that it is " glorified with the Fa-" ther and the Son." Thus this able divine adapts himself to the necessity and capacity of the prince, and does not omit to supply him with peremptory arguments, drawn from prescription, and the consent of the churches as to a formal and determined tenet.

The Emperor was so well satisfied with the letter of Athanasius, that he wished to converse with him, and ordered him to repair to Antioch. The holy bishop obeyed the more willingly, as he had already resolved to go to court; not from taste (for no bishop was ever less a courtier), but for the interests

" the opinion of Arius *, and though some contradict this " faith, we know that they cannot prejudice the whole " world." Athanasius, by reducing the Arians to so small a number, seems to differ from the common opinion; but it must be observed, 1. That the bishops who had subscribed to the council of Rimini, had recovered their fall after the death of Constantius. 2. At the very time when heresy seemed to prevail, many of those who received the forms proposed by the Arians, received them in a Catholic sense. 3. As the most determined of the Arians did not scruple to say, that Jesus Christ is God, the Christian people, who knew only the Supreme God, understood that Jesus Christ was the only and same God with his Father, and understood in a good sense the ambiguous expressions with which the error was envelopped. This occasioned the saying of a father of that time: " The ears of the people " are more holy than the hearts of the priests." B.

* This assertion was verified in the space of thirty or forty years.

GIBBON.

of the church, and from deference to the advice of his intimate friends. However advantageous his reputation was, he always gained by a personal acquaintance. Jovian liked him extremely, and gave him his confidence. It is honourable for that prince to have placed it so well. Athanasius was the greatest man of his age; and perhaps, taken all together, the church has never had a greater. God, who destined him to combat the most dreadful of heresies, armed at once with the subtleties of logic and the power of the Emperors, had endued him with all the gifts of nature and of grace, which could render him proper to fill that high destination.

He had a just, quick, and penetrating mind; a generous and disinterested heart; cool courage, and, it may be said, uniform heroism, always the same, without impetuosity or extravagance; lively faith; unbounded charity; profound humility; a christianity, strong, simple, and noble, like the gospel; a natural eloquence, abounding with penetrating strokes, strong in substance, going directly to the point, and of rare precision in the Greek writers of that time. The austerity of his life rendered his virtue respectable; the gentleness of his manners made him beloved. The calmness and serenity of his soul were painted on his face. Though he had not an advantageous person *, his external appearance had somewhat majestic and striking. He

* See note *. p. 141.

was not ignorant of the profane sciences, but he avoided making a parade of them. Skilled in the letter of the scriptures, he also possessed their spirit. Neither Greeks, nor Romans, ever loved their country so much as Athanasius loved the church, whose interests were always inseparable from his. Long experience had inured him to ecclesiastical affairs. Adversity, which enlarges and refines when it does not crush the genius, had given him admirable penetration to discover resources, even human, when every thing seemed desperate. Threatened with exile when he was in his see, and with death when he was exiled, he struggled for near fifty years against a league of men subtle in arguments, profound in intrigues, acute courtiers, masters of the prince, arbiters of favour and disgrace, indefatigable calumniators, barbarous persecutors. He disconcerted, confounded, and always escaped them, without giving them the consolation of seeing him make one false step; he made them tremble even when he was flying before them, and when he was buried alive in the tomb of his father *. He read hearts and futurity. Some Catholics were persuaded that God revealed to him the designs of his enemies; the Arians accused him of magic; and the Pagans pretended that he was

---

* Under Valens he concealed himself in the sepulchre of his father, and remained there four months. Among the ancients, particularly in Ægypt, sepulchres were buildings in the open country, so considerable that there were apartments in them. *M. Fleury*, l. XVI. 10. B.

versed

HISTORY OF JOVIAN.

versed in the science of auguries, and that he understood the language of the birds *; so true it is that his prudence was a kind of divination. No one discerned better than he the seasons to disclose or to conceal himself; those of speech or silence; of action or repose. He knew how to fix the inconstancy of the people (the Alexandrians, which is saying all), to find a new country in the places of his exile, and the same credit at the extremity of Gaul, in the city of Treves, as in Ægypt, and the very bosom of Alexandria; to keep up correspondences; to procure protections; to unite the orthodox; to encourage the most timid; of a weak friend never to make an enemy; to excuse weaknesses with a charity and goodness of heart, which shewed, that, if he condemned rigorous methods in matters of religion, it was less from interest than principle and character.

---

* This we learn from Ammianus: " It was said, that " being thoroughly skilled in soothsaying, and in what " was portended by augural birds, he sometimes foretold " future events." It is related on this subject, that as Athanasius was passing through the streets of Alexandria on the eve of a festival which the Pagans were to celebrate with great festivity, a raven was heard to croak. " What " says that bird?" exclaimed the Pagan populace. Athanasius answered smiling, " He says, *cras*" (which signifies in the Roman language, " to-morrow)," " and declares to " you that the Emperor of the Romans forbids you to cele- " brate your festival." On the morning after, the prohibition of the Emperor did not fail to arrive. SOZOMEN. B.

A prophecy, or rather a joke, is related by Sozomen, (l. iv. c. 10.) which evidently proves, if the crows speak Latin, that Athanasius understood their language. GIBBON.

VOL. II.   Z   Julian,

HISTORY OF JOVIAN.

Julian, who did not persecute the other bishops, at least openly, considered the taking away his life as a piece of great policy, thinking that the fate of Christianity was attached to that of Athanasius. This honourable distinction seemed to have completed the glory of the holy bishop, when he repaired to Jovian. He was then about seventy years old; but his career was not ready to close. After having made him triumph over three former Emperors *, God destined him to gain other victories over Valens †.

We are ignorant of the particulars of the advice which Athanasius gave to Jovian; but we may be certain, that he confirmed him in the design of labouring only in a Christian manner to re-unite Christians; and that he made him understand that it was previously necessary to inspire all parties with principles of kindness; to teach them to bear with one another; to desire and to seek peace, till it should please God to accomplish it. At the same time he disclosed to him the snares of the sectaries, some of whom at least had formed projects of conquest on a prince who was not sufficiently instructed in theological matters to distin-

---

* That is, of Constantine (in the latter years of his reign deceived by the Arians), Constantius, and Julian. B.

† The Jansenists have often compared Athanasius and Arnauld, and have expatiated with pleasure on the faith and zeal, the merit and exile, of those celebrated doctors. This concealed parallel is very dexterously managed by the Abbé de la Bleterie. GIBBON.

guish

guish by himself what characterises error, when it borrows the features of truth.

Arrian and Candidus, pure Arians, ordained bishops by the famous Ætius *, both relations of the Emperor, were gone to meet him at Edessa; and Jovian, if we may believe Philostorgius, had, in speaking to them, expressed a kind of neutrality which might give them some hope, though his answer might be only the effect of his moderation. They had followed him, without doubt, to Antioch; and it is also known that Euzoïus, bishop of that great city, and some other Arians, already practised upon the eunuchs of the palace, having not forgotten that, by that method, they had gained the favour of Constantius, and reigned in his name. All the leaders of parties besieged Jovian to obtain his permission to persecute their enemies. We may judge of their respective pretensions by the petition of the Macedonians, who demanded to be put into possession of the churches which were occupied by the pure Arians. The Emperor contented himself with replying, "I hate disputes: I love and honour those who have peaceable views, and who concur in union." These words, proceeding from the mouth of the sovereign, and coming from the bottom of his heart, were an effectual stroke, and immediately chilled the warmest disputants. They held a council in Antioch, where the Arians of the party of Acacius of Cæsarea in Palestine

* See Vol. I. p. 2. note *.

communicated with Meletius, one of the two Catholic bishops of that city, and subscribed to the form of Nice. The sincerity of their signature is questioned; but if they betrayed their conscience, it was not the fault of Jovian, who declared plainly that he would not constrain any one, and who said it sincerely. He was not so successful in terminating the schism of the Catholics of Antioch, divided between Meletius and Paulinus. Fraternal dissensions are always the most obstinate.

Though Jovian shewed very great regard for Athanasius, the Arians of Alexandria, supported clandestinely by Euzoïus, made some attempts to prevent his returning to his church. After the tragical death of their bishop, George of Cappadocia, which happened in the time of Julian *, they had cast their eyes on a priest named Lucius, a man of very bad looks, and of a still worse character, who did not fail to justify their choice by the cruelties which he committed in the persecution of Valens. The Arians of Alexandria, for some reason that is not known, had not yet caused him to be ordained. They sent deputies to Jovian, and Lucius at their head; wishing to have him for their bishop, or, at least, any other that the Emperor would give them to the exclusion of Athanasius. The Catholics of Alexandria sent deputies also on their part, to oppose the efforts of the Arians; the latter addressed the Emperor several

* See the IXth and Xth Epistles of Julian, p. 17—23.

times. We have the original relation of the different audiences which he gave them *. It is a curious remain in many respects. Above all, Jovian is there seen drawn to the life: he there shews firmness, sense, judgement, and equity, something blunt and military, a lively disposition, and, if I mistake not, a taste rather than a talent for raillery. But I am wrong to forestall the reader; let him judge for himself †.

[The Emperors, who originally were only generals of the army, were accustomed to exercise with their soldiers. There was near every city a place for exercise, called, " The field of Mars," or, " The field.]" One day, when Jovian [attended by his guard] was going on horseback through the Roman gate to the field of Mars, Lucius, Berniccus, and the other [deputies of the] Arians, approached him, saying, " We beg " your power, your majesty, your piety, to give " us audience." ' Who, and whence are you?' said Jovian. They answered, " Sir, we are Chris- " tians." ' Whence, and of what city?' added the Emperor. " Of Alexandria," replied the Arians. ' What do you desire of me?' said the Emperor. " We beseech your majesty," said they, " to give " us a bishop." ' I have ordered Athanasius,' re-

---

* *Petitio Arianorum ad Jovian. inter opera Athan.* t. I. *p.* 782. B.

† I give this account entire, having taken care to inclose within crotches all that is not in the acts themselves, and yet was necessary to facilitate the understanding them.

plied

plied Jovian, ' to return to his see.' "Sir," said the Arians, "Athanafius has been banifhed many years for crimes of which he is not cleared." Then a foldier [a Catholic, of the Emperor's guard] in the tranfport of his zeal, took the liberty to fay, ' Sir, give yourfelf the trouble to examine who are thefe people, and whence they come. They are the miferable remains of the faction of Cappadocia, the agents of George, of that villain, who defolated the city of Alexandria, and the whole world.' At thefe words, the Emperor fpurred his horfe, and went to the field.

They prefented themfelves a fecond time, and faid, ' We have feveral heads of accufation againft Athanafius, which we are able to prove. It is thirty years fince he was banifhed by Conftantine and Conftantius, of immortal memory. He has been banifhed lately by the beloved of God, the moft philofophical * and moft happy Julian.' "The accufations of ten, twenty, thirty years," faid the Emperor, " are obfolete. Speak no more to me of Athanafius. I know why he was accufed, and how he was banifhed."

[So firm an anfwer did not repulfe the Arians. They returned to the charge a third time.] "We

* It is difficult to conceive that perfons who profeffed Chriftianity, and, befides, were fpeaking to a Chriftian Emperor, fhould have been fo irreligious, fo abfurd, as to give Julian thefe epithets.

Muft there not have been fome interpolation here? B.

"have,"

HISTORY OF JOVIAN.

" have," said they," " new complaints against Atha-
" nasius." [The deputies of the Catholics of Alexandria beginning, as it seems, to speak at the same time], " Jovian said, ' When all speak together, it
' is impossible to understand who is in the right.
' Choose two persons on each side; for I cannot
' answer both of you.' The Catholics began.. " Sir,"
said they, " these men, whom you see, are the re-
" mains of the detestable George, the scourge of
" our province. They do not suffer in the cities any
" senator"... The Arians [wishing to cut short an account which would have covered them with confusion, and perceiving, besides, that Lucius, a creature of George, would never be approved by the Emperor, interrupted the Catholics by saying], ' Be so
' kind, Sir, as to set over us whomever you please,
' except Athanasius.' " I have already told you," replied the Emperor, " what concerns Athanasius is
" settled;"—and in an angry tone, he said to his guard in Latin, " *Feri, feri,*" that is to say, " Strike,
" strike *." [The order, without doubt, was not executed, as the Arians persisted.] ' Sir,' said they, ' if you send back Athanasius, our city is
' ruined; and, besides, no one associates with him.'
" I have, however,' said Jovian, " made en-
" quiries; and I am assured, that he thinks well,
" that he is orthodox, and that he teaches sound

---

* Jovian spoke Greek to the Alexandrians. It is probable that the Emperors always spoke Latin to their guard.   B.

" doctrine."

"doctrine." 'It is true,' replied the Arians, 'that he speaks well; but he thinks ill.' The Emperor said, "I require no other testimony than that which you have given him. If he thinks ill, he must give an account of it to God. We men hear words; God alone knows the bottom of the heart." 'Sir,' said the Arians, 'allow us to hold our assemblies *.' "Ah!" replied Jovian, "what hinders you?" 'But, Sir,' added they, 'Athanasius declares us heretics and dogmatists.' "His place obliges him," said Jovian. "It is the duty of those who teach the truth." 'Sir,' proceeded the Arians, 'he has taken away the lands of the churches †.' "You would make me believe," said Jovian, "that you are brought hither by other views than those of the faith. Retire, and live in peace. Go to church; you have an assembly to-morrow." [This was on a Saturday, or the eve of some festival.] "After the assembly, every one shall subscribe his profession of faith. You have here some bishops and Nemesinus ‡. Athanasius also is here. Those who are not instructed in the faith have only to apply themselves to him. I give you to-morrow, and the day after. I am now going to the field

---

* Συναγεσθαι.

† This perhaps is the meaning here of the word τα τεμενη. B.

‡ This Nemesinus is not known; he might be an officer employed by the Emperor to effectuate the re-union. Under Constantius we find *Nemesianus*, intendant of the finances, *comes largitionum.* B.

"of

" of Mars." A lawyer, a Cynic philosopher, then said to Jovian, ' Sir, on account of the bishop ' Athanasius the treasurer-general has taken some ' houses from me.' Jovian answered him, " If the " treasurer-general has taken some houses, is Atha-" nasius responsible for it?" Another lawyer, named Patalas, then said to him, ' I have a charge ' against Athanasius.' " What business," said the Emperor, " has a Pagan like thee to trouble him-" self with Christians?"

[During this time Lucius kept behind the other deputies. The bad situation in which he saw his affairs was likely to increase the confusion which his disadvantageous person might already have occasioned in him. He would have mingled in] the crowd of the people of Antioch, who were collected round the Emperor. But some seized him, and having made him advance, against his will, ' See, Sir,' said they, ' what a subject they wish to ' make a bishop!' [It must be remembered that Athanasius had a countenance full of nobleness and dignity *.]

Nevertheless the same Lucius [depending perhaps on some private recommendation] ventured to appear again before the Emperor at the gate of the palace, and begged an audience. Jovian stopped, and said to him, ' Lucius, is it ' thou to whom I am speaking? How camest thou ' hither? By sea or by land?' " By sea, Sir," replied Lucius. ' May the God of the universe, may

* See p. 141, note.

' the

'the sun * and the moon,' said the Emperor, 'punish the companions of thy voyage, for not having thrown thee into the sea! May the ship be eternally the sport of outrageous waves, and never arrive in port!' [Thus he delivered himself from that odious man by an ironical imprecation, in which the learned editors of Athanasius discover much wit †. I question whether every one discovers as much; nor do I know whether they will not be surprised at this fantastic assemblage of the sun and moon with the God of the universe in the mouth of a prince in other respects so religious.]

The Emperor, having learned that the Arian cabal were using indirect measures at court, and that Euzoïus had engaged Probatius, the great chamberlain, and the other eunuchs of the palace, to speak to him in favour of the Arians of Alexandria, was enraged to see that the successors of Eusebius and Bardion ‡, who had made a traffic of the favours of Constantius, should pretend to succeed to their credit. He made his eunuchs undergo the torture to discover the bottom of the intrigue; and said, "that he would "treat in the same manner the first [of his do-"mesticks] who should dare to solicit him against "the Christians." After having begun the work

---

* It is in the Greek Κομπῆης ηλιος, "the blazing sun." B.
† See the Latin Life of Athanasius, which is prefixed to the new edition; *et facetè quidem.* B.
‡ Braudion in the French; but in the Greek, Βαρδιων.

HISTORY OF JOVIAN.

of re-union, as far as time would permit, under the eyes and direction of Athanasius, he allowed him to return into Ægypt, and remained impressed with esteem for his virtues and talents *.

With such zeal for the Christian religion, Jovian, one would think, must have succeeded at Antioch better than his predecessor. But the city was filled with Arians, or with persons who thought themselves such; and the Arian sects deemed themselves persecuted when they could not persecute. Besides, the inhabitants of Antioch remained in possession of the faculty of despising all their sovereigns, or at least of turning them into ridicule. What prince could have found favour in their sight? They did not spare Marcus Aurelius. Some Emperors had punished those insolent people. Most had connived at their insults,

---

* Athanasius at the court of Antioch is agreeably represented by La Bleterie. He translates the singular and original conferences of the Emperor, the primate of Ægypt, and the Arian deputies. The Abbé is not satisfied with the coarse pleasantry of Jovian; but his partiality for Athanasius assumes, in his eyes, the character of justice.

GIBBON.

As soon as Athanasius had gained the confidence, and secured the faith, of the Christian Emperor, he returned in triumph to his diocese, and continued, with mature counsels and undiminished vigour, to direct, ten years longer, the ecclesiastical government of Alexandria, Ægypt, and the Catholic church. The true æra of his death is perplexed with some difficulties. But the date (A. D. 373, May 2.) which seems the most consistent with history and reason, is ratified by his authentic life (*Maffei Osservazioni Letterarie*, tom. III. p. 81.) *Ibid.*

3   Julian

Julian had lately revenged himself with his pen. But Antioch was a city that was incorrigible, was reckoned such, and abused its reputation. Jovian was not well received. The treaty of peace, and the cession of Nisibis, furnished the jokers with a thousand sarcastic strokes. They had ridiculed Julian for his beard, his diminutive stature, his temerity. As for Jovian, he was treated as a second Paris: "he has," it was said, "the good looks and per- "son of the Trojan prince. He has, like him, "ruined his nation. O that he had perished in "the war! He should be sent back into Persia "to commence another treaty. His person was "formed at the expence of his mind. The measure "of his stature is that of his folly." The walls were covered with abusive bills, the streets and squares were strewed with verses of Homer, applied, or parodied, in the most insulting manner *. In the Hippodrome a man of the dregs of the people made the spectators laugh by repeating, with a loud voice, some low jests on the stature of the Emperor; and at the idea of this wretch being apprehended, the people revolted. This sedition might have had dreadful consequences, if the præfect Sallust the second had not quelled it; and that required all his authority.

* The libels of Antioch may be admitted on very slight evidence.   GIBBON.

HISTORY OF JOVIAN.

These facts, though taken from the fragments of a Greek monk *, an historian little known, are no more than probable and suitable to the character of the inhabitants of Antioch. But what the same writer adds merits no belief. "There was," says he, "in Antioch, a small temple, of very "elegant architecture, built by Hadrian, in ho- "nour of his adoptive father, Trajan. Julian had "converted it to a library, and entrusted the care "of it to the eunuch Theophilus. Jovian, at the "instigation of his wife, reduced it to ashes, with "all the books that it contained." But, what is more surprising, the author makes Jovian march to this expedition at the head of his seraglio, with a torch in his hand †, just as Alexander formerly, with the courtesans of Greece, burned the palace of Persepolis.

I am far from suspecting the Greek monk of inventing so ridiculous a story, and of intentionally blackening Jovian. He copied, without discernment, some enemy of that prince, Eunapius perhaps, an historian very envenomed against the Christian Emperors. That the morals of Jovian

---

* John of Antioch, whose history began with the creation of the world, and closed with the reign of Phocas. B.

† Αὐτῶν τῶν παλλακίδων ὑφαπλυσῶν μίλα γιλῶτος τὴν πυρὰν. "The harlots themselves with laughter lighting the pile." SUIDAS.

He might be *edax, et vino Venerique indulgens*. But I agree with La Bleterie in rejecting the foolish report of a Bacchanalian riot (*ap. Suidam*) celebrated at Antioch, by the Emperor, his *wife*, and a troop of concubines. GIBBON.

were

were not very regular we may believe, if we please, on the word of Ammianus Marcellinus, though according to the judicious reflection of Ammianus himself, on the subject of another Emperor, the malignity, or corruption, of mankind, is accustomed to lend frailties to princes who have them not *. However, if Jovian had lived in a public and scandalous irregularity, the Christians would not have loaded him with praises at a time when no one had any thing more to hope or fear from him. The concurrence of the Empress with the mistresses of the Emperor is also something very singular. But by what caprice could the wife of Jovian, Cariton, to whom her father, Lucillian, had, without doubt, given a Roman education, suitable to the rank which he himself held in the state, have wished to burn a temple, which was no longer a temple, but a library? To annihilate the remains of profane literature is a Mussulman taste, which never prevailed among Christians, especially in the fourth century, when the most celebrated men in the church were at the same time the most conversant with the sciences of the Greeks. Besides, we shall presently see that the wife of Jovian was not then with him. In short, the silence of Ammianus and Zosimus completes the destruction of this calumny, and even renders what I have just

---

* It is supposed that they would do all that they can with impunity. *Quod crimen etiamsi non invenit malignitas, fingit in summarum licentiâ potestatum.* B.

mentioned, of the ribaldry of Antioch againſt Jovian, in ſome degree ſuſpicious.

Neither of them ſay a word of what happened during his reſidence in that city. Ammianus contents himſelf with relating ſeveral natural events which the Pagan ſuperſtition conſidered as fatal preſages. The ſtatue of Maximian, placed in the veſtibule of the palace, loſt on a ſudden the [brazen] globe (a ſymbol of the empire) which it held in its hand. A dreadful noiſe was heard in the council-room. Comets were ſeen in the day-time *. The Emperor, too intelligent to be alarmed by theſe pretended ſigns of the wrath of heaven, but filled with a thouſand anxieties on account of the provinces of the Weſt, of which he had received no intelligence, ſet out with his army in the month of December. Forced marches, and the rigour of the ſeaſon, deſtroyed a great number of men and horſes.

At Tarſus he paid the laſt duties to Julian, according to Socrates, and gave him a ſolemn funeral. Ammianus only ſays, that he ordered his

---

* Ammianus, who is very ready to diſplay his erudition, here relates the various ſentiments of the ancient philoſophers on comets, and concludes with the opinion of Pythagoras, which ſeems then to have had the preference: " that they are ſtars, like the reſt, but that we are igno-" rant of their revolutions." *Stellas eſſe quaſdam cæteris ſimiles, quarum ortus obituſque, quibus ſint temporibus præſtituti, humanis mentibus ignorari.* B.

tomb

tomb to be decorated *. This order was executed under Valentinian and Valens, with much attention, on their part, and even with sufficient magnificence. To give some idea of it, it is enough to say, that Libanius was satisfied. Thus three Christian Emperors, whom Julian had molested on account of their religion, concurred in granting him that frivolous reward of his frivolous virtues, or rather that prerogative annexed to the rank in which God had placed him in the world. Humanity, decorum, policy, and even religion authorised their conduct; and Jovian did not foresee, that, at the end of twelve centuries, his having buried the dead, and expressed some regard for the talents of the man, the Emperor, and the nephew of the great Constantine, would be imputed to him as a crime †.

Though we have no incontestible proofs of the apotheosis of Julian, there is no doubt that the

---

* Zonaras says the same in these words ; ιξ Αντιοχειας δι εις Ταρσον γεγονως, και το μνημα κοσμησας τε Ιελιανε επαινει." " Going from Antioch to Tarsus, he honoured Julian by " adorning his tomb." He also relates that the corpse of Julian was afterwards removed from Tarsus to Constantinople; which is confirmed by Cedrenus.   VALOIS.

† Baronius, in his Annals, considers the premature death of Jovian as the punishment of his having commanded the adorning the tomb of a wretch who deserved to be thrown into the highway, *hominis alioqui ne cæspititiâ quidem sepulturâ digni.*   B.

The Abbé de la Bleterie handsomely exposes the brutal bigotry of Baronius, who would have thrown Julian to the dogs.   GIBBON.

senate

senate of Rome, whose members were still almost all idolaters, paid him an honour due by right to the Emperors, unless a process was instituted against their memory. Even the Christian princes were deified. There was no medium: they must be ranked among the Gods, or numbered among the tyrants. Many cities, in which Paganism prevailed, associated Julian with their tutelar deities. Some of his credulous adorers thought that they perceived some effects of his power; while it was said by the Christians, that the ashes of that apostate stirred in the tomb. A report was even spread that the earth, by a violent shock, had discharged them from her bosom. There, however, they remained, when, writing in the reign of Theodosius, Ammianus judged the city of Tarsus little worthy of such a treasure. This historian, a soldier, wished to have seen Julian on the banks of the Tiber among the first Cæsars *; and Libanius, entirely a man of letters, would have been better pleased with him in the Academy by the side of the divine

---

* xv. 10. The passage deserves to be transcribed: *Cujus suprema et cineres . . . non Cydnus videre deberet, quamvis gratissimus amnis et liquidus; sed ad perpetuandam gloriam recte factorum præterlambere Tiberis, intersecans urbem æternam, divorúmque veterum monumenta præstringens.* B.

" Whose obsequies and ashes should not have been seen
" by the Cydnus, though a most pure and limpid stream,
" but, to perpetuate the glory of his good deeds, should
" have been laved by the Tiber, which intersects the
" eternal city, and chills the monuments of the ancient
" Gods."

Plato *. Either in the field of Mars, or in the Lyceum, Julian would have been placed with propriety. On the contrary, he would have been remarkably mifplaced, if, as the modern Greeks pretend, he had been afterwards removed from Tarfus to Conftantinople, and interred among the Chriftian princes in the church of the Holy Apoftles. Who could have made that auguft temple fo ftrange a prefent? This kind of digreffion will, I hope, be excufed. To the hiftory, that I am writing, nothing that relates to Julian is foreign.

Jovian, continuing to make long marches, paffed through Tyana in Cappadocia, where Procopius, the fecretary of ftate, and the tribune Memoridus, who had been difpatched into the Weft, brought him the following intelligence. Lucillian, his father-in-law, on arriving at Milan, had learned that Malarich, that confidential Frank appointed by the new Emperor to command the troops in Gaul, in the room of Jovinus, refufed to accept that employment. Upon that, the Count had fpeedily paffed the Alps, and repaired to Rheims, with Valentinian and the tribune Seniauchus. He

---

* *Orat. Parent.* c. 156. p. 377. Τᵘτον εδεξατο μεν το προ Ταρσων της Κιλικιας χωριον, ειχε δ' αν δικαιοτερον το της Ακαδημιας πλησιον Πλατωνος. B.

" The fuburb of Tarfus in Cilicia received him; but he had a greater right to be buried in the Academy near the tomb of Plato."

The hiftory of princes does not very frequently renew the example of a fimilar competition.   GIBBON.

HISTORY OF JOVIAN.

had found Gaul tranquil and submissive to Jovian. But without considering that the authority of his son-in-law was not sufficiently established, he undertook to proceed against some officers with a premature severity. A criminal, apprehensive of being punished for his misdemeanours, sought an asylum among some troops of Batavians *, who were probably quartered in the neighbourhood of Rheims. To induce them to take him under their protection, he assured them that Jovian was only an usurper who had revolted against Julian; but that Julian was living, and would soon make that rebel sensible of it, if he had not already; and that the most essential service which subjects could render to their lawful sovereign was to exterminate the emissaries of a tyrant, who came to surprise the fidelity of the people, and to engage them in their revolt. This Roman, indiscreet as he was, found credit among people that were simple, and besides affectionate to Julian. They took arms, and massacred Lucillian and the tribune Seniauchus. Valentinian (who in a few months was to reign) owed his life to the care which his host took to secrete him. The Batavians, having soon discovered the

---

* Ammianus only says, *ad militaria signa confugit*, without mentioning the Batavians. Zosimus names them, but extremely mutilates all this history, and places the scene at Sirmium. It appears, however, by the *Notitia* of the empire, that there were Batavians at Condren, in the second Belgic, of which Rheims was the capital. *Præfectus Laterum Batavorum Contraginenfium, Noviomago Belgicæ secundæ.* B.

imposition, returned to their duty. As, on the refusal of Malarich, Jovinus had retained the command of the troops, he dispatched the principal officers to Jovian, to assure him of the submission of the army and himself *. Procopius and Memoridus, accompanied by Valentinian, proclaimed the approaching arrival of his deputies.

The Emperor, to reward the zeal of Valentinian, gave him the second [school, or] company of targetteers, of his domestic guards, and sent Arinthæus immediately with a letter to Jovinus, by which he confirmed that general in his post, and enjoined him to punish the author of the imposition, and to send the principal leaders of the sedition to court, loaded with irons.

At the little town of Aspuna †, in Galatia, the deputies from the army of Gaul met Jovian, who having given them a public audience with extreme satisfaction, made them presents, and ordered them to return immediately to their respective employments.

He entered Ancyra ‡ at the end of the month of December; and on the first day of January, 364, he there celebrated the solemnity of his consulship. In the room of Varronian, his father,

---

* The moderation of Jovinus, master-general of the cavalry, who forgave the intention of his disgrace, soon appeased the tumult, and confirmed the uncertain minds of the soldiers.   GIBBON.

   † As he descended from mount Taurus.   *Ibid.*

   ‡ The capital of Galatia.

who

HISTORY OF JOVIAN.

who died conful elect, he had chosen for his collegue young Varronian, his son. He had been brought from Illyricum to Ancyra, where the Emperor immediately conferred upon him the title of *Nobilissimus*; a title invented for the brothers of Constantine, and afterwards given to the sons of the Emperors *. They quitted it only to assume that of Cæsar. Other princes had often raised their sons to the consulship before the time fixed by the laws; but a consul in the cradle had never yet been seen. Jovian thought it a debt to the memory of his father to substitute to that illustrious veteran an infant who bore his name. After all, this dignity, which was still called the summit of human grandeur, had no longer any functions. It served merely to denominate the years, and to perpetuate the form of the ancient government. On the day of the ceremony, when the young prince was to be placed, according to custom, in the curule chair, he expressed by obstinate cries a reluctance, which seemed a bad omen, and which was soon after considered as a kind of foresight †.

---

* The same is now the title of our dukes.

† *Cujus vagitus, pertinaciter reluctantis, ne in curuli sellâ veheretur ex more, id quod mox accidit portendebat.* Ammian. xxv. 10. Augustus, and his successors, respectfully solicited a dispensation of age for the sons or nephews, whom they raised to the consulship. But the curule chair of the first Brutus had never been dishonoured by an infant. GIBBON. See p. 290.

From Ancyra Jovian repaired to Dadaſtana, a ſmall city, or town, on the frontiers of Galatia and Bithynia, but which belonged to the firſt of theſe provinces *. There, if we credit Socrates, he received the deputies from the ſenate of Conſtantinople, who came to compliment him on his conſulſhip. Themiſtius, the chief of the deputation, there pronounced, according to the ſame hiſtorian, the panegyric of the Emperor, in which nevertheleſs are obſerved all the marks of a diſcourſe pronounced the very day that Jovian took poſſeſſion of the conſular dignity. The piece, however, is written with great elegance and dignity; but, like all that comes from the pen of Themiſtius, is rather too much loaded with learned alluſions. Some ſtrokes of flattery appear in it concerning the election of Jovian, and on the peace made with Sapor. The author extolls, with much more juſtice, the patronage with which the prince honours men of learning. The elogium principally turns on his mildneſs and equity with regard to matters of religion. The ſame orator gives him a commendation which is alone worth a panegyric; namely, that his elevation had made no change in his manner of treating mankind. He neither forgot nor ſlighted thoſe who had been his equals. He did not affect to make his ſuperiority perceived by thoſe who

---

* The Itinerary of Antoninus fixes Dadaſtana 125 Roman miles from Nice, 117 from Ancyra. Weſſeling, Itinerar. p. 142. GIBBON.

might have made him sensible of theirs. His friends, his benefactors, did not discern the change of his situation, but by the effects of his gratitude and liberality. He collected at his court the most virtuous men in the empire: he invited thither, he attached to his person, those whom disgrace, or exile, had estranged. "There were seen," according to the expression of Themistius, "watching "over the safety of his reign, the wise Nestor, the "free and generous Diomed, the Chrysantus of Cy- "rus, and the Artabazus of Xerxes." I suspect that Sallust the second is the Nestor; Valentinian might be the Diomed. I am not sufficiently acquainted with the court of Jovian to guess the two others. It is not only in modern times that orators, by way of being eloquent and figurative, express themselves in a manner sometimes ænigmatical to their contemporaries, and almost always unintelligible to posterity.

The endowments of Jovian, acknowledged by the Pagans themselves, his attention to find out persons of merit, and that talent, which in a prince may supply the place of all others, of knowing mankind, of estimating their worth, and properly employing them, announced to the Romans a wise government. Some faults, which I have not disguised, he committed. Raised on a sudden from a station of little eminence to the supreme power, to which he had never aspired even in a dream, in a manner dazzled and seduced by the fatality of circumstances,

cumstances, he made some slips on the most rugged and slippery ground in the world. But the faults of inexperience and surprise often turn to the advantage of those who commit them, when they have good sense and just intentions. Jovian was young: he might have acquired what he wanted. Ammianus could not have had a mean opinion of him, as, when he reproaches him with some vices, that author presumes that he might have corrected them through respect to his diadem. Every thing may be hoped from a monarch who respects himself so far as to find motives to become virtuous even in independence, the usual stumbling-block of virtue. The choice, which Jovian made, of his confidents and ministers, gives room to believe, that he was capable of receiving advice; and, as it is observed by one of the greatest men of the last age, " states " are generally better governed under a prince of " moderate abilities, who knows how to hear and " follow good advice, than by a sovereign of a " superior genius, who is attached to his under- " standing, and thinks himself infallible *."

The two capitals, the provinces, the armies, had acknowledged Jovian. The church was about to enjoy a profound peace: the state, united within itself, hoped to repair its losses: Jovian seemed

---

* Grotius, in his history of the war of the Netherlands, *l.* vii. under the year 1598. *Usu compertum . . . multa sæpe salubriùs gesta sub principe qui aliorum benè repertis aures et jussa commodaret, quàm si cui sapiendi fiducia contumaciam addidisset.* B.

HISTORY OF JOVIAN.

able to promise himself a long and glorious reign. Constantinople was preparing to receive him magnificently, and, impatient to possess him herself, conjured him to get the start of the prince his son. Rome, who also flattered herself with soon seeing the Emperor, was already striking medals to celebrate his arrival; his wife was coming to meet him with the pomp of an empress; when, in the night between the 16th and 17th of February [364], he was found dead in his bed, after having reigned only seven months and twenty days. This was the third Emperor who disappeared in less than three years and a half.

It is pretended that he was suffocated by the fumes of charcoal that was lighted in his chamber, to warm it, and to dry the walls which had been newly plaistered *. The danger to which Julian had been exposed at Paris †, might have put him on his guard against a like accident. Others ascribe his death to indigestion ‡, or to the attack of an apoplexy. The cause was neglected to be ascertained; without doubt, because it was thought natural: but this very negligence made many imagine it to be the effect of the wickedness of men. Am-

---

* See Ammianus Eutropius, who might likewise be present, Jerom, Orosius, Sozomen, Zosimus, and Zonaras. We cannot expect a perfect agreement, and we shall not discuss minute differences.   GIBBON.

† See the Misopogon, Vol. I. p. 236.

‡ Occasioned either by the quantity of the wine, or the quality of the mushrooms, which he had swallowed in the evening.   GIBBON.

mianus,

mianus, by saying, that "his death, like that of Scipio Æmilianus, was followed by no enquiries," insinuates, that he lost his life by some secret attack *. St. Chrysostom says expressly, that "Jovian was poisoned by his domestics." Would the eunuchs of the palace have formed a conspiracy to deprive themselves of a master who seemed not to be of a temper to suffer himself to be governed, or were they set at work by some ambitious man, such as Procopius, who, nevertheless, did not avail himself of that crime? Still it is certain, that the suspicion could not fall on the successor of Jovian. It was not till after having offered the empire to Sallust, born to deserve it, and constantly to refuse it †; it was not till after having cast their eyes on various subjects, among others on Januarius, a relation of Jovian, that the army suddenly determined [Feb. 26], in favour of Valentinian ‡, who was then absent §. The Christians

---

* Ammianus, unmindful of his usual candour and good sense, compares the death of the harmless Jovian to that of the second Africanus, who had excited the fears and resentment of the popular faction.   GIBBON.

† He enjoyed the glory of a second refusal; and when the virtues of the father were alleged in favour of his son, the præfect, with the firmness of a disinterested patriot, declared to the electors, that the feeble age of the one, and the unexperienced youth of the other, were equally incapable of the laborious duties of government.   *Ibid*.

‡ Valentinian was the son of Count Gratian, a native of Cibalis, in Pannonia, who, from an obscure condition, had raised himself, by matchless strength and dexterity, to the military commands of Africa and Britain; from which

he

tians bitterly lamented Jovian, and thought that God had only shewn him to the world, becaufe the world was not worthy of him *. A proof that it was not the fpirit of party that caufed their tears to flow, is the good that is faid of him by the Pagans. Valentinian and Valens did not prevent the fenate of Rome from placing him among the Gods †. His corpfe was carried to Conftantinople into the church of the Holy Apoftles ‡, where, long after, his tomb was feen among thofe of the other Augufti.

His wife furvived him feveral years; an inftance as memorable, but ftill more ftriking, of the infignificance of what is ftyled grandeur. She had loft in a few months a father-in law, a father, a hufband, of whofe elevation fhe only heard to feel more poignantly his lofs. That which is the refource of all other mothers, completed her unhappinefs. She had a fon; but a fon deprived of the higheft hopes, and fufpicious to the government.

---

he retired with an ample fortune and fufpicious integrity. The city of Nice in Bithynia was chofen for the place of election. Valentinian affociated his brother Valens in the empire, in one of the fuburbs of Conftantinople, thirty days after his own elevation. GIBBON.

§ In his quarters at Ancyra.

* *Oftendunt terris hunc tantum fata, neque ultra Effe finunt.* VIRG.

† This feems to me the meaning of thefe words of Eutropius: *benignitate principum qui ei fucceffierunt inter Divos relatus eft.* B.

‡ The fad proceffion was met on the road by his wife Charito. GIBBON.

The

HISTORY OF JOVIAN.

The empire was elective, and young Varronian not having been chosen Cæsar, had no right to pretend to it. Besides, Jovian had not had time to ingratiate many dependents. It was feared, however, that Varronian would sooner or later aspire to the place which his father had filled. He was still living in the year 380. A barbarous policy had already deprived him of an eye; and his mother constantly trembled for the life of that unfortunate child, who had no crime but that of being the son of an Emperor *. She was, without doubt, a Christian, and no one had ever more need of the solid consolations which Christianity alone can give. It is not certain that Jovian had conferred on her the title of *Augusta*. No medal of this princess now exists, though those of Jovian are not scarce. She was placed, after her death, in the tomb of her husband.

---

* Chrysostom, *tom.* I. *p.* 336. 344. *edit. Montfaucon.* The Christian orator attempts to comfort the widow by the examples of illustrious misfortunes; and observes, that " of " nine Emperors (including the Cæsar Gallus) who had " reigned in his time, only two (Constantine and Con-" stantius) died a natural death." Such vague consolations have never wiped away a single tear. GIBBON.

An ABSTRACT of an ESSAY,

By the Abbé de la BLETERIE,

On the Rank and Power of the ROMAN EMPERORS, in the Senate *.

From *Les Memoires de l'Academie des Sciences et Belles Lettres,* at Paris, tom. XXIV.

THE object of this Memoir is to shew the error of those who consider the imperial government as a monarchy, and to prove that it was in fact an aristocracy, the head of which, invested with the power of the civil and military magistrates, the consuls, tribunes, and generals of the ancient republic, was, after all, only the first magistrate; powerful enough indeed to oppress his country, when willing to expose himself to the risk of acting the tyrant, but also liable to be punished as such whenever she could assert her rights. Without admitting this point, the history of the Emperors must appear a heap of the grossest contradictions, a confused chaos of unaccountable facts and events, a downright school of fanaticism and rebellion; whereas, by adopting it, every obscurity vanishes, every difficulty is removed; and we

* The Abbé de la Bleterie delights to pursue the vestiges of the old constitution, and sometimes finds them in his copious fancy.   GIBBON.

are no longer surprised at seeing the senate proceed judicially against a Nero, and other such monsters, both before and after their deaths.

In the senate the Emperor sat between the two Consuls. His curule chair did not, by any thing that appears, differ in any respect from theirs. The privilege, granted to Caius [*], of sitting on a tribunal so high that it was impossible to reach him, did not descend to his successors. Neither Tiberius nor Augustus had ever any guards in the senate. Tiberius, indeed, in the twentieth year of his reign, asked leave to introduce with him Macro, Præfect of the Prætorium, accompanied by a small number of other officers; and the senate permitted him to bring in as many military men as he thought proper; but this concession, of which that prince, as he never returned to Rome, never had occasion to avail himself, became so precarious, as to be renewed for Caius, and then for Claudius, after whom the Emperors generally appeared in the senate with one or two Præfects of the Prætorium.

The meetings of the senate were either ordinary, the number of which was fixed to two for every month, or extraordinary, being called, as the exigence of affairs seemed to require, by the Consul in possession of the *fasces*, the Prætor, in the absence of the Consuls, or the Tribune, in certain

---

[*] Caligula.

cases, which it is not easy to determine. The Emperors, without being Consuls for the year, had the privilege of calling extraordinary meetings of the senate; first, as invested with the tribunitian power; secondly, by virtue of the concession made to Augustus, A. U. C. 732; thirdly, as perpetual Consuls. Most of the Emperors, when at Rome, were present in the senate; and all, or almost all of them, acknowledged themselves inferior to it, at least in some respects. They addressed it as suppliants or petitioners. " I pray you, I conjure " you, I beseech you, conscript Fathers," are their common expressions. Some of them style the senators their lords and their patrons; others call them the princes of the world, and give them the title of " Your clemency, your majesty," &c. The Emperors chosen by the army always applied to the senate to confirm their election. But what were the prerogatives of the Emperor in this august assembly?

Either the Emperor was Consul for the time being, or Consul elect, or neither the one nor the other. In quality of Consul for the time being, he convened the senate, presided in it, proposed the affairs upon which it was to deliberate, collected the suffrages, and finally dismissed it; all functions attached to the consular dignity; but it was only alternately with the other Consul, his collegue, that he performed them. For a long time, the Prince, when in the exercise of the consular

sular power, wore the same kind of robes as the other Consuls *; which robes were kept in the capitol, to shew that both one and the other held from Heaven, and their fellow-citizens, the powers of which those robes were the ensigns †.

As Consul-elect, the Prince performed the functions attached to that dignity. The Consuls elect gave their votes first, and it appears that the Emperor submitted to this custom. In the early days of Rome, the Consuls for the time being never gave their votes in affairs of their own proposing; and if they sometimes voted during the Imperial goverment, it was never but in matters which the Emperor himself had laid before the senate.

The Emperor seldom presided in the senate, though actually present, unless invested with the ordinary consular dignity. This the Abbé de la Bleterie proves by a passage in Pliny the younger, who, speaking of Marcus Priscus, says, that Trajan then presided in the senate, "for he was "Consul." The Prince was often present only in quality of senator. We read that several Emperors reckoned it an honour to be members of the Senate, and to pay the tax called *glebæ senatoriæ præstatio*.

---

* That dress was a robe of purple, embroidered with silk and gold, and sometimes ornamented with costly gems.
GIBBON.

† The Emperors themselves, who disdained the faint shadow of the republic, were conscious that they acquired an additional splendor and majesty as often as they assumed the annual honours of the consular dignity. *Ibid.*

They

They never left the house till the Consul had dismissed the senators in the usual form, by the words " *Nihil vos moramur, Patres conscripti.*" There are many instances to prove, that the Emperor used to give his opinion in the senate; and that the Consul called upon him for it. This is sufficient to shew the error of Salmasius and Muret, who, from the Emperor's collecting the votes, concluded, that he never gave any himself; it being an established custom, that whatever member collected the votes never gave any himself, and the prince was, besides, superior to all the other magistrates. But, as the prince did not always preside, neither did he always collect the votes, nor was he superior to the state, of which the Consul was both the organ and the representative, when, as president of the assembly, he called upon the members for their votes. Accordingly, the senate often decided against the opinion of the Emperor, and its decrees were always considered as the voice of the state. Sometimes, it is true, the will of despotic princes was blindly followed by the senators; but even then the senate deliberated and decided sovereignly. On this occasion M. de la Bleterie observes, that authors, in general, are too apt to exaggerate the abuse which the Roman Emperors made of their authority. From the year of Rome 727, the epocha of the lawful authority of Augustus, to the first year of Diocletian, and U. C. 1037, there elapsed 310 years. Now let us, us, on the one hand, add together the reigns of all the bad Emperors, and, on the other hand, the reigns of those who were sometimes good and sometimes bad, and we shall not be able to make out above 120 years of oppression for the Romans; and even in this interval we shall find proofs of the Roman liberty subsisting, at least *de jure,* though oppressed *de facto;* so that there remain 190 years, during which the government was conformable to law, and favourable to liberty. This learned Academician has, besides, observed, in order to invalidate a fact related by Tertullian, that authors are apt to insist too much on the slavish subjection of the senate to the will of Tiberius. That Emperor, having received from Palestine an account of the miracles performed by Jesus Christ, wrote to the senate to propose placing him among the Gods; which proposal was rejected. It is true, indeed, that the senate was, at that time, both the instrument and the victim of that Emperor's cruelty, and that, therefore, it would not have refused to comply with his desire, had he discovered such earnestness to have it granted as might have been deemed an order. But the senate, no doubt, was aware, that, in order to amuse the people with a shadow of liberty, he asked, with little earnestness, what he was not solicitous to have granted. Nor was much resolution requisite to humour this grimace.

But

But if, on the one hand, the senate had a right to decide against the opinion of the Emperor, the Emperor, on the other, by virtue of his tribunitian power, had a right, by his *veto*, to hinder the decisions of the senate from being carried into execution. Besides, he presided " extraordinarily," without being Consul, by virtue of a special concession, which constituted one of the most considerable branches of the Imperial power. This prerogative is known by the name of *jus relationis*, or " right of proposing matters in the senate." This was primitively the ordinary function of the Consuls, in the absence of the Prætors, and, in certain cases, of the Tribunes. When, in the year of Rome 731, Augustus divested himself of the Consulship, which he then exercised for the eleventh time, he likewise resigned that consular prerogative. Upon which, the senate confirmed to him, in perpetuity, the tribunitian power, with the privilege of proposing, at every sitting, any one subject that he thought proper; whereas the Consul had an unlimited authority of proposing as many as he pleased. Soon after, the senate conferred upon him the right of convening it as often as he thought proper. In 735, the senate offered him, for life, the ordinary and extraordinary powers of the consulship, and he accepted them, but without assuming any title that indicated such perpetual consulship; without depriving the annual Consul of the right of performing the
public

public ceremonies, and proposing affairs to the deliberation of the senate, and perhaps too, without accepting the lictors and fasces, that were likewise offered to him. He accepted, however, first, the precedence in the senate; secondly, a tribunal, with a right of trying causes, and, probably, the general inspection of the finances; and, thirdly, the prerogative of acting as he thought proper in the pressing exigencies of the state, without waiting for the orders of the senate.

Augustus confined himself to the prerogative, that had been granted him, of proposing any one subject he thought proper, at every meeting, so that neither he, nor his successors, unless they happened to be annual Consuls, ever enjoyed an unlimited right of proposing matters to the deliberation of the senate. Accordingly we find this right conferred at every change, with fixed bounds, *jus tertiæ, quartæ, quintæ relationis*. As often as the Emperor proposed any affair to the deliberation of the senate, he became President of it, if he was not so already in quality of annual Consul, and used to ask the votes as a mere Consul might have done, but with one remarkable difference. Originally, and even under the Emperors, the magistrates in office never gave their opinion in affairs of their own proposing. The Consul who presided, and proposed the business on which the senate was to deliberate, did not call upon his collegue, nor the Prætors, nor any of the Curule magistrates,

magistrates, for their opinion. He first addressed himself to the Consuls elect, to the Prince of the senate, or first senator, to the Prætors, and other magistrates, elect, in short, to all the members of the senate not actually in office. He might indeed re-capitulate the arguments on both sides, and weigh them one against another, but without pretending to conclude upon them; which precautions were, no doubt, employed to secure to all the members a proper liberty of speech. But when the Emperor proposed any affair, the Consul and other magistrates were allowed to give their opinion. This is expressly observed by Tacitus, (*Ann*. III. 17.) in speaking of the charge brought against Piso, and his wife Placina, for the murder of Germanicus. The Abbé de la Bleterie is of opinion, that this concession, to the Consuls, of voting, was by way of compensation for the two special privileges they had before, one, of proposing any affair they thought proper, the other, of hindering the senate from deliberating upon it; and that this concession extended by degrees to the other magistrates.

This entertaining and instructive Memoir is followed by another, containing " an answer to some " objections." The first objection is, that the decisions of the Roman senate might be, and were sometimes, actually amended, and even rescinded, by the judgements of the Emperor; and that the Emperor continued in the possession of this prerogative till the reign of Hadrian, which began 140 years after that of Augustus. This we find in the Digest, *sciendum est appellari à senatu non posse principem; idque oratione Divi Hadriani effectum* *. Till then, therefore, the decrees of the senate were subject to the revision of the prince, whose authority, of course, must have been superior to that of the senate, and the whole nation.

This prohibition of Hadrian, says the Abbé de la Bleterie, proves indeed that appeals used sometimes to be made from the senate to the Emperor, and that the Emperor finally decided upon these appeals; but it does not prove, that these appeals, or the decisions given upon them, were according to law. The legal authority of the Emperor resulted entirely from his power as both Consul and Tribune. Now, neither the ordinary power of the Consul, nor even the extraordinary power, by virtue of which the Consuls might act, in pressing emergencies, without consulting the senate, gave him any right to alter the decrees of the senate, not even while the republic subsisted in its primitive form, when the senate was only the national council, and still less under its new form, when the senate represented the whole nation. As Tribune, the Emperor had a right first, to interpose both judicially and by force in favour of the oppressed, and obstruct the execution of all sentences, even those that were national: secondly, a

---

* *Lib.* XLIX. *Tit.* 2. *a quibus appellare.*

new right of trying all caufes brought into his court, either in the firft inftance, or by appeal, and of pardoning thofe who had been condemned at any other tribunal whatever. But the author has elfewhere proved, that the only appeals that could be made from the fenate to the Emperor, were thofe which preceded a final fentence. Befides, to pardon and to abfolve are different things, and, in general, inftead of giving it himfelf, he ufed to afk the fenate for the pardon of criminals.

Suetonius, it is true, feems to fay, that Tiberius cancelled fome decrees of the fenate, *conftitutiones quafdam fenatûs refcidit*; but, perhaps, thefe decrees had not as yet gone through the ufual forms. For example, a *fenatûs confultum* was confidered as little better than the project of a law, till it had been depofited in the *Ærarium*. In fuch cafes, therefore, the oppofition of the Emperor did not exceed the bounds of his authority as Tribune. Perhaps too the hiftorian means no more than that Tiberius engaged the fenators to alter fome of its decrees; an interpretation which no way clafhes either with the text or the ftyle of Suetonius. For example, he tells us, in another place *, that Vitellius, uncle to the Emperor of the fame name, " accufed Pifo of the murder of Germanicus, and " condemned him," *accufavit, condemnavitque*. Now, the fame perfon could not be both judge and accufer; and it is, befides, well known that Pifo was

* *In Vitell. c.* II. 2.

condemned by the senate on the accusation of Vitellius. This therefore must have been the meaning of Suetonius; and the word *rescidit* will admit of the same latitude. Besides, the passage of Suetonius can only be understood of the beginning of the reign of Tiberius, who not being as yet firmly seated on the throne, and being, besides, under apprehensions from Germanicus, would hardly have ventured to give any umbrage to the senate by annulling its decrees.

Suetonius, likewise tells us, that Vespasian cancelled the decree *, by which the senate had voted divine honours to Galba † : *decretum Vespasianus abolevit*. The Abbé de la Bleterie, by combining what Tacitus and Suetonius have said on this subject, proves, that, at the request of the younger Domitian, the senate by way of reparation for the

---

* Here we may observe that the superiority of the senate over the Emperor, if we may trust to Father Hardouin, is proved by the decrees of that body granting divine honours to these princes. *Neque enim consecrat*, says he, *aut in Divos reponit, nisi potestas superior eo qui consecratur*; a principle, from which he has drawn the following conclusion, which M. de la Bleterie has corroborated by so many other proofs: *Atque hinc intelligis id, quod multis aliunde constat argumentis, Imperatores Romanos senatui fuisse subjectos, a quo utique consecrabantur ii, qui hunc sibi post obitum deferri honorem in vitâ meruissent.* Note 18. on the xxxvith book of Pliny, Sect. 14.

This argument scarce proves the superiority of the senate to the living reigning prince. All that can well be deduced from it is, that the senate was superior to the Emperors when they were dead, according to the old adage, *A living dog*, &c.

† Galba, c. xxiii.

infults offered to Galba, ordered, firſt, that his ſtatues ſhould be erected again; and, ſecondly, that a column and a new ſtatue ſhould be erected to him in the forum: that Tacitus mentions only the firſt of theſe orders, and Suetonius only the ſecond. The firſt was executed; the ſecond required time; and Veſpaſian, who ſuſpected Galba of having formed a deſign upon his life, gave himſelf no trouble to haſten the execution of it; and the ſenate, being informed of the Emperor's ſuſpicions, ſuffered the project of the ſtatue and the column to drop; ſo that this part of its decree was aboliſhed by the mere non-execution of it; and the term employed by Suetonius may ſignify no more, and not a formal abrogation.

By a ſhort view, which our learned author takes, of all the Emperors before Hadrian, it appears that Caligula was the only one among them who can be proved to have made any encroachment on the juriſdiction of the ſenate; and it was, no doubt, in order to prevent ſuch encroachments for the future, that Hadrian, who was perfectly well acquainted with the rights of the Roman people, and never decided any important queſtion without the advice of the ſenate, whoſe intereſt he had very much at heart, brought in the law mentioned in the Digeſt. After all, this law only forbade appeals, after judgement had been formally given by the ſenate; till then, the parties might appeal from the ſenate to the Emperor, who, in quality of of Tribune, might interpose, of himself, *ex officio*, so as to hinder the senate from ever proceeding to judgement, though he had no right to judge himself, or call the affair to his own tribunal.

The second objection to this doctrine of the Abbé de la Bleterie is drawn from an epistle quoted by Julius Capitolinus. Macrinus, Præfect of the Prætorium, having caused Antoninus Caracalla to be assassinated, was chosen Emperor by the army [*], who did not believe him accessary to that murder. This election required confirmation by a national act. The decree of the senate, as representing the nation, that conferred on the new prince all the prerogatives of which the Imperial authority was the result, was styled, first, *lex imperii*, and afterwards, under Justinian, *lex regia*. Macrinus, therefore, wrote to the senate, requesting them to ratify what had been done by the army. He says, in his epistle, that in conjunction with the troops, he had decreed divine honours to Caracalla, adding, "You will likewise decree them to him, conscript Fathers: we have a right, as Emperor, to command you to do it; nevertheless, we only request it of you." *Et vos, Patres conscripti, ut decernatis, cum possimus imperatorio jure præcipere, tamen rogamus.*

But this epistle bears so many marks of forgery, that it is surprising M. de Tillemont should have been the only one who has discovered the imposture;

---

[*] See the Cæsars, Vol. I. p. 163.

though Tillemont, neverthelefs, for want of having narrowly examined the nature of the Imperial government, confidered the Emperors as real monarchs.

Our learned Academician fhews, that this pretended epiftle is full of contradictions, and of expreffions, which not only clafh with probability, but cuftom, and even truth. He alfo proves, that it muft have been forged by fome friend of Elagabalus, an implacable enemy of Macrinus and his fon Diadumenus. We likewife find, in the hiftory of Auguftus, two epiftles afcribed to the laft, though it is evident that they were forged with a defign to blacken Diadumenus, and to make him pafs for a monfter, of which Elagabalus did well to rid the world.

For farther particulars the reader muft be referred to the Memoir itfelf, in which he will meet with deep refearches, folid reflections, and great purity of ftyle.

ADDITIONAL NOTES.

VOLUME I.

P. 14. l. 18. Carterius. *
* Libanius, in his Life, p. 59, mentions a Carterius, who was in many respects notorious for his folly, particularly in daring to offend the august Emperors. The person above-named must probably have offended Constantius, or he would not have wanted the interest of Julian, and the assistance of Araxius. Libanius also mentions another Carterius, in his CCXLVIIIth Epistle (probably the son of the former) as an orator whom the senators of Arce in Phœnicia had enrolled among them. And in his DLXXth he apologises to Maximus for his deserting the Muses, and following Mars. Araxius was præfect of Palestine. Libanius has six Epistles to him.

P. 121. note †.
To the " Rhodian shower of gold" Libanius also alludes in his DCCCLXXIIId Epistle; and Ammianus, XVII. 7.

P. 149. To note * may be substituted this.
* Julian has here in view that passage of Homer, in the first book of the Iliad, [ver. 607.] where he says, that " every God has his mansion and throne † fabricated by " Vulcan with his own hands;" and which he repeats in another place.   SPANHEIM.

Ib. l. 18. When therefore they rise at the entrance of their Father ‡ &c.

‡ This is also taken from a passage of Homer, in the same book [ver. 533.] to this effect; that " at the approach " of their Father Jupiter all the Gods rise from their " seats, and go to meet him, and that no one waits for " him." I find, however, that the poet says the same thing of Apollo, in the Hymn which is ascribed to him, in praise of that God.   *Ibid.*

---

† In this passage Homer mentions only their mansion, or house, &c.
———— their starry domes ——
The shining monuments of Vulcan's art,   POPE, 778.

The

The shining synod of th' immortals wait
The coming God, and from their thrones of state
Arising silent, wrapt in holy fear,
Before the majesty of heaven appear, &c.   POPE, 696.

P. 151. To note † add.

† The authority of Julian, no doubt, is highly respectable; but if a person in youth carry the marks of a bad disposition, and deliberately commit atrocious actions, when his interest required them, we are still warranted to question the sincerity of his conversion, though, in a different state of his interest, even the whole tenor of his life should change.   FERGUSON.

P. 290. To note † add.

These Abantes are also mentioned by Libanius in his Orat. XIX.

P. 305. To note † add.

The Jupiter, who laments with tears of blood the death of Sarpedon, his son, had a very imperfect notion of happiness, or glory, beyond the grave.   GIBBON.

Libanius, "on hearing of the death of Julian," repeats this allusion, by saying, "I looked up to heaven, expecting "tears mixed with blood, such as Jupiter shed upon Sar- "pedon; but I did not see them; though perhaps he "poured them on the corpse, and, like the dust and blood "attendant on a battle, they were seen by few." *In Jul. Imp. Necem.*

P. 312. note ‡. Ουτ' εν λογω ατ' εν αριθμω. Substitute this.

Libanius quotes this oracle again in his MCXVIth Epistle: "But now he who is ignorant of the laws is truly an "Ægian *, of no name or rank." On which the translator has the following note:

* Αιγιευς.] In the MS incorrectly Αιγιευς, called Αιγιευς, from Αιγιον, a city of Achaia, as we learn from Stephens de Urbibus, p. 36, who quotes this oracle given to them,

Υμεις δ' Αιγιεις, ετε τριτοι, ετε τιταρτοι,

to which others add the following,

Ουτε δυωδεκατοι, ετ' εν λογω, ετ' εν αριθμω.

Compare Th. de Pinedo on this passage, p. 36. To this our author refers. Erasmus, in his Adages, p. 393, applies this to the Æginensians, deceived by the similitude of the name.   WOLFIUS.

The scholiast on Theocritus applies it to the inhabitants of Megara.

Υμεις δ' ω Μεγαρεις, κ. τ. λ.

P. 316.

ADDITIONAL NOTES.

P. 316. note *.

Calliopius, it appears from several other Epistles, was also an assistant to Libanius in his instruction of youth, one of his ushers.

P. 324. l. 8. Calliope is also honoured, &c.

† See Vol. II. p. 251. note *.

VOLUME II.

P. 14. Epistle VIII. " You are come, Telemachus.'

Libanius begins his Legation to Julian (πρεσβευτικος προς Ιουλιανον) with the same quotation.

P. 45. Epistle XXII. To LEONTIUS *.

* Consular of Palestine in 363, as appears by the title of a law, XII Cod. Theod. tit. 55. *De Decurionibus.*

This Leontius seems to be that governor of Palestine whom at that time, together with Alypius, Julian is said by Ammianus to have given a fruitless commission to re-build the temple of Jerusalem. [See p. 74. note.] To the same there are several Epistles of Libanius. He afterwards governed Palestine as Pro-consul under Theodosius the Great.

GODEFROI.

P. 46. Epistle XXIII. To HERMOGENES †.

† Libanius often mentions an Hermogenes, as Prætor of Syria, and styles him in his Life, p. 39, " the best of " magistrates." He has also two Epistles to him, viz. the MDXLIXth of Wolfius, and the XIIth of Zambicari, l. III. By the latter he appears to have had a house at Corinth. Ammianus too mentions him, XIX. 12. See Valois on the passage, and Godefroi in the prosopographia of his Theodosian Code, p. 365.

P. 69. l. 16. The garden *.

* The short description, which Julian here gives, of this Syrian garden, may be added to the few particulars of ancient gardens which Mr. Burgh has collected in a note on Mr. Mason's English Garden, p. 130. The extent is not mentioned, but by its comparison to that of Laërtes it must have been small. Of its disposition, however, we are informed, which was far from happy. The pot-herbs and fruit-trees were planted in the middle, the latter, in that

hot

hot climate, not requiring walls to force them, and there was not only a grove of cypresses, but a row of those trees was also ranged along the walls, it being, like the Italian gardens described by Bishop Burnet, walled round, and by this double fortification, as it were, completely excluded from a view of the country.

P. 90. l. 2.

"Diogenes," says Libanius, "was a native of Synope, and the uncle of Aristophanes." See Vol. I. p. 317.

P. 148. l. 7. swallows.†

† In like manner his master Libanius (Ep. XLIV.) compares chattering and long letters to swallows, birds that are noisy in the summer, and fly to and fro. WOLFIUS.

P. 199. Add to note *.

By the Epistles above-mentioned of Libanius, Eutherius appears to have been præfect of Armenia, and to have had a son under his tuition.

P. 227. Add to the second paragraph of the note:

In a subsequent work Libanius deems both these events presages of the death of Julian. "This," says he, "was predicted by the temple of Apollo destroyed by fire. The God forsook the earth, as it was soon to be polluted. This was also foretold by the earthquakes convulsing all the ground as harbingers of approaching disturbance and confusion." *In Jul. Imp. Necem*, p. 258.

P. 246. Among the gardens of antiquity to which Milton, b. iv. compares and prefers his "Paradise of Eden," is

"That sweet grove
"Of Daphne by Orontes."

P. 247. Add to note *.

Libanius in his Life, p. 47, 8. mentions the Olympics which were celebrated on his 50th birth-day; which must have been in the year 364, the year after the death of Julian. "At these," says he, "I had an ardent desire to be present; but on the first day was imprisoned, not by the Prætor, but by a severe attack of the gout."

INDEX.

INDEX
TO
VOLUME II.

A.
                                                Page

ÆTIUS, bishop, Julian writes to him   78
       a note on that Epistle, by Fabricius   200
Alexander, the Great, his figure in miniature 15. the founder of Alexandria 20. his esteem for Homer 30. (note) conspired against by Hermolaus 166. his cruelties   167
Alexandrians, Julian writes to them   19. 64. 136. 155.
Alypius, of Antioch, Julian writes to him   73. 76
    —— commissioned by Julian to re-build the temple of Jerusalem   74 (note)
    —— banished by Valens   *ibid.* 220 (note)
    —— author of a geographical work   76
Amerius, Julian writes to him   93
Amida, city of, is enlarged. Jovian builds a suburb there for the inhabitants of Nisibis   308
Ammianus, Marcellinus, his opinion of the treaty of Dura   289
Amogila, Julian intercedes for her   200
Amphion, fragment on   207
Anacreon, quotation from   38
Ancyra, Jovian celebrates there the solemnity of his consulship   356
Antioch, people of, Julian writes to them 189. rejoice at his death 293. the stay that Jovian makes there 311. schism of the church 314. their unworthy treatment of Jovian   348

Vol. II.   C c   *Antiochus,*

INDEX.

	Page
Antiochus, tutor of Julian's sons (so called)	196
Apis, grief at his death	241
Apollo, Daphnæan, statue of described 249. destroyed	250
Areus, a friend of Augustus	139
Argives, Julian intercedes for them	83
Arianism, a cruel and persecuting sect	314
Arintheus, a great general, sent by Jovian to Sapor	276
—— receives baptism	277 (note)
Aristænetus, præfect of Bithynia 218. Monody on by Libanius 227 (note) his death	237
Aristomenes, Julian writes to him	7
Aristophanes, quotation from	47
—— of Corinth	193
Aristotle, quotation from	49
Arsaces, satrap of Armenia, Julian writes to him	186
this epistle probably is spurious 187 (note) deserved to be disgraced by Julian, and why	281
is abandoned by Jovian *ibid.* his death *ibid.* (note)	
Arsacius, high-priest of Galatia, Julian writes to him	127
Artabius, Julian writes to him	13
Astydamas, proverbially, a self-commender	27. 159
Athanasius, archbishop of Alexandria, banished by Julian 64, 5. recalled by Jovian, who writes to him 330. answers Jovian 333. comes to Antioch 334. his character 335. compared to Arnauld 338. — (note) returns to Alexandria 347. his death *ib.* (note)	
Athens, its foundation by Cecrops 232. named by Minerva	233 (note)
Augustus, the tribunitian power confirmed to him in perpetuity	371

B.

Baronius, his brutal bigotry exploded	352 (note)
Basil (not the Great), Julian writes to him	26
Batnæ described	68, 69. 383
Berea, city of, Julian arrives there 66. attempts in vain to pervert the senate 67. firmness of one of the chief citizens	*ibid.* (note)
Besançon, city of	97 (note)
Bineses, a Persian satrap 282 (note) takes possession of Nisibis	297, 8
Bleterie, John Philip René de la, account of	397

Bostre-

INDEX.

	Page
Bostrenians, Julian writes to them	242

Boys, ordered by Julian to be instructed in sacred
    music   153
Byzantines, Julian writes to them 24. Perhaps Bisanthians   25 (note)

C.

Caligula, the only Emperor who encroached on the
    jurisdiction of the senate   377
Callimachus, quotation from   77
Callippus, the Athenian, deceived Plato   161
Callixene, priestess of Ceres. Julian writes to her   43
Cappadocians, Julian is disgusted with them, and why 8 (note)
    their religion   9 (note)
Carrhæ, inhabitants of, murder the messenger who
    announced the death of Julian   291, 2
Celts, explained   31 (note)
Chabrias, a fable of   160
Chamber of justice   46 (note) 59 (note)
Charito, wife of Jovian 349, 50. goes to meet him
    361. it is not thought that he gave her the title
    of *Augusta*   364
Christians practise all virtues by the confession of Julian 128. long abstained from blood, and from
    things strangled 182 (note) their joy at the death
    of Julian 292. their divisions 313. their disputes
    are renewed 317. lament Jovian   363
Christianity, necessary to mankind   131 (note)
Church, state of, when Jovian came to the empire   314, &c.
Cimmerian darkness   149
Cimon, a natural son of Libanius   222 (note)
Constans, Emperor   159
Constantinople, people of Julian, writes to them   184
    this epistle ascribed by Wolfius to Libanius *ib*. (note)
Constantius, Emperor   28. 46. 78. 197
Consuls, their functions   368
Corduenne, its situation   260
Corinth, its origin and destruction   231, 2
Corinthians oppress the Argives   85, &c.
Council of Antioch   339

INDEX.

D.
	Page
Dadastana, city of, Jovian receives there the deputies from the senate of Constantinople	358
Damascus, praises of	51
Daniel, a prophecy of, perverted perhaps by Julian 58 (note)	
Daphnæan temple of Apollo burnt 243 (note) 250, &c. described	249, &c.
Daphne, its beauty	68. 246
Dead, custom of the Pagans in funerals	309
Delany, Dr.	286 (note)
Democritus, his consolation of Darius	94
Didymæan oracle, quoted	177
Diodorus, bishop of Tarsus	205
Diogenes, the philosopher 90. Julian writes to him	201
Dionysius, Julian writes to him 158. his cowardice	160
his drunken abuse 165. his blunders 169. perhaps commander in Greece	210 (note)
Divination of Heathens under Valens 219. inquisition into it	ib. (note)
Donatists, furious schismatics	316
Dositheus, Julian writes to him	79
Dura, city of, Julian loses four days there 272. ignominious treaty of	280

E.
Ecdicius, præfect of Ægypt, Julian writes to him	11. 17. 134. 153
Ecebolus, the sophist, Julian writes to him	39
——— chief magistrate of Edessa, Julian writes to him	118
Echo, the wife of Pan	151
Edessa, city of, persecuted by Julian 118. zeal of its inhabitants for the Christian religion 119 (note) Jovian arrives there	310
Edict of Julian relating to physicians 63. to professors 110 forbidding the Christians to teach polite literature 111 relating to profaners of tombs, and concerning funerals	189
Eleusinian pontiff	50 (note)
Elpidius, the philosopher, Julian writes to him	154
Ethnarchs, chiefs of the Jews till the beginning of the Vth century	58 (note)
Enagrius, Julian writes to him	122

INDEX.

	Page
Euclid, the philosopher, Julian writes to him	204
Eugenius, the philosopher, Julian writes to him	38
Eumenius and Pharianus, Julian writes to them	152
Euripides, quotations from 164 (note) 237 (note)	247
Eusebius and Bardion, eunuchs of Constantius	346
Euzoius, an Arian bishop of Antioch	339

F.

Fabricius John Albert, his *Lux Evangelii* 193 (note) 196 (note) his Life of Libanius translated 216—226
Fame, a Dæmon   163
Fragments of Epistles   207—211
Florentius, præfect of Gaul, Julian complains of him   36

G.

Galen, quotation from   49 (note)
Gaul, army of sends deputies to Jovian   356
George, archbishop of Alexandria, his library 17. 92. his massacre   18 (note)
———— the Catholic, Julian writes to him   14. 151
Grasshoppers described 110 (note) loquacious   165
Greeks, the ten thousand, retreat of   259. 283 (note)
Gregory, duke, Julian writes to him   73
———— Nazianzen, his discourse against Julian   291. 312

H.

Hadrian, Emperor, builds a temple to Trajan   349
Hatra, city of, Jovian arrives there   285
———— its history   286
Hector, son of Parmenio, drowned   167
Hercynian forest, fragment on   211
Hermogenes, late præfect of Ægypt, Julian writes to him 46. prætor of Syria   383
Herodotus, quotations from 45. 47. fragment on 208. account of   ibid. (note)
Hesiod, quotations from   41. 87.
Hippocrates, quotations from 49. 161. mistaken by Julian   161 (note)

Homer,

INDEX.

              Page

Homer, quotations from 14. 16. 33. 39. 40. 41. 45. 48. 51. 54. 55. 56. 82. 94. 100. 106. 108 (note) 110 (note) 114 (note) 121. 124. 130. 133. 148. 149 (note) 150 (note) 164 (note) 168. 195. 203. 229 (note) 230 (note) 238 (note) 247 (note) 249 (note).

Hundred, preferable to all other numbers, and why   53

J. and I.

Jamblichus, Julian writes to him 80. 101. 107. 148. 171. 174. Two philosophers must be distinguished of that name 70 (note) 80 (note).

Januarius, a relation of Jovian, thought of for Emperor 362

Jerusalem, temple of, attempt to re-build, defeated 61, 62 (note) 74 (note)

Jews, community of, Julian addresses them 57. less odious to the Pagans than the Christians, and why   183 (note)

Imperial government, an aristocracy   365

John of Antioch, his history   349

JOVIAN, conducts the corpse of Constantius to Constantinople, 262. rather chooses to quit the service than renounce his faith, 263. His character, 264. chosen Emperor, 265. declares that he cannot command Pagans, 266. listens to the proposals of Sapor, 276. reasons which induce him to accept the peace, 281, 2. passes the Tigris, 284. causes his election to be announced to the provinces of the West, 289. encamps under the walls of Nisibis, and obliges the inhabitants to evacuate it, 296, &c. enters Antioch, 311. regulates matters of religion, 319. makes a law to allow liberty of conscience, *ibid.* restrictions which he puts upon that liberty, 322, 3. treats with some respect the philosophers who were in the train of Julian, 325. writes in favour of the Christians, 327. recalls those who were banished on account of religion, and restores to the churches their privileges, 328. makes a law in favour of the virgins consecrated to God, *ibid.* writes to Athanasius, and invites him to court, 330, &c. gives three audiences to the

              Arians,

INDEX.

                                          Page

Arians, 341-5. is despised by the inhabitants of Antioch, 348. celebrates the funeral of Julian at Tarsus, 351. orders his tomb to be decorated, 352. passes through Tyana, in Cappadocia, and hears news from the West, 354. enters Ancyra, and celebrates the solemnity of his consulship, having taken his son Varronian for his collegue, 356, &c. his death, 361. his apotheosis, 363.

Jovianus, a distinguished officer, his tragical death   297

Jovians, a body of troops   263

Jovinus, commander of the troops in the Gauls 289. 356

Isthmian games supported by the Corinthians   86

JULIAN, Emperor, collects the library of George, 17. 92 believes in dreams, 34. attempts in vain to rebuild the temple of Jerusalem 61, 2 (note) 74 (note) leaves Antioch, passes through Litarbo, Berea, and Batnæ, and arrives at Hierapolis, 65—71. an accident which happened to him at Hierapolis 72 (note) believes in theurgy, 98 confiscates the effects of the church of Edessa, 118. makes a present of a country-house to one of his friends, 122. pays an honourable testimony to Christians, 128. wishes to establish in Paganism the discipline of the church, *ibid*. attacks Christianity with weak arguments, 137, &c. persecutes the Christians, 145. sends for an obelisk to decorate Constantinople, 155. believes the immortality of the soul, detests the materialists and free-thinkers, 159, 80. ill treats Ahaces king of Armenia, 186 (note) destroys his own fleet, 258. state of his army at his death, 260. idea that the Persians had of him, 267. various opinions of his death, 269. his funeral, 309. bad consequences of his government, 312. he is interred at Tarsus, 351. his tomb is decorated by three Christian princes, 352. he is placed in the number of the Gods   353

Julian Count. The Emperor Julian writes to him   27

Julus, Patriarch of the Jews 60. mistaken by Fabricius   200 (note)

                                                                              Labarum,

INDEX.

L.

Labarum, Jovian replaces in it the monogram of Jesus Christ 327. described ibid. (note)
Lardner, Dr. doubts the truth of the fiery eruption 62 (note) his reasons ibid.
Lemnian misfortunes 240. proverbial ib. (note)
Leontius, Julian writes to him 45. consular of Palestine 383
Libanius, the sophist, Julian writes to him 6. 28. 65. 120. 195. 203. his life by Fabricius 216—226. his monody on Nicomedia 227—242. his monody on Daphne 243—251. his thoughts on the death of Julian 269. is inclined to kill himself 290. composes two discourses in honour of Julian 291. complains of the severities exercised against the Pagans 323
Lucian, the sophist, Julian writes to him 79
Lucillian, Count, father in law of Jovian, his defence of Nisibis 304. sent to Milan 289. 354. is killed at Rheims 355
Lucius, an Arian bishop, chosen to succeed George 340. sent to Jovian ibid. Jovian extricates himself from him 340

M.

Macedonians (heretics) their request to Jovian 339
Macrinus, Emperor, a forged epistle of 378
Magnentius, his usurpation 159 (note) 288
Magnus, Count, burns the church of Beryta 329. is pardoned 330. his character ibid. his cruelties ibid. (note)
Malarich, a Frank officer, appointed commander of the troops in the Gauls 289. refuses that employment 354
Markland, Mr. refers to a passage of Julian 50 (note)
Maximus, the perverter of Julian, that prince writes to him 29. 31. 96. 100. is persecuted under Valens, and put to death, 30 (note) 220 (note) 324 (note)
Meletius and Paulinus, bishops of Antioch 315 (note)
Memoridus, a tribune, sent into the West 288. gives an account of his commission 354

Momus,

INDEX.

	Page
Momus, his sarcasm on the sandal of Venus	166
Morell, Frederick, his translation of Libanius faulty	223
(note) 233 (note) 236 (note) his intense application to it 223 (note) his plagiarism	224 (note
Muret, error of	369
Musonius, fragment on	210

N.

Nemean games, defrayed by the Argives 86
Neptune, his destruction of the Grecian wall 230. reprimanded by Libanius 230. 232
Nevitta, a general 47 (note) 261
Newton, bishop, defends the fiery eruption 62 (note)
Nicomedes I. founder of Nicomedia 230, 1
Nicomedia described 227 (note) 233, &c. history of 231
destroyed by an earthquake 228 (note) 237, &c.
Nile, the rising of 134. cause of it 135 (note)
Nisibis, city of, its history 299. consternation of its inhabitants on being forced by Jovian to quit it 304. they ask but are refused permission to defend themselves 305. they retire to Amida 308
Novatians (heretics) their tenets 316

O.

Olympic games, supported by the Eleans 86
———— of Antioch 247
Oribasius, physician to Julian, that prince writes to him 33. his works 34 (note)

P.

Paganism had no morality 131 (note) properly speaking, had no dogmas 322. the methods Constantine employed to undermine it *ibid.*
Pagans, virtues rare among them 131 (note) their despair at the death of Julian 292
Painter, Julian writes to one 185
Patriarch (of Antioch) Julian writes to him 200
Paul, his calumny and punishment 194 (note)
Phædon of Elis 161
Phædrus of Plato 203
Phalaris, his epistles, fabricated perhaps by Libanius 226 (note)
Phidias,

INDEX.

	Page
Phidias, the sculptor, his excellence	15
Philip, Julian writes to him	197
Philosophers, alarmed at the accession of Jovian	312
persecuted under Valens 323 (note) well treated by Jovian	325
Photinum, Juliani Epistola ad, 205. bishop of Sirmium, his temerity and degradation	ibid. (note)
Physicians, exemptions granted to them	63
Pindar, quotations from	39. 55. 104. 125
Plato, referred to 160, 161. deceived by Dionysius	161
Pocock, Dr. his description of Nicomedia	234 (note)
Porphyry, treasurer-general of Ægypt, Julian writes to him	92
Priest, a heathen, censured and suspended by Julian	177
Priscus, the philosopher 6. Julian writes to him	202
Probatius, great chamberlain to Jovian	346
Procopius, a relation of Julian, commands in Mesopotamia, is suspected by Jovian 276, &c. acknowledges Jovian 296. conducts the corpse of Julian to Tarsus 309. secretes himself 310. his revolt and death	221 (note)
———— secretary of state	288
Professors, regulated, and Christians forbidden to teach	112
Proharesius, a Christian sophist, Julian writes to him	5
Proteus, an impostor	81
Pythian games, supported by the Delphians	65

R.

Rheims, city of	355
Rhine, the people bordering on that river plunge their infants into it, and why	31
Rhodian shower of gold	381
Rostgaard, Frederick, his collections 193 (note) 225 (note)	

S.

Sabinus, a citizen of Nisibis, speaks boldly to Jovian 305
Sallust (afterwards Præfect of Gaul) extolled by Julian 37
———— the second (afterwards Præfect of the East) president of the council of Chalcedon 47 (note) refuses the empire after the death of Julian 261. is sent
to

INDEX.

	Page
to Sapor 276. quells a tumult at Antioch	348
refuses the empire again after the death of Jovian	362
Salmasius, an error of	369
Sappho, quotations from 39. 40.	173
Sapor I. king of Persia, burnt Antioch	245
Sapor II. hears of the death of Julian 267. attacks the Roman army *ibid.* makes the first overtures for a peace 275. thinks it strange that the death of Julian is not revenged	277
Sebastian, Count, comes to pay his duty to Jovian	296
Sepulchres, punishment of those who profaned them, excesses of some Christians, laws on that subject 190, &c. (note)	
Serapion, a senator, Julian writes to him	47
Simonides, an expression of	55
Singara, city of, demanded by Sapor 280. Jovian makes the inhabitants quit it	308
Sopater, the disciple of Jamblichus 76.	149
Sosipater, (probably the same) Julian writes to him	196
Sozomen, the historian, his murderous doctrine	271
Suetonius, a passage of explained	377
Sun, his blessings	139
Surena, the general of the Persian cavalry, sent to Jovian by Sapor	275
Swan-song, a poetical idea	37 (note)
Sylofon, ill rewarded by Darius	73
Symmachus, a Roman orator, extolled by Julian	163

T.

Telchin, a name for Apollo	248
Telchines, inhabitants of Rhodes, their ingenuity *ib.* (note)	
Temenus, the eldest of the Heraclidæ	84
Tertullian, a fact related by him invalidated	370
Themistius, senator of Constantinople, pronounces the panegyric of Jovian 319. part of that elogium *ibid.* &c. substance of it	321
Theocritus, quotation from	7
Theodora, Julian writes to her 10. a letter to her from Libanius	*ibid.* (note)
Theodore, a high priest, Julian writes to him	178

Theodorus,

INDEX.

Theodorus, named in a divination, and put to death 220 (note)
Theophrastus, quotation from 50
Therapeutæ, their superstition 156 (note)
Thisalphata, the name of the place where Jovian re-entered the Roman territories 296
Thracians, Julian writes to them 125
Tiberius, Emperor, his proposal for placing Jesus Christ among the Gods rejected 370
Titus, bishop of Bostraa, Julian endeavours to prejudice him in the minds of the people 145. his tenets ibid. (note)
Trajan, Emperor 286. 349

V. and U.

Valentinian accompanies Lucillian into the Gauls 354 is in danger of his life 355. is made captain of the guards 356. succeeds Jovian 362. associates his brother Valens in the empire 363 (note)
Valentinians, heretics 118
Varronian, Count, father of Jovian 263, dies consul elect 290
——— an infant, son of Jovian, chosen consul in the room of his grandfather 357. his unhappy fate 364
Vehicles, public, their danger and inconvenience 203
Vesontio (now Besançon) described 97
Vetranio, his revolt 288 (note)
Ur, a castle of Mesopotamia 287

W.

Warburton, bishop, his "Julian" 61 (note) 62 (note)
Wolfius, John Christopher, his edition of the Epistles of Libanius 225 (note)

Z.

Zambicari, Francis, his Latin Epistles of Libanius 225 (note)
Zeno, a celebrated physician, Julian writes to him 121

⁎ Since this work has been printed off, I am enabled, by the *Nouveau Dictionnaire Historique* *, (4me edition, 6 tomes, 8vo, à Caen, 1779), to add the following account of a writer to whom I am much obliged.

BLETERIE (JOHN PHILIP RENE de la), born at Rennes, died in an advanced age, in 1772. He was a man of learning, was much attached to religion, and his morals did not belie his principles. His knowledge, being solid and diversified, rendered his conversation interesting and improving. He published several works, which have been well received by the public. 1. *The History of Julian the Apostate* †, Paris, 1735. 1746. 12mo. a curious performance, well written, and distinguished at once by its impartiality, precision, elegance, and judgement. 2. *The History of the Emperor Jovian*, with translations of some works of the Emperor Julian, Paris, 1748, 2 vols. 12mo. &c. &c.

* The work so styled, *ou Histoire abregée de tous les hommes qui se sont fait un nomme par le Genie, les Talens, les Vertus, les Erreurs, &c. depuis le commencement du monde jusqu'à nos jours, par une Societé de Gens de lettres*, is of itself a library.

† This work, it is observable, is not so entitled by the author, but solely *Vie de l'Empereur Julien*.

VOL. II.   D d

ERRATA in VOL. II.

Page
17. note † l. 1. r. "Julian was truly"
26. note † l. 6. r. 'χρυσων'
31. note * l. 2. r. "common reading"
65. l. 13. r. 'Chalcis'
66. is mispaged
82. note * l. 3. r. 'ευρῃ ποιλω'
95. note * l. 7. r. 'δυσωπεισ- θαι'
97. note † l. 7. 'F. Martinius,' &c. belongs to the next note
102. note † l. 1. r. 'παιδιων.'
124. l. 13. After 'friends' add ‡ and prefix the same reference to the note beginning "Julian, it appears," &c.

Page
159. l. 5. r. 'Constans'
165. note * l. 3. r. 'Phædon'
169. note * l. 1. r. 'Φαιδων'
206. l. the last, r. 'confectam'
214. l. 4. r. (21)
240. note * l. the last, r. 'Chiliades'
259. is mispaged
279. note * l. 3. r. 'to whom'
284. l. 3. fr. the bottom, r. 'as were'
291. note † l. 3. r. 'a Latin'
333. note † l. 3. r. 'πασι'
341. l. 17. r. 'Bernicius' to note † add B.
361. note * l. 1. after 'Ammianus', add a comma

www.ingramcontent.com/pod-product-compliance
Lightning Source LLC
Chambersburg PA
CBHW030423300426
44112CB00009B/820